Visual Reference

KU-053-335

Microsoft Windows NT Workstation 4.0

At a Glance

Microsoft Press

PUBLISHED BY
Microsoft Press
A Division of Microsoft Corporation
One Microsoft Way
Redmond, Washington 98052-6399

Copyright © 1997 by Gerald Joyce and Marianne Moon

All rights reserved. No part of the contents of this book may be reproduced or transmitted in any form or by any means without the written permission of the publisher.

Library of Congress Cataloging-in-Publication Data
Joyce, Jerry, 1950–

    Microsoft Windows NT workstation 4.0 at a glance / Jerry Joyce and Marianne Moon.
      p. cm.
    Includes index.
    ISBN 1-57231-574-1
    1. Microsoft Windows NT. 2. Operating systems (Computers).
    3. Microcomputer workstations. I. Moon, Marianne. II. Title.
    QA76.76.063J694 1997
    005.4'469—dc21
                                   6-29985
                                    CIP

Printed and bound in the United States of America.

1 2 3 4 5 6 7 8 9 QEQE 2 0 1 9 8 7

Distributed to the book trade in Canada by Macmillan of Canada, a division of Canada Publishing Corporation.

A CIP catalogue record for this book is available from the British Library.

Microsoft Press books are available through booksellers and distributors worldwide. For further information about international editions, contact your local Microsoft Corporation office. Or contact Microsoft Press International directly at fax (206) 936-7329.

IntelliMouse, Internet Explorer, Microsoft, Microsoft Network (MSN), MS-DOS, Outlook, Windows, the Windows logo, Windows NT, and the Windows Start logo are either registered trademarks or trademarks of Microsoft Corporation in the United States and/or other countries. Other product and company names herein may be the trademarks of their respective owners.

Companies, names, and/or data used in screens and sample output are fictitious unless otherwise noted.

Acquisitions Editor: Kim Fryer
Project Editor: Lucinda Rowley

Technical Editor: Michael T. Bunney
Manuscript Editor: Marianne Moon

Contents

Windows NT is your working headquarters.

See page 6

Jump to any location
See page 26

Find a folder or a file
See pages 30–33

4 **Working with Programs** **53**

Meet Windows NT
Explorer
See page 45

Create a picture
See page 64

Welcome to the
Network Neighborhood!
See page 81

*"Stop the
presses!"*

See page 100

Work in MS-DOS
See pages 111–132

Change the size
of the MS-DOS window
See page 125

Associate a sound
with an event
See page 148

Clean up your Desktop!
See page 184

*"How do I add
items to the
Start menu?"*

See page 195

Schedule Mail Delivery...

Let Windows NT
schedule your remote
mail delivery
See page 224

Add fonts
See pages 236–237

*The newest
generation
of pointing
devices...*

See pages 249–254

Connect to a newsgroup
See page 266

"Help!"

See pages 279–289

*"Where can
I find free
software?"*

See page 290

Acknowledgments

This book is the result of the combined efforts of people whose work we trust and admire and whose friendship we value highly. Kari Becker, our talented typographer, meticulously laid out the complex design. Michael Bunney, our eagle-eyed technical editor, double-checked every procedure and every graphic to verify that things worked as described. Herbert Payton refined and produced the interior graphics. We worked with Susan Bishop on the *Microsoft Publisher Companion,* and we're happy to have her distinctive drawings in our book. We've worked with Alice Copp Smith on other books. She does so much more than proofread: her gentle and humorous chiding teaches us to write better. And our indexer, Kari Bero, seems to inhale the soul of a book and magically exhale an extensive index. Thanks also to Jeanne Lewis, Todd Emery, and Paul Ampadu for their help with the graphics, and to our old friend, Ken Sanchez, for moral and technical support and lots of laughs.

At Microsoft Press, first and foremost we thank Lucinda Rowley for making it possible for us to write this book. Thanks also to Judith Bloch, Kim Eggleston, Kim Fryer, Mary DeJong, Nancy Jacobs, and Jim Kramer, all of whom provided help and valuable advice along the way.

On the home front, Roberta Moon-Krause and Rick Krause allowed their puppies, Baiser and Pierre, to roam freely on our virtual and literal desktops. Pierre decided not to appear in this book, but Baiser graces some of our pages with her furry little image. Roberta brought us many a wonderful home-cooked dinner as we toiled long into the night, and Rick helped with details too numerous to mention. Thanks, kids—you're the greatest!

About This Book

Microsoft Windows NT Workstation 4.0 At a Glance is for everyone who wants to get the most from their computer and their software with the least amount of time and effort. Whether you do your work in a giant corporate network whose network administrator recently installed Microsoft Windows NT Workstation 4.0 on all the computers, in a small workgroup, or at a stand-alone computer, you'll find this book to be a straightforward, easy-to-read reference tool. With the premise that your computer should work for you, not you for it, this book's purpose is to help you get your work done quickly and efficiently so that you can get away from the computer and live your life.

No Computerese!

Let's face it—when there's a task you don't know how to do but you need to get it done in a hurry, or when you're stuck in the middle of a task and can't figure out what to do next, there's nothing more frustrating than having to read page after page of technical background material. You want the information you need—nothing more, nothing less—and you want it now! *And* it should be easy to find and understand. That's what this book is all about. It's written in plain English—no technical jargon and no computerese. No single task in the book takes more than two pages. Just look up the task in the index or the table of contents, turn to the page, and there's the information, laid out step by step and accompanied by graphics that add visual clarity. You don't get bogged down by the whys and wherefores: just follow the steps, look at the illustrations, and get your work done with a minimum of hassle.

Occasionally you might have to turn to another page if the procedure you're working on has a "See Also" in the left column. That's because there's a lot of overlap among tasks, and we didn't want to keep repeating ourselves. We've also scattered some useful tips here and there, and thrown in a "Try This" once in a while, but by and large we've tried to remain true to the heart and soul of the book, which is that the information you need should be available to you at a glance.

Useful Tasks...

Whether you use Windows NT for routine tasks or you find yourself doing something new each day, we've tried to pack this book with procedures for everything we could think of that you might want to do, from the simplest tasks to some of the more esoteric ones.

...And the Easiest Way to Do Them

Another thing we've tried to do in *Windows NT Workstation 4.0 At a Glance* is to find and document the easiest way to accomplish a task. Windows NT often provides a multitude of methods to accomplish a single result—which can be daunting or delightful, depending on the way you like to work. If you tend to stick with one favorite and familiar approach, we think the methods

described in this book are the way to go. If you like trying out alternative techniques, go ahead! The intuitiveness of Windows NT invites exploration, and you're likely to discover ways of doing things that you think are easier or that you like better than ours. If you do, that's great! It's exactly what the creators of Windows NT had in mind when they provided so many alternatives.

We haven't covered everything you can do with Windows NT Workstation, because it's really designed to be administered by a systems professional. For example, we haven't dealt with the different platforms on which Windows NT can be run, the different file systems you can use, or the different levels of access that can be granted by an administrator. A few of the procedures we discuss might require different access rights from the ones you have—and, of course, we have no way of knowing how access rights have been defined in your workgroup. However, if you don't have the appropriate access rights, Windows NT will let you know. Then you can either ask your system administrator to grant you the access rights you need, or find a coworker who does have those access rights and tell him or her exactly what you want to do.

A Quick Overview

This book isn't meant to be read in any particular order. It's designed so that you can jump in, get the information you need, and then close the book and keep it near your computer until the next time you need to know how to get something done. But that doesn't mean we scattered the information about with wild abandon. If you were to read the book from front to back, you'd find a logical progression from the simple tasks to the more complex ones. Here's a quick overview.

First, because Windows NT Workstation 4.0 is preinstalled on so many computers or is installed company-wide by a network administrator, we're going to assume that Windows NT is already installed on your machine. If it's not, the Setup Wizard makes installation so simple that you won't need our help anyway. So, unlike most computer books, this one doesn't start out with installation instructions and a list of system requirements. You've already got that under control.

Sections 2 through 5 of the book cover the basics: starting Windows NT; starting programs; using shortcut menus; creating, finding, and organizing files and folders on your computer or on the network; and working with programs, including some of the programs that come with Windows NT.

Sections 6 through 8 describe tasks that are a little bit more technical but are really useful: printing; working in the MS-DOS environment and using MS-DOS programs; and working with multimedia, including sound and video.

Section 9 is all about communicating with your coworkers: sending and receiving e-mail, transferring files by modem, and even making telephone calls through your computer.

Sections 10 through 13 deal with more advanced topics that will let you get the most from your computer by customizing it: adding and removing software components, changing settings, using special tools so

that you can work at different locations, and even adding full fax capabilities to your computer.

The final two sections, 14 and 15, are about using Windows NT as your window on the world at large: surfing the net and using all the tools that go along with working and playing in cyberspace, including easy ways to telecommute and videoconference directly from your computer. And you'll find out how to get all sorts of information, help, and tools directly from Microsoft.

A Final Word (or Two)

We had three goals in writing this book, and here they are.

- ◆ Whatever you *want* to do, we want the book to help you get it done.

- ◆ We want the book to help you discover how to do things you *didn't* know you wanted to do.

- ◆ And, finally, if we've achieved the first two goals, we'll be well on the way to the third: we want the book to help you *enjoy* doing your work with Windows NT. We think that would be the best gift we could give you as a "thank you" for buying our book.

We hope you'll have as much fun using this book as we've had writing it. The best way to learn is by *doing*, and that's how we hope you'll use *Windows NT Workstation 4.0 At a Glance*.

Jump right in!

Jump Right In

Microsoft Windows NT Workstation 4.0 is designed to work for you, not you for it. Don't be afraid to jump right in and try out some features. You'll find that there are often several ways to accomplish one task. Why? Because people work differently. Because different tasks have different requirements. And so that you can find the way that works best for you, get your work done quickly, and get away from the computer!

You'll find that most of the procedures are simple and straightforward and that Windows NT often uses automated methods to help you get the more complex chores done easily. This doesn't mean that you can't get stuck or get into trouble, but there are so many safeguards built into Windows NT and so many places to get help that you'll have to work pretty hard to get into *real* trouble.

This section of the book covers the really basic stuff, from starting up Windows NT through shutting it down.

Don't change or delete anything just yet, though—you want to feel comfortable with the basics before you do any customizing. The best way to learn about starting Windows NT, running programs, managing windows, and getting help if you *do* get into trouble is to jump right in and try it.

Windows NT at a Glance

Windows NT is your working headquarters—the *operating system* that makes it possible for you to run different programs simultaneously and share information between programs if you need to. Most of the programs you'll use have common characteristics that were designed to work together in the Windows NT environment—meaning that once you learn how to do something in one program, you know how to do it in other programs.

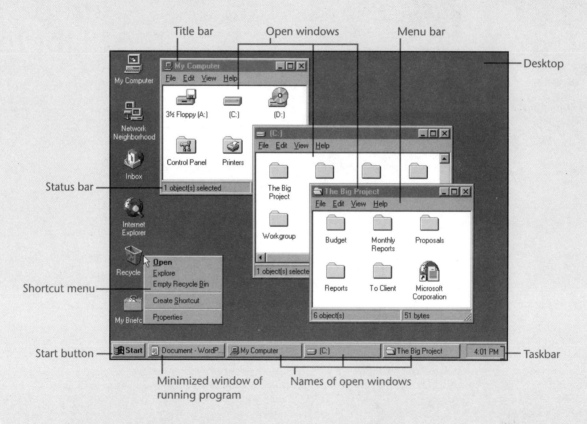

Take a look at the different parts of the Windows NT environment that are displayed on these two pages—what they do and what they're called—and you'll be on the road to complete mastery! Windows NT is so intuitive that you'll learn by doing, but you can always come back to this visual glossary for a quick refresher on Windows NT terminology.

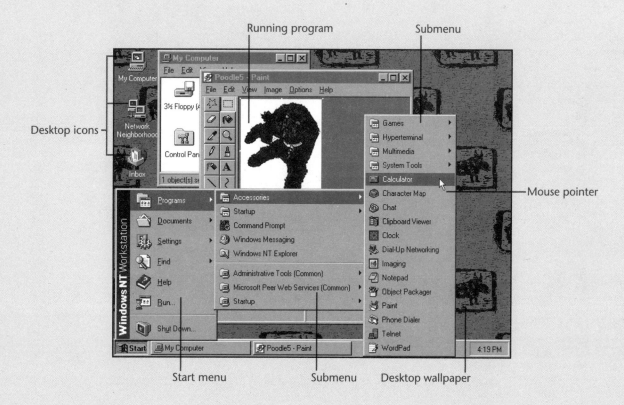

Running program

Submenu

Desktop icons

Mouse pointer

Start menu

Submenu

Desktop wallpaper

Starting Up

When you turn on your computer, you're also starting Windows NT. When Windows NT starts, it loads programs and files into the computer's memory. The time your computer takes to start up depends on its speed and configuration (including network connections) and on the programs that are set up to start when Windows NT starts.

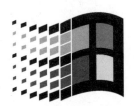

TIP

Pressing Ctrl+Alt+Delete to start logging on is a security feature that has been built in to Windows NT to prevent unauthorized people from using their own program to create a fake Logon Information dialog box and steal your password. If you don't log on immediately, you'll need to press Ctrl+Alt+Delete again to restart the logon procedure.

Start Windows NT

1 Turn on your monitor.

2 Turn on your computer.

3 Turn on any peripheral devices—your printer, for example.

4 Press Enter to start the default version of Windows NT, or use the direction keys to select a different version of Windows NT or another operating system. Press Enter.

5 If you have different hardware profiles, select the profile you want to use.

6 Wait while Windows NT loads.

7 Press and then release the Ctrl, Alt, and Delete keys simultaneously.

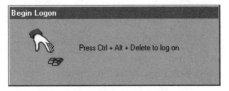

TIP

Windows NT gives you 30 seconds to select a different version of Windows NT or another operating system before it starts the default version. You can change the default operating system, and you can change the time Windows NT waits for your response.

SEE ALSO

"Dialog Box Decisions" on page 19 for information about using a dialog box.

"Changing Your Password" on page 95 for information about changing your password.

"Changing the Way Windows NT Starts" on page 214 for information about changing the startup options.

TIP

If your computer is set up as a workgroup computer, you probably won't see the Domain text box.

Enter Your Password

1 Type the name you've been assigned in the User Name text box if it's not already there, and press the Tab key.

2 Type your password in the Password text box. Be sure to use the correct capitalization!

3 Confirm that the domain name is filled in and that it's correct. If not, press Tab again, and type the network domain name— or, if you're logging on locally, the computer name—in the Domain text box.

4 Click OK.

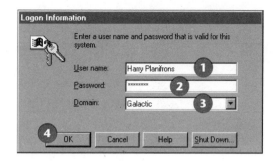

Starting a Program

Despite all the hype, the real work of an operating system is to run your software programs. Windows NT usually gives you several different ways to start up your programs, so you can choose the way that's easiest for you or that you like the best.

SEE ALSO

"Mouse Maneuvers" on page 14 for detailed information about pointing, clicking, and double-clicking with a mouse.

"Accessing Documents from the Desktop" on page 198 for more information about accessing your programs from the Windows NT Desktop.

Start a Program from the Start Menu

1. Click the Start button.

2. Point to the Programs menu item.

3. Continue pointing to groups as the submenus cascade out. If you don't see the program you want, point to a group where it might be located.

4. When you see the program you want, point to it and click to choose it.

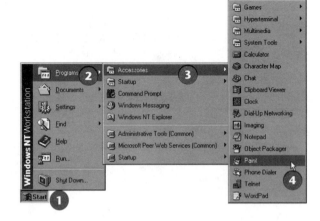

Start a Program from the Desktop

Point to the program icon and double-click.

TIP

Start a Program from a CD.
Many CDs have a feature called AutoPlay—you simply insert the CD into the CD-ROM drive and Windows NT starts the program automatically. If you want to grab some files from the CD without starting the program, hold down the Shift key while inserting the CD. (You might need to hold the Shift key down for a while to allow the CD drive to start up.)

SEE ALSO

"Exploring with Windows NT Explorer" on page 46 if you want to try another way of navigating through your drives and folders to start programs.

Start a Program from My Computer

1 Double-click the My Computer icon.

2 Double-click the drive that contains the program you want to start.

3 Double-click the folder that contains the program. If the program is in a subfolder, continue double-clicking the subfolders until you reach the program you want.

4 Double-click the program icon.

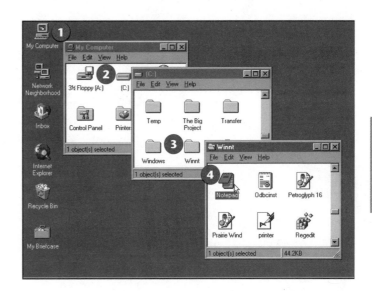

Managing a Program Window

"Managing" a window means that you can boss it around: you can move it, change its size, and open and close it. Most programs are contained in windows. Although these windows might have some different features, most program windows have more similarities than differences.

SEE ALSO

"Mouse Maneuvers" on page 14 for information about dragging and dropping.

Move a Window

1 Point to the title bar.

2 Drag the window and drop it at a new location.

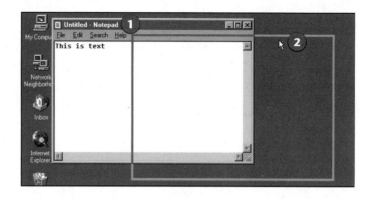

Use the Buttons to Switch Between Sizes

1 Click the Maximize button, and the window enlarges and fills the screen. (If the window is already maximized, you won't see the Maximize button.)

2 Click the Restore button, and the window gets smaller. (If the window is already restored, you won't see the Restore button.)

3 Click the Minimize button, and the window disappears but you see its name on a button on the Windows NT taskbar.

4 Click the window's name on the taskbar, and the window zooms back to the size it was before you minimized it.

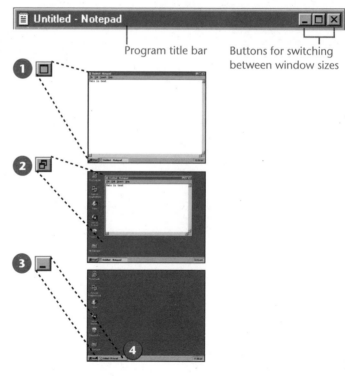

Program title bar

Buttons for switching between window sizes

SEE ALSO

"Arranging Windows on the Desktop" on page 28 for information about automatically arranging all your program Windows.

TIP

Save, Save, Save! *Don't wait until you quit a program to save your work. You never know what disaster is about to befall you, so be cautious and save your work frequently.*

TIP

Move Your Mouse...*over a side border to change the window's width; over a top or bottom border to change the window's height; over a corner to change both height and width.*

Use the Mouse to Resize a Window

1 Click the Restore button if the window is currently maximized. (You can't manually size a maximized window.)

2 Move the mouse over one of the borders of the window until the mouse pointer changes into a two-headed arrow. The directions of the arrowheads show you the directions in which you can move the window border.

3 Drag the window border and drop it when the window is the size you want.

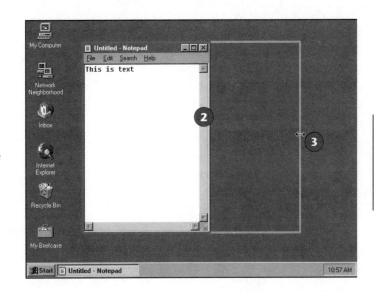

Close a Window

1 Click the Close button.

2 If there's work that you haven't yet saved, the program asks you whether you want to save it. Click Yes to save it, No to discard it, or Cancel if you've changed your mind about closing both the window and the program.

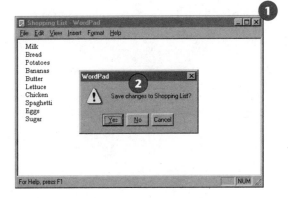

Mouse Maneuvers

Navigating with a mouse is like traveling in a helicopter: you can lift off from any spot, fly a straight line over hills and canyons, and set down wherever you want. Using the keyboard to navigate is like taking the scenic route: you'll run into detours in a program's topography, and you might need a good map to navigate through menus and shortcut keys to reach your destination. You might prefer the longer keyboard route—you get to explore the road less traveled, and you might even come across features and techniques that are new to you. But to finish your tasks as quickly as possible—and to take advantage of some of Windows NT's best features—give your mouse the job!

Before you fly off on your mouse wings, though, you might need some Mouse Basics. At Mouse School, we believe there are no bad mice (okay, mouse devices)—only bad mouse operators. Here you'll learn to point, click, double-click, right-click, select, and drag and drop.

Point: Move the mouse until the mouse pointer (the small arrow-shaped pointer on the screen) is pointing to the item you want.

Click: Point to the item you want, and then quickly press down and release the left mouse button.

Double-click: Point to the item you want, and then quickly press down and release the left mouse button twice, making sure that you don't move the mouse between clicks.

Right-click: Point to the item you want, and then quickly press down and release the right mouse button.

Select: Click the item you want. A selected item is usually a different color from other similar items, or is surrounded by a frame.

Drag and drop: Select the item you want. Then, keeping the mouse pointer on the selected item, hold down the left mouse button, move the mouse until the item is at the desired location, and then release the left mouse button to "drop" the item.

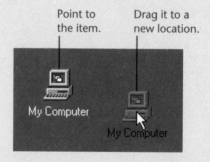

Point to the item. Drag it to a new location.

You can customize the way your mouse works, including switching the roles of the left and right mouse buttons (but you'll have to remember to reverse left and right in the previous instructions). For more information on customizing your mouse settings, see "Customizing Mouse Operations" on page 200. If you have an IntelliMouse, you'll want to read pages 249–254.

Using Shortcut Menus for Quick Results

Windows NT and the programs that work with it were designed to be intuitive—that is, they anticipate what you're likely to want to do when you're working on a particular task, and they place the appropriate commands on a shortcut menu that you open by clicking the right mouse button. These shortcut menus are *dynamic*, which means that they change depending on the task in progress.

TIP

If in Doubt, Right-Click.
If you're not sure how to accomplish something, right-click, and you'll often see the appropriate command on the shortcut menu.

Use a Shortcut Menu Command

1 Right-click an item.

2 Choose a command from the shortcut menu to accomplish the task at hand. (A few items and the shortcut menus they produce when right-clicked are shown here.)

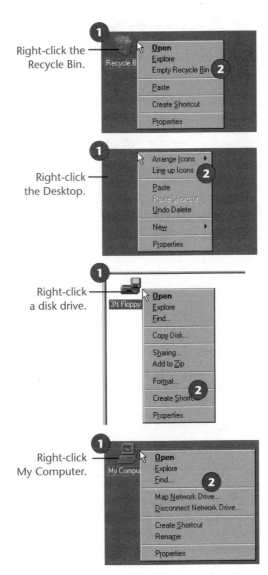

Right-click the Recycle Bin.

Right-click the Desktop.

Right-click a disk drive.

Right-click My Computer.

Getting Help

What's big and colorful; packed with information, procedures, tools, and videos; and sadly under-utilized? The Help programs! Of course, they couldn't possibly replace this book, but you can use them to find the concise step-by-step procedures you need to diagnose and overcome problems, see demonstrations on how to work in Windows NT, and learn how to accomplish your tasks faster and more easily than you ever imagined.

Read a Procedure from Windows NT Help

1 Click the Start button, and choose Help.

2 Click the Index tab.

3 Type a word that describes what you want to do.

4 Double-click the related word or phrase in the list box.

5 Read the topic.

6 Click the Help Topics button to see more topics.

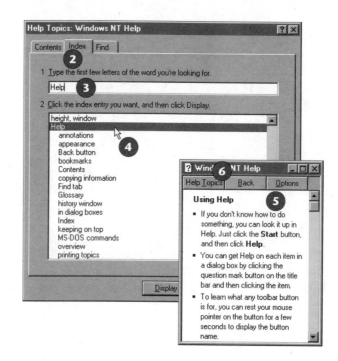

TIP

That's No Help! *Sometimes Help, or parts of it, are not installed. If you get a message that Help or a Help component is not installed, you can easily install whatever's missing.*

SEE ALSO

"Dialog Box Decisions" on page 19 for information about using a dialog box.

"Adding or Removing Windows NT Components" on page 232 for information about installing Windows NT components.

TIP

Fast Learner. *The first time you run Help, it has to compile a list of topics and index words, so you'll have to wait for a few moments while it gets itself ready—but it's worth the wait! After that, Help is the place to go for quick answers to any problems.*

Getting Background Information

1 Click the Contents tab.

2 Double-click a closed book to open it.

3 If necessary, double-click a book that's contained within the first book to open it.

4 Double-click a topic to open it.

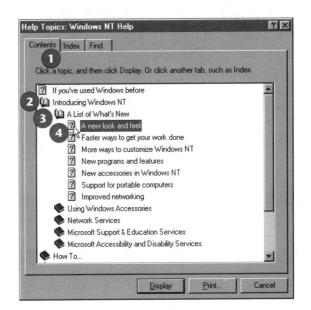

Use "What's This?" Help

1 In a Windows NT dialog box, click the "What's This?" Help button.

2 Click the item you want more information about.

3 Read the Help information, and then click anywhere to close Help.

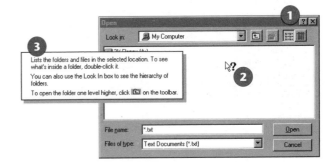

Quitting Windows NT

Shutting down your computer used to be a simple matter—you just turned it *off!* But in Windows NT, just as starting the computer takes longer, shutting it down takes more time while Windows NT closes any open programs and saves all your current settings.

TIP

Some computers with advanced power-management features shut off automatically after you confirm that you want to shut down the computer.

TIP

You'll want to restart Windows NT if you have software problems or when you've made changes to the configuration.

SEE ALSO

"Quitting When You're Stuck" on page 78 if you have problems when you try to quit Windows NT.

Shut Down and Turn Off Your Computer

1. Click the Start button, and choose Shut Down.

2. Click the appropriate option.

3. Click Yes.

4. Wait while Windows NT shuts down and records any changes you've made to your system.

Reboots the computer so that you can start a different operating system or reload Windows NT.

Exits Windows NT. Wait for a message telling you that it's safe to turn off your computer.

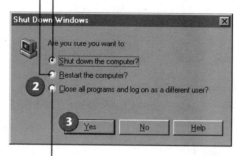

Resets Windows NT for a new user to log on.

Dialog Box Decisions

You're going to be seeing a lot of *dialog boxes* as you use Windows NT, and if you're not familiar with them now, you soon will be. Dialog boxes appear when Windows NT or a program (WordPad, let's say) needs you to make one or more decisions about what you want to do. Sometimes all you have to do is click a Yes or No button; at other times, there'll be quite a few decisions to make in one dialog box. The Print dialog box, shown below, is one you'll probably be seeing frequently, so take a look at its components and how they work.

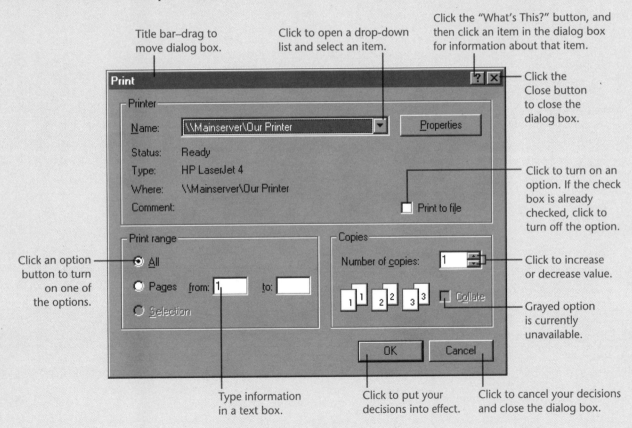

2

Title bar–drag to move dialog box.

Click to open a drop-down list and select an item.

Click the "What's This?" button, and then click an item in the dialog box for information about that item.

Click the Close button to close the dialog box.

Click to turn on an option. If the check box is already checked, click to turn off the option.

Click an option button to turn on one of the options.

Click to increase or decrease value.

Grayed option is currently unavailable.

Type information in a text box.

Click to put your decisions into effect.

Click to cancel your decisions and close the dialog box.

3

Navigating Windows NT

Using Windows NT is like having a super-efficient office assistant. When you open a folder on the Windows NT Desktop, Windows NT shows you an inventory of every document, or file, in the folder. When you tell Windows NT what you want to do, it hurries off to do your bidding—fetch a file, copy a document and put the copy away in another folder, toss old files into the Recycle Bin, and so on.

The filing system in Windows NT is structured like a paper-filing system, with its equivalents of filing cabinets, drawers, folders, and documents. The My Computer icon on the Windows NT Desktop is the gateway to this system. You can open any drawer, dig through any folder, and pull out any document.

If you prefer to work with files and folders using the basic "tree-structure" filing system that you're familiar with from MS-DOS or from earlier versions of Windows, you can do that too. With Windows NT Explorer, you can gain direct access to any file, folder, or drive without having to step through a series of other folders.

Whether you use My Computer, Windows NT Explorer, or both methods simultaneously depends on the type of work you do, the way you work, and your personal preference. We'll explore both systems so that you can decide which system is better for you.

Exploring Windows NT

Sitting on the Windows NT Desktop is an icon that's the gateway (okay, it's a window) to your computer. The icon is called, appropriately enough, My Computer. Using My Computer, you open windows to the world of *your* computer, and you can move to any folder and find any file anywhere on your computer.

TIP

To move back to the previous window, press Backspace.

SEE ALSO

"Mouse Maneuvers" on page 14 for information about pointing, clicking, double-clicking, and dragging with the mouse.

Open a Folder

1. Double-click My Computer on the Windows NT Desktop.

2. Double-click a drive icon (for example, [C:]) to open a window for that drive.

3. Double-click a folder icon (for example, Assembled Documents) to open a window for that folder.

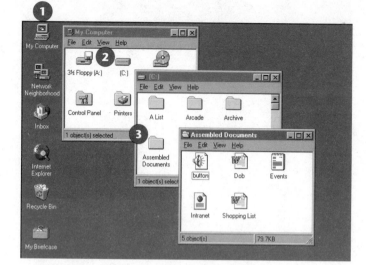

Move an Icon

1. Point to the file icon.

2. Drag the file icon and drop it at a new location.

3. Whether you're using Small Icons view or Large Icons view, choose Line Up Icons from the window's View menu to keep those icons in line!

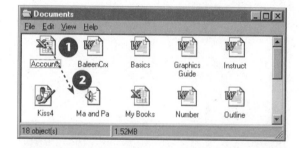

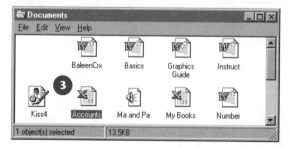

SEE ALSO

"Managing Files with Windows NT Explorer" on page 48 for information about managing folders and files with Windows NT Explorer.

TRY THIS

Window Treatments. *Point to Arrange Icons on the window's View menu, and then choose Auto Arrange from the submenu (if there's not already a check mark next to it) to turn on Auto Arrange mode. Then, in Large Icons or Small Icons view, move some icons. Auto Arrange mode moves the icons to fill any gaps left when an icon is moved or deleted, adds space if the icons become too crowded, and rearranges the icons to fit a window that has been resized.*

TIP

If you want to close a series of windows in one fell swoop, hold down the Shift key while you click the Close button on the last window opened—all the windows that are on the direct route back from that last window to My Computer will close.

Change the Display

1 Click the View menu.

2 Choose a view:

◆ Large Icons, to see files or folders with large representative icons

◆ Small Icons, to see small representative icons arranged from left to right

◆ List, to see small representative icons arranged from top to bottom

◆ Details, to see small representative icons and full file information

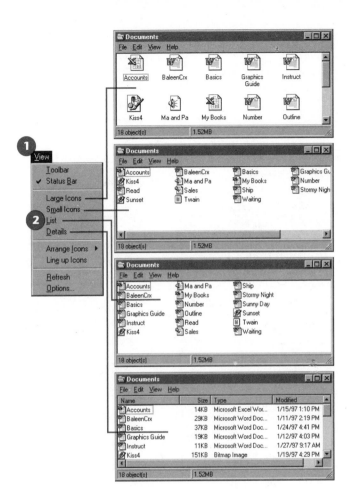

Sorting the File Listings

Depending on the contents of your files and your own idiosyncrasies, you might want Windows NT to list files alphabetically, by date of most recent edit, by size, or by some other criterion. Windows NT can also reverse the sorting order—listing names from Z to A, for example—in an opened window.

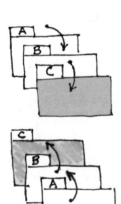

Sort the Files

1 Double-click My Computer on the Windows NT Desktop.

2 Open the folder you want to examine.

3 Click the View menu and point to Arrange Icons.

4 From the submenu, choose the type of sorting you want:

- ◆ By Name, to order the files by their filenames

- ◆ By Type, to order the files by their type—Paint, Excel, Word, and so on

- ◆ By Size, to order the files by their size in kilobytes

- ◆ By Date, to order the files by the date they were created or most recently modified

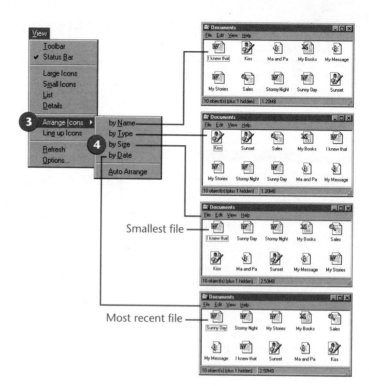

Smallest file

Most recent file

SEE ALSO

"Locating a File by Name" on page 30 and "Locating a File by Date or Content" on page 32 for information about finding files.

TRY THIS

If you don't have a folder open, double-click the My Computer icon, double-click the C: drive, double-click My Documents, and choose Details from the View menu. Click the Type button to see all the files grouped by their types. Then click the Name button to list the files alphabetically.

Reverse the Sort Order

1. Choose Details from the View menu.

2. Click a label button (Name, Size, Type, or Modified) to choose the type of sorting you want.

3. Click the same label button to reverse the sort order.

Smallest file   Click the Size button to sort by file size.

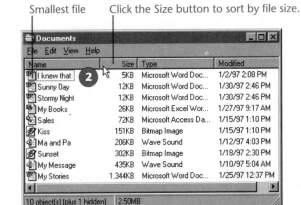

Largest file

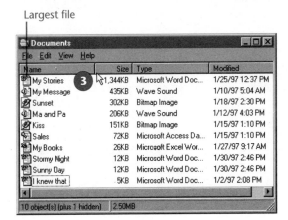

Gaining Access to Everything

The My Computer window gives you easy access to the drives on your computer, but you can also use it to access the contents of your Windows NT Desktop, of other computers in your workgroup, and even of your network resources.

Display the Toolbar

1 Double-click My Computer on the Windows NT Desktop.

2 Choose Toolbar from the View menu to display the toolbar.

Copy item to Clipboard.
Undo last action.
Move up one level.
Display properties of selected item.
Go to a different folder.

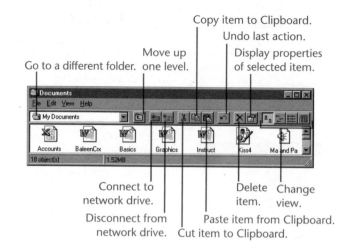

Connect to network drive.
Disconnect from network drive.
Cut item to Clipboard.
Delete item.
Change view.
Paste item from Clipboard.

Choose a Different Location

1 Click the down arrow at the right of the Go To A Different Folder box to open the drop-down list.

2 Click the new location to display it in the current window.

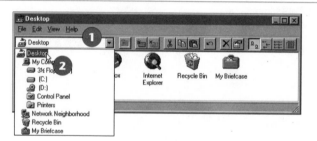

Folders and the File Structure

As we mentioned at the beginning of this section, the filing system in Windows NT is structured very much like a paper-filing system: My Computer is the filing cabinet; the drives are the drawers of the filing cabinet; the folders in the drives are the folders in the drawers, and sometimes, in each system, there are folders inside folders. And, just as with the paper-filing system, you store your documents, or files, inside the folders. Windows NT maintains the basic structure for you—My Computer, the drives, and the folders for your programs and documents. You can organize your files in whatever fashion you want by creating your own series of folders to define your own structure.

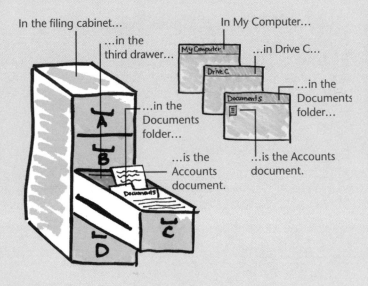

In the filing cabinet...

...in the third drawer...

...in the Documents folder...

...is the Accounts document.

In My Computer...

...in Drive C...

...in the Documents folder...

...is the Accounts document.

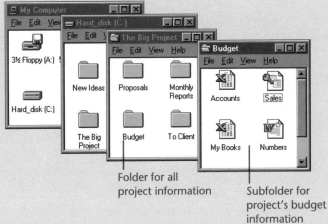

Folder for all project information

Subfolder for project's budget information

Arranging Windows on the Desktop

When you open a series of windows to get to a specific file or folder, your Desktop can become littered with overlapping windows. You can close each window that you don't need and arrange the open windows for easy access. If you want to be *really* neat, set My Computer to use only one window, which changes as it displays each folder.

TIP

Use a single window if you keep all your documents for a project in one folder and usually work in one folder at a time. Use a separate window for each folder if you use documents from different folders or if you frequently copy documents between folders.

Arrange Your Open Windows

1. Minimize any windows other than the ones you want displayed.

2. Point to an empty spot on the Windows NT taskbar and right-click.

3. Choose Cascade Windows, Tile Windows Horizontally, or Tile Windows Vertically to arrange all the open windows.

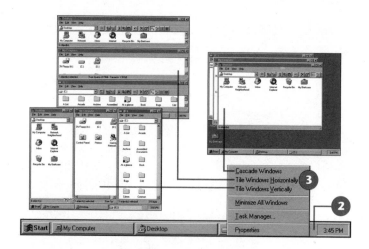

Use a Single Window

1. Choose Options from the View menu.

2. Click the Folder tab.

3. Select the Browsing option that lets you use a single window that changes as you open each folder.

4. Click OK.

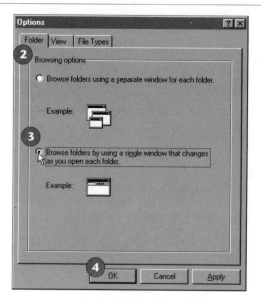

Getting More Information About a File or Folder

Windows NT records information and statistics on every file and folder that you can access from Windows NT. The information depends on the type of file or what's contained in the folder. This information is called the file's or the folder's *properties*.

TIP

Unless you have a good reason to do so, don't change the Attributes settings. Programs use this information in their own file-management processes, and changes can cause unexpected results.

SEE ALSO

"Find a Folder or a File Somewhere on Your Computer" on page 30 for information about locating files or folders.

Review the Properties of a File or Folder

1. Find the file or folder you want to examine.

2. Right-click the file or folder.

3. Choose Properties from the submenu.

4. Review the information in the Properties dialog box.

5. Click OK.

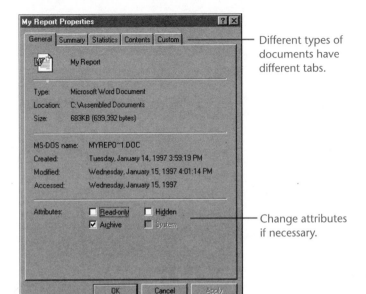

Different types of documents have different tabs.

Change attributes if necessary.

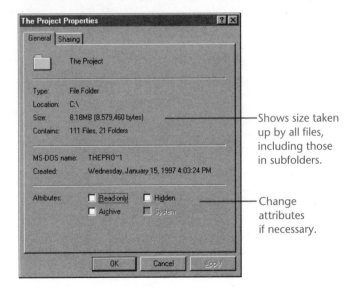

Shows size taken up by all files, including those in subfolders.

Change attributes if necessary.

Locating a File by Name

If you don't know where a file is located, you can waste a lot of time trying to find it no matter which method you use to explore your windows. Fortunately, Windows NT can find it for you.

TIP

If you don't know the full name of the file or folder you're looking for, enter as much as you know, and Windows NT will find files whose names contain the characters you typed.

TIP

Depending on the programs you have installed, you can use the Find command to search other locations. For example, you can use it to search the network for a specific computer, or you can use Outlook for advanced searches if you have Microsoft Office 97 installed.

Find a Folder or a File Somewhere on Your Computer

1 Click the Start button, point to Find, and choose Files Or Folders from the submenu.

2 Type the name, or as much of it as you can remember.

3 Select the location to be searched.

4 Turn on the Include Subfolders check box to search all subfolders.

5 Click Find Now.

6 Examine the results.

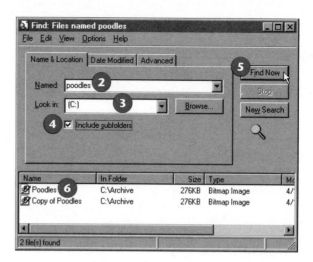

Limit the Search to a Specific Location

1 Click the Browse button.

2 Select the folder to search, and click OK.

3 Turn off the Include Subfolders check box unless you want to include the subfolders in the folder you specified.

4 Click Find Now.

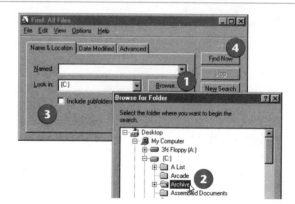

TIP

Shut Out! *You might be unable to locate some files on a network even though you know those files are there. Access privileges set on the workgroup host computer or by the network administrator might make these files inaccessible to you.*

SEE ALSO

"Creating Shortcuts" on page 40 for information about creating shortcuts.

"Editing Text Documents in WordPad" on page 60 for information about cutting and copying text.

"Viewing a Document Quickly" on page 75 for information about Quick View.

Find a File on a Network

1 Click the Browse button.

2 Select a server, a workgroup computer, or a folder on the server or workgroup computer, and click OK.

3 Click Find Now.

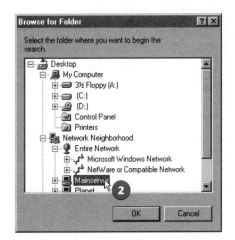

Use the Found File

1 Point to the file and right-click.

2 Choose the appropriate command:

   ◆ Open, to open the file in its associated program

   ◆ Print, to print the file to the default printer

   ◆ Quick View, to review the file using a viewer

   ◆ Send To, to send a copy of the file to another location

   ◆ The other commands, to perform standard file-management procedures

Locating a File by Date or Content

You can search for a file by the date when it was last saved, by text contained in the file, or by file type. You can use any of these as your sole search criterion, or use them in conjunction with the file's name and location.

SEE ALSO

"Locating a File by Name" on page 30 for information about specifying the name and location, and "Conducting and Reusing a Search" on the opposite page for information about saving searches and search results.

TIP

A Sensitive Case. *If you want to search for content that exactly matches the uppercase and lowercase letters you typed in the Containing Text field, choose the Case Sensitive command from the Options menu.*

Find a File by Its Date

1 Click the Start button, point to Find, and choose Files Or Folders.

2 Click the Date Modified tab.

3 Select the range of dates to search.

4 Click Find Now.

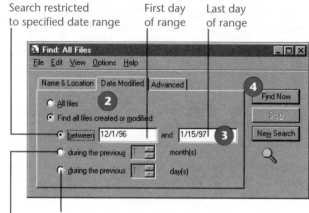

Search restricted to specified date range

First day of range

Last day of range

Search restricted to range from current date to specified number of days ago

Search restricted to range from current date to specified number of months ago

Find a File by Its Type, Content, or Size

1 Click the Advanced tab.

2 Enter the search information.

3 Click Find Now.

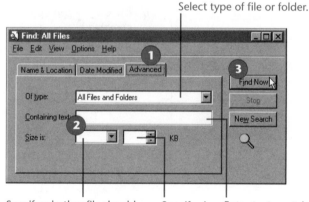

Select type of file or folder.

Specify whether file should be larger or smaller than specified value.

Specify size threshold.

Enter text contained in the file.

Conducting and Reusing a Search

If you conduct a search and want to use the search results at a later time, or if you frequently conduct a search using the same criteria, you can save the search and its results for later use.

TIP

Specify as much information as possible to limit the search; otherwise, you might end up wading through a long list of possibilities.

Set Up and Conduct a Search

1 Click the Start button, point to Find, and choose Files Or Folders.

2 Enter your search criteria in the Find dialog box and click Find Now.

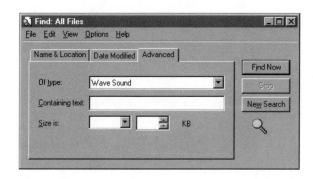

Save the Search and Its Results

1 Choose Save Results from the Options menu if there's not already a check mark next to it.

2 Choose Save Search from the File menu.

Check mark shows that search results will be saved with search.

Reuse a Search

1 Double-click the search results on the Windows NT Desktop.

2 Use the results of the previous search or rerun the search to update the list.

3

Organizing Your Folders

Windows NT provides the basic filing structure for you—drives and ready-made folders such as Personal and Printers. You can customize the filing system by adding your own folders, or even adding folders inside folders (subfolders).

TIP

Off Limits! *There are some locations in which you can't create your own folders—for example, the My Computer window, the Printers and Control Panel folders, or any network folder to which you don't have full access. In these cases, the New command won't be on the submenu.*

Create a Folder

1. Open the folder or drive that is to contain the new folder.

2. Point to an empty part of the window and right-click.

3. Point to New.

4. Choose Folder.

5. Type a name, and press Enter.

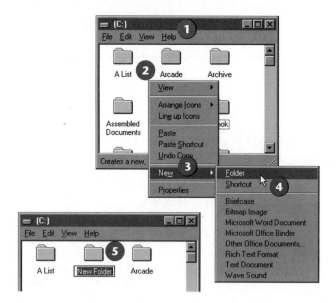

Move or Copy a Folder into Another Folder

1. Open the window containing the folder to be moved or copied.

2. Open the destination folder.

3. Select the folder to be moved or copied.

4. To move the folder, drag it and drop it in the destination-folder window. To copy a folder, hold down the Ctrl key while you drag the folder.

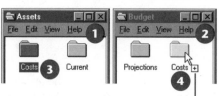

Plus sign shows the folder is being copied.

Renaming or Deleting a Folder

It's quick and easy to rename your folders, or to edit a misspelled folder name. Deleting a folder is even easier—in fact, it's *so* easy that Windows NT asks you for confirmation. However, if you *do* accidentally delete a folder from your hard disk, don't panic—you can usually retrieve it from the Recycle Bin.

SEE ALSO

"Recovering a Deleted Item" on page 42 for information about retrieving a deleted folder from the Recycle Bin.

TIP

Take the Windows NT confirmation check seriously. If you delete a folder or a file from a floppy disk or a network location, you won't be able to recover it. Lose an important file this way just once, and you'll quickly become a believer in routine backups!

Rename a Folder

1. Click the folder to select it.

2. Click the folder name (not the folder icon).

3. With the name selected, type a new name, or click to position the insertion point and then edit the name.

4. Press Enter.

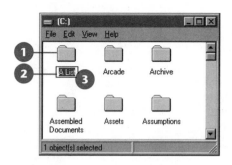

Delete a Folder

1. Open the drive or folder containing the folder to be deleted.

2. Select the folder.

3. Press the Delete key.

4. Click Yes to delete the folder or file and send it to the Recycle Bin.

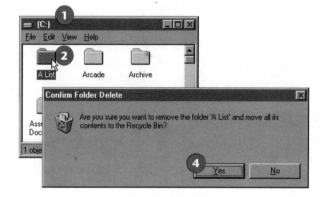

Organizing Your Files

If you work with a limited number of files, you can easily keep them all in the Personal folder that Windows NT provides. However, if you have many files or files dealing with different projects, you'll probably want to organize them by placing them in individual folders.

TIP

Use the Shift to Shift!
When you drag a file to a folder that's on a different drive, Windows NT copies the file but doesn't move it. To move it, hold down the Shift key while you drag the file.

Move a File into a Subfolder

1 Open the window containing the file and the subfolder.

2 Select the file to be moved.

3 Drag the file and drop it on top of the subfolder.

Move a File into Another Folder

1 Open the window containing the file to be moved.

2 Open the destination folder.

3 Select the file to be moved.

4 Drag the file to the destination folder and drop it on a blank spot.

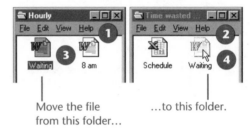

Move the file from this folder...

...to this folder.

TIP

To select a series of contiguous files, click the first file, hold down the Shift key, and then click the last file. To deselect one of the files, hold down the Ctrl key and click the selected file.

SEE ALSO

"Exploring with Windows NT Explorer" on page 46 for information about moving files among several different folders.

Copy a File into a Folder

1 Open the window containing the file to be copied.

2 Open the destination folder.

3 Select the file to be copied.

4 Hold down the Ctrl key, drag the file to the destination folder, and drop the file's copy on a blank spot.

 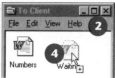

Move or Copy Several Files

1 Select the files to be moved or copied.

2 Point to any one of the selected files, holding down the Ctrl key if the files are to be copied, and then drag the files and drop them at the new location.

Select the files you want to move or copy. Hold down the Ctrl key and click to select multiple files.

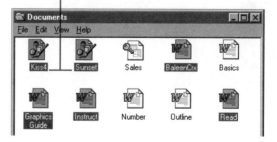

Storing Information on a Floppy Disk

If you use floppy disks to transport or archive information, Windows NT provides easy access to your disks. If you have a disk that's not preformatted, or if you want to quickly erase and reuse a disk, you'll need to format the disk before you can use it.

Format a Floppy Disk

1 Place the disk in your floppy drive.

2 Double-click My Computer on the Windows NT Desktop.

3 Right-click the floppy drive.

4 Choose Format from the shortcut menu.

5 Select the formatting options you want.

6 Click Start.

7 Click OK to confirm that it's safe to format the disk, and click OK after the disk has been formatted.

8 Click Close when you've finished.

Select the correct density for the disk.

Select the filing system for the files and the destination system.

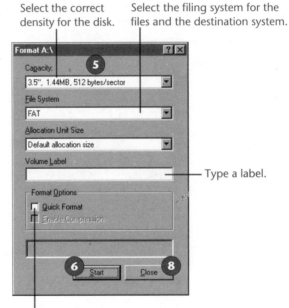

Type a label.

Turn on if you simply want to erase the directory (provides quicker formatting but does not fully clean the disk).

TIP

Look Before You Delete!

When you're duplicating a disk, any existing information on the destination disk will be deleted, so check the contents of the disk before using it.

TRY THIS

To see how much free space you have on a floppy disk, place the disk in the drive, open your My Computer window, right-click the floppy drive, and choose Properties from the shortcut menu. The General tab displays the amounts of used and free space.

TIP

Always label both disks before you duplicate a disk, to make sure that you don't use the same disk as both source and destination disk.

Copy Files or Folders to a Floppy Disk

1. Place a disk in your floppy drive.

2. Open the window containing the files or folders to be copied.

3. Select the files or folders to be copied.

4. Right-click a selected file or folder.

5. Point to Send To on the shortcut menu.

6. Click the floppy drive that contains the disk.

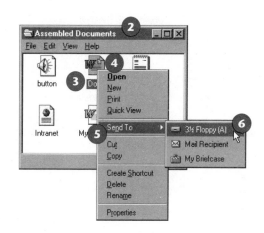

Duplicate a Floppy Disk

1. Place the disk to be duplicated in your floppy drive.

2. Open the My Computer window, right-click the drive containing the disk, and point to Copy Disk.

3. Select the drives to be used.

4. Click Start.

5. Click Close when copying has been completed.

You can copy only between drives of the same type. If you're using a single drive, switch disks when requested.

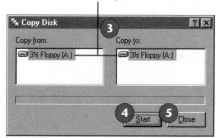

Creating Shortcuts

Windows NT provides quick access to programs, documents, and folders by using shortcuts. Shortcuts are little files that contain the information that's needed to locate and start a program, to locate and open a file, or to locate and open a window for a folder. Because shortcuts use so little space, you can create as many as you want—placing several shortcuts to the same document in different locations, for example—so that you can get to almost anything from almost anywhere.

TIP

You can also create shortcuts to network, intranet, and Internet locations.

SEE ALSO

"Creating Quick Access to a Network Resource" on page 87 for information about creating a shortcut to a network location.

Create a Shortcut

1 Open the window containing the folder, document, or program.

2 Right-click its icon.

3 Choose Create Shortcut from the shortcut menu.

4 Drag the shortcut to the location you want. Hold down the Ctrl key if you want to copy the shortcut.

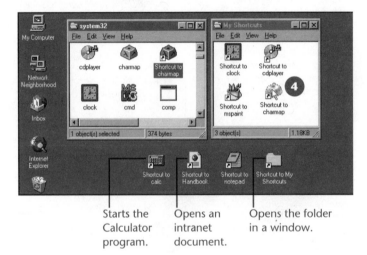

Starts the Calculator program.

Opens an intranet document.

Opens the folder in a window.

TRY THIS

Create a folder and fill it with shortcuts to your favorite locations. Then create a shortcut to this folder and place it on your Desktop. Without cluttering up your Desktop, you now have access to many shortcuts.

TIP

You can create different shortcuts to the same item, but you should set different properties for each shortcut. For example, in one shortcut you might add some command-line switches to start your word processor with no document loaded, whereas in another shortcut you might have the word processor start with a blank document. Shortcuts are easy and powerful methods to modify the way a program starts. (See your program's documentation for alternative ways of starting the program with command-line switches.)

Customize a Shortcut

1 Right-click the shortcut whose setting you want to change.

2 Choose Properties from the shortcut menu.

3 Click the Shortcut tab.

4 Change the settings.

5 Click OK.

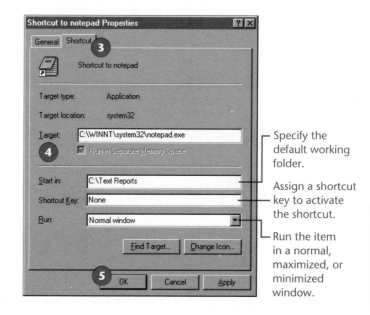

Specify the default working folder.

Assign a shortcut key to activate the shortcut.

Run the item in a normal, maximized, or minimized window.

3

Recovering a Deleted Item

If you mistakenly delete a file, folder, or shortcut from your computer's hard disk you can quickly recover the deleted item by either undoing your action or restoring the deleted item from the Recycle Bin. The Recycle Bin holds all the files you've deleted from your hard disk until you empty the bin or until it gets so full that the oldest files are automatically deleted.

Undo a Deletion

1. Point to an empty part of the Windows NT Desktop or to an empty part of any folder window, and right-click.

2. Choose Undo Delete from the shortcut menu.

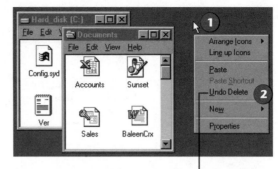

Available only if the deletion was your last action

Restore an Item from the Recycle Bin

1. Double-click the Recycle Bin icon on the Windows NT Desktop.

2. Select the item or items to be recovered, and right-click.

3. Choose Restore from the shortcut menu.

4. Click the Close button to close the Recycle Bin.

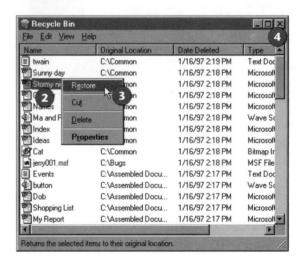

Displaying MS-DOS Paths and Filename Extensions

If you miss seeing all that familiar MS-DOS information—paths and filename extensions—you can have Windows NT display the path to the active folder, and list the file extensions for every file.

TIP

If the filename extension is displayed when you rename a file, make sure you include the original extension in the new filename. If you omit it, Windows NT won't know what type of file it is. When the filename extension isn't displayed, Windows NT automatically attaches the original extension to the file.

SEE ALSO

Section 7, "Running MS-DOS," starting on page 111, for information about working in MS-DOS.

Display MS-DOS Information

1. Double-click My Computer on the Windows NT Desktop.

2. Choose Options from the View menu.

3. Click the View tab.

4. Turn on the Display The Full Path In The Title Bar check box.

5. Turn off the Hide File Extensions For Known File Types check box.

6. Click OK.

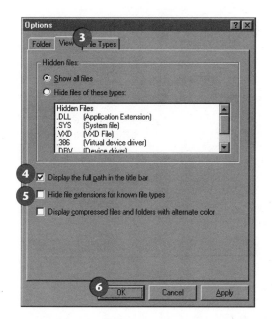

MS-DOS path in title bar

Filename includes MS-DOS filename extension.

Hiding or Displaying System Files

System files are those files with strange names that occupy many of the folders used by the operating system and by some of your programs. You'll rarely—*if ever*—want to move, delete, or rename any system files. By hiding them, you protect yourself from the horrors that can occur when a critical file is accidentally deleted. Although the files are hidden from view, they still exist in their folders, the programs that need to access them can still find them, and you and your computer will be happy. However, if you need to do some system maintenance, *and* if you really know what you're doing, you can manually replace some system files.

Hide or Display System Files

1 Choose Options from the View menu.

2 Click the View tab.

3 Click the Hide Files Of These Types option button to hide the system files, or click Show All Files to display the system files. (When you set Windows NT to show all files, you also display any files or folders that have the Hidden attribute turned on.)

4 Click OK.

System files displayed

System files hidden

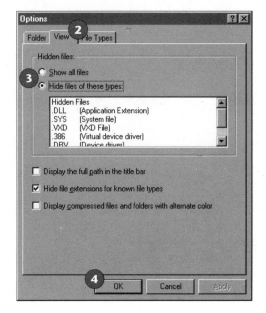

Meet Windows NT Explorer

Windows NT Explorer has functions similar to those of the folder windows that you reach from My Computer. The list of computers, disks, and folders (often called a *directory tree*) in the left pane gives you direct access to any drive or folder on your computer or on a network. You can click the plus sign next to a drive or folder name to expand that branch of the tree structure and see the subfolders, and then click the minus sign to collapse the branch and hide the subfolders again. The right pane shows you the contents of whatever item you select in the left pane.

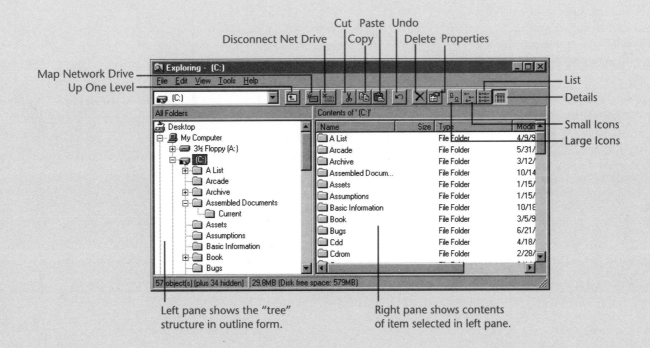

Left pane shows the "tree" structure in outline form.

Right pane shows contents of item selected in left pane.

Exploring with Windows NT Explorer

If you're new to Windows NT, take a few minutes to go exploring with Windows NT Explorer. If you're a long-time Windows or Windows NT user and you liked using File Manager in earlier versions, you'll feel right at home with Windows NT Explorer.

SEE ALSO

"Managing Files with Windows NT Explorer" on page 48 for information about copying and moving files and folders with Windows NT Explorer.

Explore

1. Click the Start button, point to Programs, and choose Windows NT Explorer from the submenu.

2. Click through the drives and folders in the left pane to reach the folder you want to explore. Use the plus or minus signs to display or hide subfolders.

3. Click any folder to see a listing of its contents displayed in the right pane.

Click a plus sign to expand the listing and display the folders it contains.

Click a minus sign to collapse the listing and hide the folders it contains.

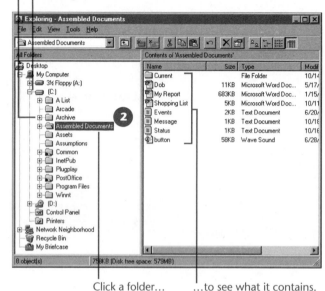

Click a folder...   ...to see what it contains.

Searching for a File with Windows NT Explorer

If you want to find a file but don't know its exact location, you can search for it in Windows NT Explorer. By starting in a specific folder, you can narrow down the search and save a bit of time.

TRY THIS

Open a folder that contains subfolders. Open the Find dialog box, leave the Named box blank, turn on the Include Subfolders check box, and run the search. The returned results include a full list of all the files in the folder and all the files in the subfolders.

SEE ALSO

"Locating a File by Date or Content" on page 32 for information about completing the different tabs.

Search for a File

1. In the left pane, open the drive or folder that you know contains the file.

2. Choose Find from the Tools menu, and then choose Files Or Folders from the submenu.

3. Type the name of the file, or as much of it as you can remember.

4. Fill in as much information as you can on the Date Modified and Advanced tabs.

5. Click Find Now.

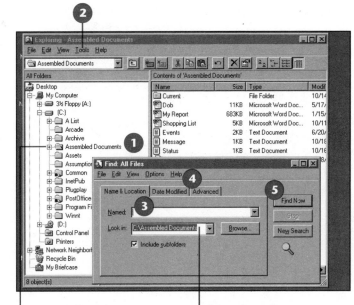

The open folder... ...determines where the search is started.

Managing Files with Windows NT Explorer

With Windows NT Explorer you can quickly and easily copy or move any files or folders on any drive that is accessible to your computer.

TIP

To select several contiguous files to be copied, moved, or deleted, click the first filename, hold down the Shift key, and then click the last filename in the series. To select non-contiguous files, hold down the Ctrl key and click each filename.

Copy or Move Files and Folders

1 Expand the drive and any folders to display the folder containing the files or folders to be moved or copied.

2 Click the folder to display its contents in the right pane.

3 Select the files or folders.

4 Drag and drop the files or folders into the destination folder. However:

◆ If you want to copy a file or folder to a folder on the same drive, hold down the Ctrl key while dragging.

◆ If you want to move a file or folder to another drive, hold down the Shift key while dragging.

Drop when destination folder becomes selected.

Multiple selected files to be copied

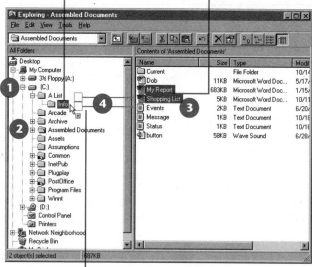

Files are being copied.

TRY THIS

If you miss the double-pane functionality of File Manager that you had in previous versions of Windows, you can re-create it. With Windows NT Explorer running, start Windows NT Explorer again from the Start menu. You now have two Windows NT Explorer windows on your Desktop. Arrange the windows so that one window is above the other. Voilà! The arrangement of File Manager with the power of Windows NT Explorer!

TIP

Still miss the real thing? Well, File Manager is still around. You can run it by starting the WinFile program in the System 32 folder, but you'll soon find that it isn't nearly as powerful as Windows NT Explorer.

Create a Folder

1 Select the drive or folder that is to contain the new folder.

2 Right-click any blank spot in the right pane.

3 Choose New from the shortcut menu.

4 Choose Folder.

5 Type a name for the new folder, and press Enter.

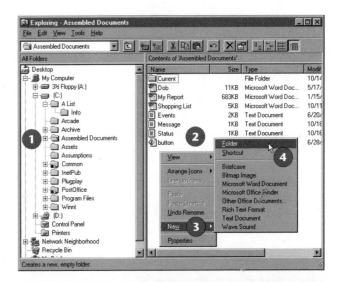

Deleting Files or Folders in Windows NT Explorer

You can quickly and easily delete any file or folder on any drive that is accessible to your computer. If you're deleting a file or folder from your hard disk, the file is sent to the Recycle Bin. If you're deleting a file or folder from a floppy disk or from a network location, the file or folder is *permanently* deleted—so be careful!

Delete a File or Folder

1 In the right pane of Windows NT Explorer, select the file or folder on your computer to be deleted.

2 Press the Delete key.

3 Click Yes to delete the item(s) and send it to the Recycle Bin, or click No if you change your mind and decide not to delete the item(s).

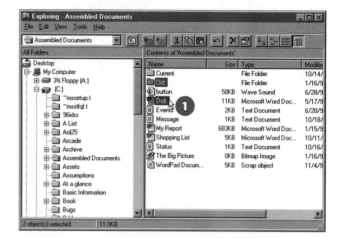

When you delete items from the hard disk, Windows NT tells you how many items you're deleting and then stores the deleted items in the Recycle Bin.

When you delete items from a network drive or from a floppy disk, Windows NT tells you how many items you're deleting and reminds you that the items will be permanently deleted.

Customizing Windows NT Explorer

Just as you can customize the folder windows that you access from My Computer, you can change the look of Windows NT Explorer. By displaying only the window components that you use and changing the view, you can maximize your access to information.

SEE ALSO

"Displaying MS-DOS Paths and Filename Extensions" on page 43 for information about displaying MS-DOS paths and filename extensions.

TIP

The type of view you choose affects only the right pane. You can't modify the view in the left pane.

Display or Hide Components

1 Click the View menu.

2 Choose a command to change the appearance of the window:

  ◆ Turn the Toolbar or Status Bar command on or off to display or hide the toolbar or status bar.

  ◆ Click a view to change the type of view.

3 Choose Options from the View menu, and on the View tab, turn the Include Description Bar For Right And Left Panes option on or off to display or hide the description bar.

Resize the Panes

1 Position the mouse pointer over the border that separates the left and right panes, until the mouse pointer changes into the Resize pointer.

2 Drag the border to the left or right and drop it at a new location.

Bullet indicates that List view is displayed.

Check mark indicates that status bar is displayed.

Description bar

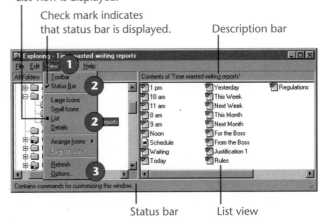

Status bar   List view

Drag the border to a new location.

Working with Programs

Getting to know the programs that come with Windows NT is a bit like moving into a new house or apartment. Just as your new abode has the basics—stove, refrigerator, bathtub, and (dare we say it?) windows—the Windows NT operating system comes with several useful accessories and tools. Just as you'll add dishes, furniture, rugs, and all the other accoutrements that turn empty rooms into a home, you'll add other programs to Windows NT to utilize its full potential as you work (and play).

But take a look at the basics first. There's WordPad, a handy little word processor for quick notes, and Paint, an easy-to-use graphics program. Windows NT comes with other goodies, too—mail capabilities, multimedia, and lots of accessory programs—but we'll save those for later. Right now we'll cover some quick ways to accomplish everyday tasks—switching between multiple programs with a single mouse-click, for example, and copying items between documents that were created in different programs.

And, just as you might customize the walls of your living quarters with paintings or wallpaper, you can have some fun redecorating your Windows NT Desktop with your own highly individual "wallpaper" creations.

Managing Multiple Programs

Windows NT lets you run several programs at the same time. You can have more than one open program window on your screen and can easily switch between programs. If you prefer, you can park your running programs neatly on the taskbar, where they'll sit snoozing quietly until you need them. To make one or all of them instantly spring back to life on your screen, just click their program buttons.

TRY THIS

Look, Ma, I'm Multitasking!
Arrange your program windows by tiling them. To make the full screen available as you work, click the Maximize button. When you want to switch to another program, just click the Restore button, and the first program will return to its tiled position.

Switch Between Program Windows

1 If you have several overlapping program windows on your screen, click in any visible part of an open window to bring it to the front of your screen and make it the active program— that is, the program you're working on now.

2 If the program window is minimized or is obscured by other windows, click the program button on the taskbar.

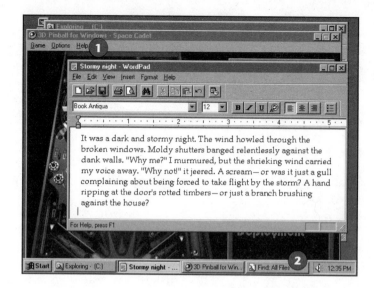

Creating a Document

You can create and name a blank document for any of the programs you have installed. When you're ready to get to work, you simply double-click the document, and it opens, ready for you to add content. This way, the document is named and located in the correct folder—and you don't need to look around for the program and open it.

TRY THIS

Get Organized! *When you're starting a new project, or adding information to an existing one, try creating blank word-processor documents for correspondence, blank spreadsheet documents for financial records or schedules, and so on. Put them all in the main project folder. Then just double-click each one and drop in your information—quick, easy, and so well organized! You concentrate on what to put in the documents and let Windows NT worry about which programs to run.*

Create a Document

1. Open the folder that is to contain the new document.

2. Point to an empty part of the window and right-click.

3. Choose New from the shortcut menu.

4. Click a document type.

5. Type a name for the new document, and press Enter.

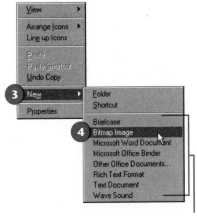

Windows lists documents only for programs that are installed.

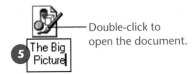

Double-click to open the document.

4

Creating a WordPad Document with Formatted Text

WordPad—a program that comes with the Windows NT operating system—can create and open Microsoft Word 6 documents, Microsoft Write documents, Rich Text Format (RTF) documents, and text documents. It can open but not create Microsoft Write documents. WordPad isn't a full-featured word processor, but it's ideal for quick notes. For anything more ambitious, you'll want to use a program such as Word.

TIP

If WordPad isn't on your Start menu, you can add it using Add/Remove Programs in the Control Panel.

Start WordPad, and Format the Page

1. Click the Start button, point to Programs and then to Accessories, and choose WordPad.

2. Choose Page Setup from the File menu to display the Page Setup dialog box.

3. Specify paper size, paper source, orientation, and margins.

4. Click OK.

5. Save the document.

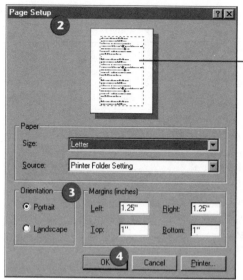

Portrait orientation, shown here, is a page that's longer than it is wide. Landscape orientation is a page that's wider than it is long.

Enter and Format Text

1. Use the View menu to display the Standard and the Formatting toolbars if they're not already visible.

2. Use the drop-down lists and buttons to format the text you're going to type.

3. Type your text.

4. Select any text you want to reformat, and use the formatting tools.

5. Save the document.

Click a "pushed-in" button to turn off formatting.

Click a button to turn on formatting.

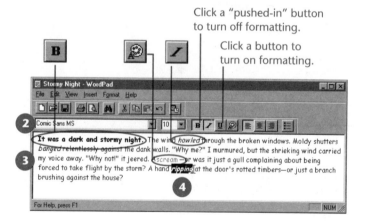

SEE ALSO

"Adding or Removing Windows NT Components" on page 232 for information about installing Windows components.

TIP

How Do You Measure Up?
You can use units other than inches. To set a different unit of measurement as the default, choose Options from the View menu and, on the Options tab, select the unit of measure you want.

TIP

Point to a button on any toolbar, and wait for a tooltip to appear to identify the button.

Format the Paragraphs

1 Choose Ruler from the View menu if the ruler isn't displayed.

2 Click in the paragraph to be formatted, or select all the paragraphs that you want to have the same formatting.

3 Use any of the formatting tools:

   ◆ Alignment buttons

   ◆ Bullets button

   ◆ Indent markers

   ◆ Tab markers

4 Save the document.

Drag for left indent.

Drag for first-line indent.

Click to set tab.

Click to set alignment.

Drag for right indent.

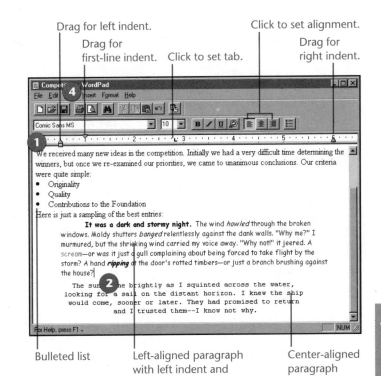

Bulleted list

Left-aligned paragraph with left indent and first-line indent

Center-aligned paragraph

Adding a Picture to a WordPad Document

You can create a picture in a program such as Paint and add it to a WordPad document, or you can add an existing picture from a picture file to a WordPad document. Either way, the picture is placed in WordPad as an object.

TIP

You can insert different types of objects, depending on the programs that are installed on your computer. The Object Type list in the Insert Object dialog box shows the various types of objects supported by your system.

Create and Insert a Picture

1 Start WordPad, add and format your text, and position the insertion point where you want to place the picture.

2 Choose Object from the Insert menu to display the Insert Object dialog box.

3 Select the Create New option.

4 Select Bitmap Image as the Object Type.

5 Click OK.

6 Create a picture in the frame, using Paint's menus and controls, which temporarily replace WordPad's menus and controls.

7 Click outside the frame to deselect the object and return to WordPad.

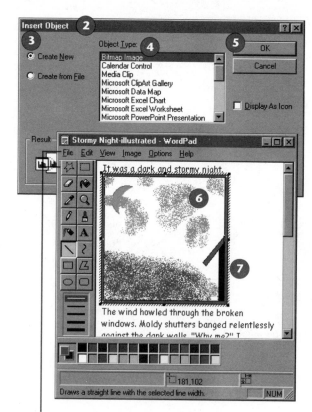

Paint's tools and menus are displayed in the WordPad window.

SEE ALSO

"Creating a WordPad Document with Formatted Text" on page 56 for information about basic text formatting.

"Creating a Picture" on page 64 for information about creating a picture in Paint.

"Copying Material Between Documents" on page 70 for information about including part of an existing picture.

"Linking to Information That Changes" on page 72 for information about linking to a document.

TIP

After you've inserted a picture, choose Print Preview from the File menu to verify that the layout of the page is correct.

Resize a Picture

1. Click the picture to select it.

2. Drag and drop a sizing handle to change the size of the picture. If you change only the height or only the width, the picture becomes distorted.

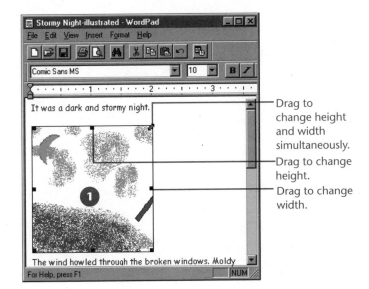

Drag to change height and width simultaneously.

Drag to change height.

Drag to change width.

Editing Text Documents in WordPad

You can use WordPad to edit Microsoft Word, Microsoft Write, Rich Text Format (RTF), or text-only (ANSI and ASCII) documents.

TIP

When you use WordPad to edit a document that was created in Word, you'll lose any special formatting that WordPad doesn't support.

TIP

To keep a copy of the original document as well as your edited version, use the Save As command on the File menu to save the document under a different filename.

Open a Document

1. Start WordPad if it's not already running.
2. Click the Open button on the Toolbar.
3. Select the type of document to be opened.
4. Find and select the document.
5. Click Open.

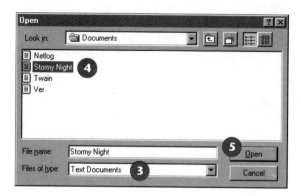

Insert or Delete Text

1. Click where you want to insert the text.
2. Type the text.
3. Select text to be deleted by dragging the mouse pointer over the text.
4. Press the Delete key to delete the text.

It was a dark night. The wind nearly howled through the broken windows. Moldy shutters banged relentlessly against the dank walls. "Why me?" I murmured, but the

It was a dark and stormy night. The wind nearly howled through the broken windows. Moldy shutters banged relentlessly against the dank walls. "Why me?" I murmured,

It was a dark and stormy night. The wind nearly howled through the broken windows. Moldy shutters banged relentlessly against the dank walls. "Why me?" I murmured,

It was a dark and stormy night. The wind howled through the broken windows. Moldy shutters banged relentlessly against the dank walls. "Why me?" I murmured, but the

TIP

Presto Change-o. *To replace repetitive words or phrases throughout the document, use the Replace command on the Edit menu.*

SEE ALSO

"Creating a WordPad Document with Formatted Text" on page 56 for information about changing the format of text.

"Print a Document Using a Specific Printer" on page 98 to print your document using a printer other than the default printer.

Replace Text

1 Select the text to be replaced by dragging the mouse pointer over the text.

2 Type the new text. The selected text is deleted.

Selected text is replaced...

It was a dark and stormy night. The wind howled through the broken windows. Moldy shutters banged relentlessly against the wet walls. "Why me?" I murmured, but the

...when you type new text.

It was a dark and stormy night. The wind howled through the broken windows. Moldy shutters banged relentlessly against the dank walls. "Why me?" I murmured, but the

Move Text

1 Select the text to be moved by dragging the mouse pointer over the text.

2 Point to the selected text.

3 Drag the text and drop it in a new location.

Drag the selected text to a new location.

It was a dark and stormy night. The wind howled through the broken windows. Moldy shutters banged relentlessly against the dank walls. "Why me?" I murmured, but the wind shrieking carried my voice away. "Why not!" it jeered. A scream—or was it just a gull complaining about

It was a dark and stormy night. The wind howled through the broken windows. Moldy shutters banged relentlessly against the dank walls. "Why me?" I murmured, but the shrieking wind carried my voice away. "Why not!" it jeered. A scream—or was it just a gull complaining about

Save and Print a Document

1 Click the Save button to save the document in the same format and with the same name.

2 Click the Print button to print the document using the default printer.

Creating a Text-Only Document

Text-only documents are useful in many circumstances. They are often used in program files (the well-known and dreaded INI and BAT files, for example), and they are useful when you're transferring information between documents that were created in different programs, because almost all word processors, editors, and viewers can read text-only files. A text-only document is exactly that: bare-bones text with no formatting information. If you want to indent the paragraphs or apply bold or italic formatting, you'll need to save the document as a Word document or as an RTF document.

TIP

All for Naught. *Any formatting or inserted objects will be lost if you save the document as a text document.*

Start WordPad for Text

1 Start WordPad.

2 Choose New from the File menu to display the New dialog box.

3 Select Text Document.

4 Click OK.

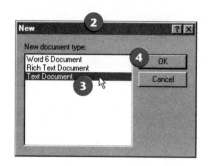

Customize Your View

1 Choose Options from the View menu to display the Options dialog box.

2 Click the Text tab.

3 Select the options for your display. (Any line wrapping you set changes the display of the file but doesn't change the contents of the file.)

4 Click OK.

Select to see line breaks as they appear in the file.

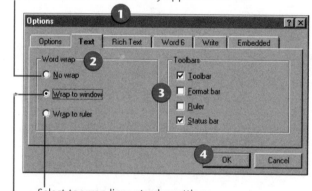

Select to wrap lines at ruler settings.

Select to wrap lines at the right edge of the window.

TIP

To remove the temptation to add formatting to your text-only documents, keep the Formatting toolbar turned off.

TIP

Notepad is the traditional Windows program for working with text, but WordPad provides an easier and friendlier environment. However, if you need to save your text as Unicode text for compatibility with other programs, use Notepad rather than WordPad.

SEE ALSO

"Specifying Which Program Opens a Document" on page 210 for information about making WordPad the default text editor.

Create and Save Your Text

1. Type your text, pressing Enter when you want to start a new line.

2. Click the Save button.

3. Open the folder where the document will be stored.

4. Type a filename. You can use up to 250 characters, including spaces, but you can't use the \ / * ? < > and | characters.

5. Save the document.

Shows folder that is open.

Keep double-clicking folders until you open the one you want.

Creating a Picture

If you're feeling artistic, you can create a picture in Paint. The Paint program comes with Windows NT and was designed to create and edit bitmap pictures. (A bitmap is just that: a map created from small dots, or bits. It's a lot like a piece of graph paper with some squares filled in and others left blank to create a picture.) Although you can print your picture if you want to, Paint pictures are usually inserted into other documents as *embedded* or *linked* objects. You can also create a Paint picture and use it as the wallpaper for your Windows NT Desktop.

SEE ALSO

"Copying Material Between Documents" on page 70 for information about embedding an object in a document.

"Linking to Information That Changes" on page 72 for information about linking an object.

Create a Picture

1. Click the Start button, point to Programs and then Accessories, and choose Paint.

2. Click a drawing tool.

3. Click the color you want to use.

4. Click an option for the selected tool.

5. Click to start the drawing.

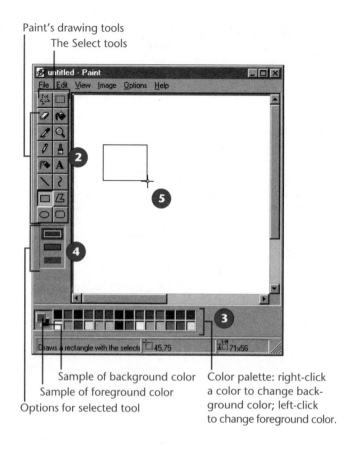

Paint's drawing tools

The Select tools

Sample of background color

Sample of foreground color

Options for selected tool

Color palette: right-click a color to change background color; left-click to change foreground color.

TIP

Bitmaps or Drawings?

A bitmap is a picture in which each line, circle, or shape is an integrated part of the picture—just like a picture drawn on paper. A drawing is a picture in which each line, circle, or shape is treated as an individually drawn object—like a collage assembled with cutout shapes. The Paint program creates bitmaps and is nice because of its simplicity. Drawing programs are useful for complex drawings and for pictures that need extensive editing.

TIP

Bitmap documents can be quite large. You can limit their size by saving the file at the lowest color depth that doesn't compromise the picture's quality. Unless it is a very high quality image, a 256-color bitmap is usually sufficient.

TIP

Use the Undo command on the Edit menu if you want to remove your last drawing action. Use the Undo command again to remove the previous drawing action.

Use the Tools

1 Hold down a mouse button and drag the shapes you want:

- ◆ Hold down the left mouse button to draw with the foreground color.

- ◆ Hold down the right mouse button to draw with the background color.

2 Hold down the Shift key for special effects when drawing shapes:

- ◆ Ellipse tool creates a circle.

- ◆ Rectangle tool creates a square.

- ◆ Rounded Rectangle tool creates a square with rounded corners.

- ◆ Line tool draws a horizontal, vertical, or diagonal line.

3 Keep choosing appropriate tools, colors, and options to complete your picture.

4 Save the picture periodically.

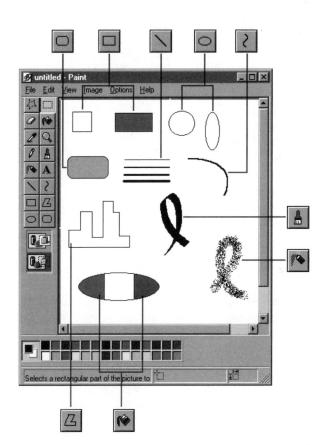

4

Editing a Picture

It's easy and fun to modify an existing bitmap picture to customize it, or to create a new picture using only part of the original picture. However, the picture must be a bitmap; if it isn't, you'll need a different program (rather than Paint) in which to edit it.

> **TIP**
>
> *To replace one color with another, set the foreground color to the color to be replaced and the background color to the replacement color. Select the Eraser tool, and then hold down the right mouse button and drag the Eraser over the area where you want to replace the color.*

> **TIP**
>
> *If you don't see a thumbnail version of your picture, choose Zoom from the View menu, and then choose Show Thumbnail.*

Edit a Picture

1. Start Paint if it isn't already running.

2. Choose Open from the File menu, locate the bitmap picture to be edited, and click Open.

3. Use the drawing tools to edit the picture.

4. Use the Magnifier tool to magnify the details so that you can fine-tune your edits.

5. Press Ctrl+G to turn on the grid if it's not already turned on. (The grid isn't visible in Normal Size or at 2x magnification.)

6. Click the Magnifier tool again to restore the view to Normal Size.

7. Save the picture.

8. If you want to rename the file, choose Save As from the File menu, and type a new name for the picture.

Use the Magnifier tool.

Thumbnail shows context for the magnified area.

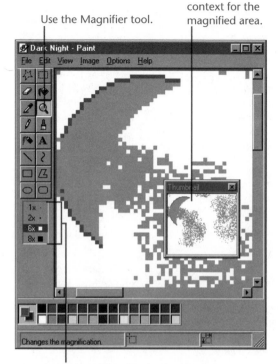

Select the level of magnification.

SEE ALSO

"Editing Inserted Material" on page 74 for information about editing a picture that is contained in another document.

"Changing the Look of the Desktop" on page 182 for information about using the patterns and pictures that come with Windows NT.

TRY THIS

Not So Opaque. *Click a Select tool. Click the Opaque Paste option and paste in a picture. With the inserted picture still selected, in the Color Box right-click the color that is the main background color in the inserted picture. Then, with the picture still selected, click the Transparent Paste option.*

Modify the Picture

1 Use one of the Select tools to select the part of the picture you want to work on. The illustration at the right shows a few examples of what you can do.

2 Use the Eraser tool to replace all colors with the background color.

Drag a handle... ...to resize the selection.

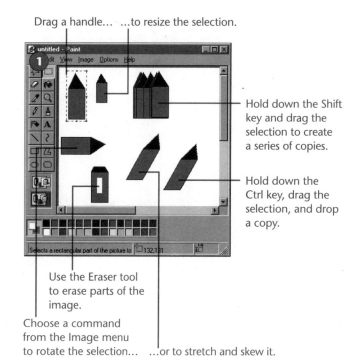

Hold down the Shift key and drag the selection to create a series of copies.

Hold down the Ctrl key, drag the selection, and drop a copy.

Use the Eraser tool to erase parts of the image.

Choose a command from the Image menu to rotate the selection... ...or to stretch and skew it.

4

Adding a Picture to a Picture

By combining all or part of one bitmap picture with another bitmap picture, you can create an interesting and complex drawing.

TIP

You can have the Paint program running in more than one window at a time. That way, you can switch between the pictures, copying and pasting the parts you want to use.

TRY THIS

To use a picture that isn't a bitmap, capture it as a bitmap. Here's how. Open the picture in a program that displays it. Press the Print Screen key to capture the picture, switch to Paint, and paste the picture. Select the part of the picture you want, and copy it to a file. (Whenever you copy a picture, be sure that you're not violating any copyright rules.)

Get a Part of a Picture

1 Open the picture in Paint.

2 Use one of the Select tools to select the area to be saved.

3 Choose Copy To from the Edit menu.

4 In the Copy To dialog box, open the folder that will contain the picture, type a filename, and select the type of bitmap to be used.

Copy the selection to a new document.

Combine the Pictures

1 Open the picture that is to include another picture.

2 Click one of the Select tools.

3 Click Opaque Paste or Transparent Paste.

4 Choose Paste From from the Edit menu.

5 Locate the picture to be copied, and click Open.

6 Drag the pasted picture and drop it where you want it. Click outside the selection to deselect the pasted picture.

Drop the pasted picture where you want it.

Transparent Paste

Use Opaque Paste to include the pasted picture's background.

Adding Text to a Picture

You can add text to your picture, using any of the fonts on your system, by putting the text in a text box. While the text box is open, you can format and edit the text; but once you move on to another part of the picture, the text becomes part of the picture and you can't edit the text any further.

TIP

When you click outside the text box, the text characters are converted into bitmap images, so the lettering will look more jagged than normal text does. Edit the text as you would edit any other picture elements.

Add Text

1 Click the Text tool.

2 Drag out a text box for the text.

3 Choose the font, font size, and any emphasis you want to apply.

4 Type the text, and make any editing and formatting changes you want.

5 Click outside the text box to deselect it.

6 Save the picture.

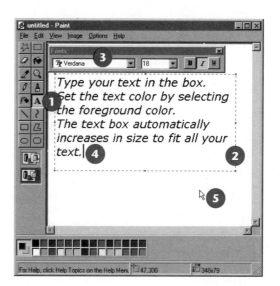

4

Copying Material Between Documents

It's easy to copy material from a document that was created in one program to a document that was created in another program. How you insert the material depends on what it is and which programs you're using. If the item is similar to and compatible with the receiving document—text copied into a Word document, for example—it's usually inserted as is and can be edited in the receiving document's program. If the item is dissimilar— a sound clip, say, inserted into a Word document—it's either *encapsulated*, or isolated, as an object and can be edited in the originating program only, or you simply are not able to paste that item into your document.

Copy and Insert Material

1. In the source document, select the material to be copied.

2. Choose Copy from the Edit menu. Windows NT places copied items on the Clipboard. The Clipboard can hold only one item at a time, so always paste the Clipboard contents into your document before you copy anything else, or you'll lose whatever was on the Clipboard.

3. Switch to the destination document.

4. Click at the location where you want to insert the material.

5. Choose Paste from the Edit menu.

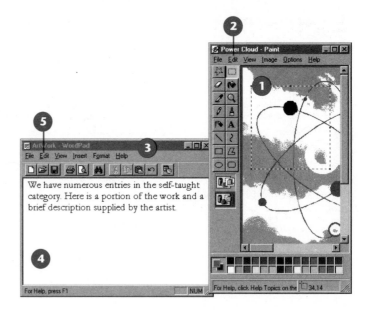

TIP

The formats listed depend on the different formats that are available for the source document and on which formats the destination document can accept.

TIP

Objects are either embedded or linked. An embedded object places all its information, or data, in the document in which it is placed. A linked object keeps most of its information in a separate file, and inserts only enough information so that the linked file can be located when necessary.

SEE ALSO

"Linking to Information that Changes" on page 72 for information about linking to files whose content changes.

Use a Different Format

1 Copy the material from the source document, and click in the destination document.

2 Choose Paste Special from the Edit menu.

3 Select the type of format in which you want the material to be inserted.

4 Click OK.

The source document and its program

The different formats available

Description of the result when you use the selected format

Copy and Insert an Entire Document

1 Use My Computer to locate and select the document to be copied.

2 Drag the document to the destination document, and drop it where you want it to appear.

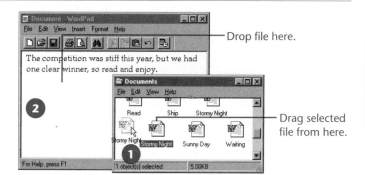

Drop file here.

Drag selected file from here.

4

Linking to Information That Changes

When the content of an item you've inserted into your document is likely to change in the source document, you can make sure that those changes are automatically updated in your document. You do this by linking to the source document. When the content of the source document changes, the changes appear in your document. But because the content resides in the source document and not in your document, the source document must be available whenever you work in your document. If you change the location of the source document, you must change the link, because the link contains the full path to the document.

Link to a Source Document

1. Locate the source document and right-click it.

2. Choose Copy from the shortcut menu.

3. Switch to the destination document.

4. Click at the location where you want to insert the item.

5. Choose Paste Special from the Edit menu.

6. Select the Paste Link option.

7. Click OK.

Source document

Check to display icon instead of content.

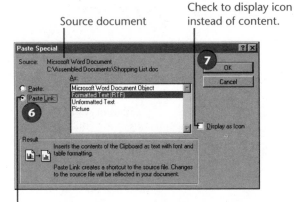

Links the inserted content to an external document.

TIP

Some programs don't support linking—check your program documentation.

TIP

If you include many large items in a document—several graphics in a Word document, for example—you can make the files easier to transfer by linking to the graphics documents instead of embedding the graphics. Files with embedded graphics can become so large that they are often difficult to fit on a single floppy disk.

TIP

What happens if the source document is no longer available depends on your program. If the linked item remains in your document but its content is never updated, your program converted the item into an embedded object; you'll need to relink the item to the source document. If you get a message telling you that the file can't be found, or if a different document appears, use the Change Source button in the Links dialog box to locate the source document and reestablish the link to the correct document at the correct location.

Change the Link

1 In your document, select the linked information.

2 Choose Links from the Edit menu.

3 Select the current link.

4 Make the changes.

Click to browse and locate moved document, or to use different document.

Click to edit document in its source program.

Click to update content from source document.

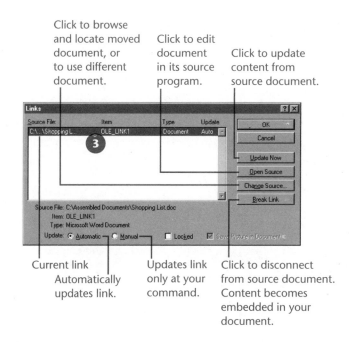

Current link
Automatically updates link.

Updates link only at your command.

Click to disconnect from source document. Content becomes embedded in your document.

Editing Inserted Material

When material from a document that was created in a different program has been inserted in your document as an *embedded object,* you can edit the inserted item *in place*—that is, in your document—using the tools of the program it which it was created.

TIP

Some programs won't let you edit inserted material in place. Instead, the source program opens automatically and you can make your edits there. When you've finished, choose the Update command from the source program's File menu to update the information in the embedded object before you exit the source program.

Edit Embedded Material in Place

1 Double-click the inserted item.

2 Use the toolbar buttons, menu commands, and any other tools that are provided by the source program to make your editing changes.

3 Click outside the selected area to return the edited material back into an object in your program and to restore your program's toolbars, menus, and other tools.

Paint menus

Paint tools

WordPad window

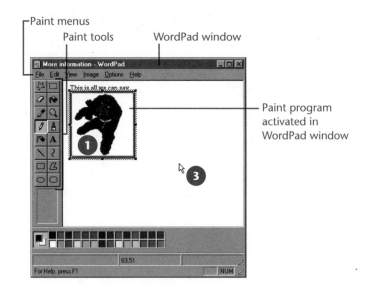

Paint program activated in WordPad window

Viewing a Document Quickly

You can view the contents of many different types of documents to verify that you've found the document you're looking for, and you can do so without spending the time it takes to start the document's program. Quick View lives up to its name!

SEE ALSO

"Adding or Removing Windows NT Components" on page 232 for information about installing Quick View.

TIP

If you've installed a viewer for a specific program—Microsoft Word Viewer, for example— that viewer will be listed on a shortcut menu instead of Quick View. This type of program-specific viewer has more capabilities than Quick View and also has the ability to print a document.

View a Document

1 Right-click the document you want to view.

2 Choose Quick View from the shortcut menu.

3 Use the Increase Font Size or Decrease Font Size button to change your view of the document. Font size changes affect only your view of a document— they don't change any information in the file.

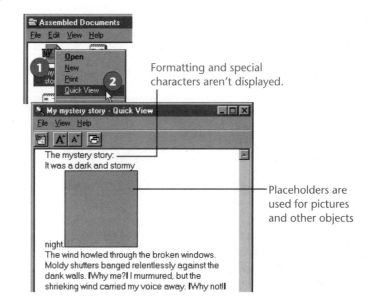

Formatting and special characters aren't displayed.

Placeholders are used for pictures and other objects

View and Open a Different Document

1 Drag the document icon and drop it in the Quick View window to display the document.

2 Choose Open File For Editing from the File menu to open the document in its source program.

Click to open the document for editing.

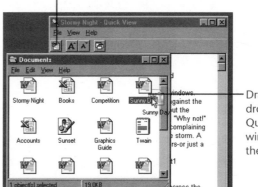

Drag the icon and drop it in the Quick View window to display the document.

4

Inserting Special Characters

Windows NT has a special accessory program called Character Map that lets you insert into your programs characters and symbols that aren't available on your keyboard. Character Map displays all the characters that are available for each of the fonts on your computer. Although Character Map shows all the characters available from Unicode fonts, you can use the Unicode characters only in programs that work with Unicode.

TIP

Unicode is a standard that's currently being adopted in many programs. It gives you a much-larger-than-normal character set, providing multi-language support within each font. If you get black boxes instead of the characters when you insert Unicode characters, however, your program probably does not support Unicode characters.

Insert Special Characters

1 Open the Start menu, point to Accessories, and click Character Map.

2 Select the font you want to use.

3 Select the character subset.

4 Click the character you want.

5 Click Select.

6 Repeat steps 4 and 5 until all the characters you want are selected.

7 Click Copy to place the characters on the Windows NT Clipboard.

8 Click Close.

9 Switch to your document, click where you want the special characters inserted, and paste them from the Clipboard.

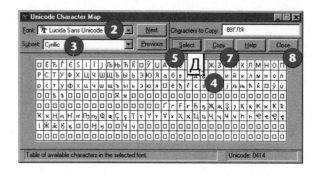

Creating Your Own Desktop Wallpaper

If you'd like to create your own Desktop wallpaper rather than using one of the ready-made patterns that come with Windows NT, you can use Paint to develop a design that expresses your personality or your mood of the day.

TIP

"Changing the Look of the Desktop" on page 182 for information about using the patterns and pictures that come with Windows NT.

Create Your Desktop Wallpaper

1 Start Paint.

2 Choose Attributes from the Image menu, and specify Width and Height.

3 Draw and save your picture.

4 Choose one of the Set As Wallpaper commands from the File menu:

◆ Choose Centered for a single full-screen picture.

◆ Choose Tiled for multiple instances of the same picture.

Set the values equal to your screen resolution for a single full-screen picture, or set them to a small value for the tiled wallpaper.

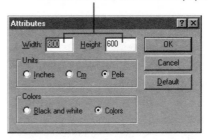

This wallpaper was created... ...by tiling this picture.

Quitting When You're Stuck

If a program isn't working properly and doesn't respond when you try to close it, Windows NT gives you an alternative course of action, which is known as "ending the task." If that doesn't work, you can log off and reset Windows NT or you can completely shut down and start anew. Whatever you do, you'll probably lose any work that you hadn't saved in the problem program. If your system locks up and you can't shut down the problem program only, you'll probably lose any unsaved work in other programs and even some Windows NT settings that you made during this session.

End the Task

1 Right-click in the taskbar, choose Task Manager from the shortcut menu, and click the Applications tab.

2 Select the program that's misbehaving.

3 Click the End Task button. If Windows NT asks if you want to wait, click End Task.

Force the End

1 If Windows NT doesn't respond when you right-click in the taskbar, press Ctrl+Alt+Delete.

2 Click the Task Manager button.

3 Select the program that's misbehaving.

4 Click the End Task button.

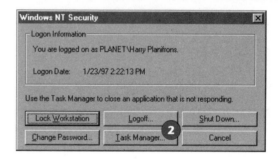

SEE ALSO

"Getting System Information" on pages 282–283 for information about using the Dr. Watson utility, which records system information when a program stops functioning correctly.

TIP

If you shut down the computer by turning off the power, you'll lose any unsaved work in all your open programs and any Windows NT settings you made in this session.

Log Off

1 If the program doesn't shut down, or if Windows NT still seems unstable, press Ctrl+Alt+Delete.

2 Click the Logoff button.

3 Click OK to confirm that you want to end the session.

4 After all programs are closed, log on to the system again.

Shut Down

1 If Windows NT doesn't close all the programs, or if it still seems unstable, press Ctrl+Alt+Delete.

2 Click the Shut Down button.

3 Select the Shutdown And Restart option, and click OK.

4 After the computer restarts, log on again.

5 If Windows NT doesn't shut down, turn off the computer, wait a few seconds, and restart the computer.

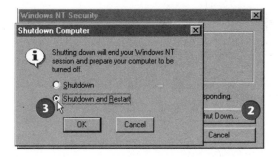

4

Windows NT, and
Windows in Windows NT

Windows NT is called "Windows" because everything in Windows NT is contained in a window. Well, almost everything. In Windows NT, the icons on the Desktop have escaped from their windows, and the taskbar and the Start menu are free of window restraints. There are a few other items that work outside of windows, too—some toolbars and dialog boxes, and the Setup wizards that Windows NT uses to install new hardware and change system settings. But, by and large, every program lives in a window. Some programs even have windows inside their window.

WordPad and Microsoft Word are good examples of the difference between a program that uses a single window and one that uses document windows.

Document windows work just like program windows, except that when you close a document window, you're closing only the document or the file that lives in that window; the main program window stays open. Likewise, when you move, size, maximize, or minimize a document window, it is still contained within the program window.

Most programs that have document windows also have a Window menu that you can use to arrange the windows and to switch between them.

WordPad can display only one document at a time.

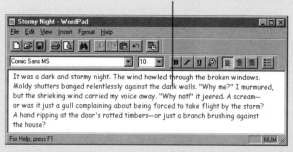

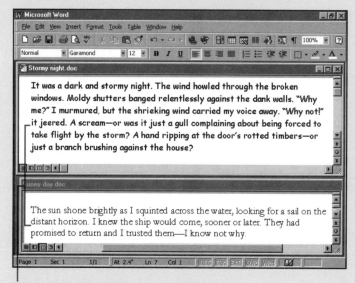

Word can display different documents in separate windows within the Word window.

5

Networking

No, this isn't about the kind of networking that involves schmoozing with people at power breakfasts or "working the tables" at luncheons, handing out business cards and trying to get the inside track on everything. This is a lot better!

From your computer network, you can reach out and communicate with people in your immediate group or, if you work for a company that has national or international branches, with people in distant parts of the country or on the other side of the world. You're all part of the Network Neighborhood, which makes it possible for you exchange information quickly and productively with coworkers in Athens, Georgia or Athens, Greece. Although the type of network you're connected to affects exactly what you can do, the way in which you do everything is fairly standardized.

When you first enter the world of networks, you might run into a few walls that seem to make simple acts difficult. Most of these walls are security features that are designed to reduce the damage—unintentional or intentional—that someone could do to the network and to the computers that are a part of it. If you play by the rules, however, and if the system has been set up to minimize the roadblocks, you'll be able to work efficiently and take advantage of all the network has to offer.

Different Ways
of Networking

Working with networks means that you could be dealing with a *client-server* network system, a *peer-to-peer* network system, or both. What's the difference?

A client-server network is the conventional corporate-type network in which a computer (the server) *hosts,* or provides network services to, other computers (the clients). Almost everything on the network has to pass through the server, which is at the center of this networking universe. The server is managed by a tyrannical overlord known as the *network administrator,* who dictates what each client is allowed to do on the network and can sometimes even prescribe how each client computer is set up.

Servers in a client-server network are often linked so that users have access to other servers. A collection of servers is usually grouped into a management unit called a *domain.* When you log on to a domain, one of the servers verifies your name and password, and grants you specific access rights to servers and computers that are part of that domain. Because so many different programs are used to run networks, and because the network administrator can customize the system, you need to refer to your company's network guides for the technical details about using your network.

A peer-to-peer network, as its name implies, is a more democratic network structure. In this kind of network, all computers are created equal and the users of the computers decide whether and what they will share with others. Any computer in the group can be a server (sharing its printer, for example), a client (using someone else's files), or both. When you connect to another computer workstation, you are using peer-to-peer networking.

Why the different systems? A peer-to-peer system uses Windows NT Workstation software, whereas a client-server network uses dedicated server software such as NT Server, which provides many additional services. Peer-to-peer systems are easier to use but are limited by the number of computers that can be connected. A client-server system with one or more powerful server computers and sophisticated management software is designed to handle large volumes of traffic and provides a higher level of security. So, for a small office with 10 or fewer computers, you'll probably want a stand-alone peer-to-peer network, unless you need the added security and services of a server. For a company with more than 10 computers, you'll need a client-server network.

Client-Server Network

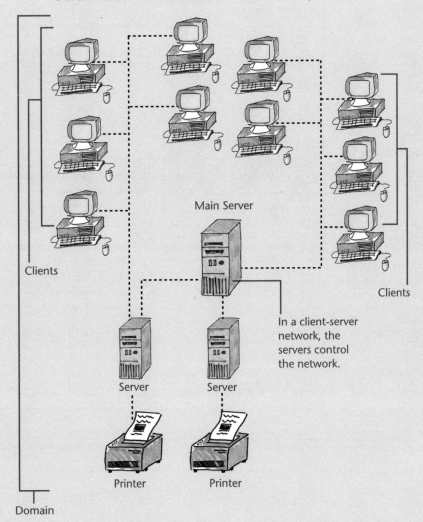

Clients

Main Server

Server

Server

Printer

Printer

Clients

In a client-server network, the servers control the network.

Domain

Peer-to-Peer Network

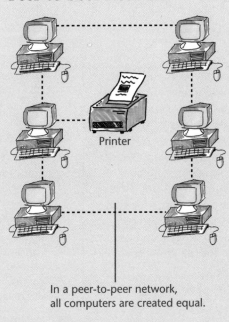

Printer

In a peer-to-peer network, all computers are created equal.

5

Accessing a Document on Another Computer

Just as My Computer is the gateway to everything that resides on your computer, Network Neighborhood is the gateway to everything you need on your network. The computers in your domain or workgroup are ready and waiting for you, and the computers that reside in other domains are there for the finding.

Access a Computer

1 Double-click the Network Neighborhood icon on your Windows Desktop to display the Network Neighborhood window.

2 Double-click the computer you want to access.

Access Another Workgroup or Domain

1 In the Network Neighborhood window, double-click Entire Network.

2 If more than one network exists, double-click the network that contains the computer you're looking for.

3 Double-click the workgroup or domain.

4 Double-click the computer you want to access.

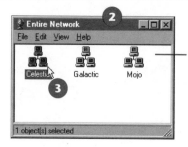

The Entire Network window shows the domains and workgroups on the network.

TIP

You can't access folders on other computers unless the folders have been set up to be shared.

SEE ALSO

"Locating a File by Name" on page 30 and "Locating a File by Date or Content" on page 32 for information about finding files and folders.

TRY THIS

Double-click Network Neighborhood, find your own computer, and double-click it. You'll see what everyone else on the network sees—that is, only the folders that are shared.

Access a Folder

1 Navigate to find the folder, if necessary.

2 Double-click the folder.

3 If asked, supply the user name and password to access the folder, and click OK.

4 Use the folder just as if it were a folder on your own computer. If you try to do something that isn't permitted, you'll be notified.

Window for the Luna computer in the Celestial domain

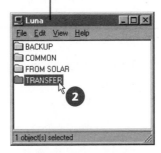

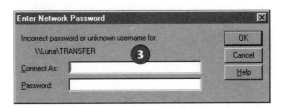

5

Finding a Computer

If you know the name of a computer that you want to connect to, you can search for that computer by name instead of wandering around the network hoping to stumble across it.

TIP

Because of the way some networks are set up, you might not be able to find a computer that is connected to the network. In such a situation, you might be able to find the computer by typing its full address, in the form \\computer\share (where computer is the identifying name of the computer and share is the name of the shared folder you want to access), in the Named box.

SEE ALSO

"Creating Quick Access to a Network Resource" on the facing page for information about creating a shortcut to a computer.

Search for a Computer

1. Click the Start button, point to Find, and choose Computer from the submenu.

2. Type the name of the computer.

3. Click Find Now.

4. Double-click the found computer to access it, or drag it onto the Windows NT Desktop and create a shortcut to the computer.

Searching for a computer by its name...

...locates the computer...   ...and shows you its location.

Creating Quick Access to a Network Resource

If you frequently need access to another computer, or to a folder that's on another computer, you can either create a shortcut to the folder or assign a drive letter to the folder. Although the shortcut is the easiest connection, you might want to assign a drive letter when you're using certain programs. How do you know which way to go? When you want direct access to a folder, create a shortcut. When you're working with a program that requires a drive letter to access network resources, assign a drive letter.

Create a Shortcut

1. Double-click the Network Neighborhood icon on your Windows NT Desktop.

2. Locate the computer and the folder you want.

3. Click the folder to select it.

4. Hold down the right mouse button, drag the folder, and drop it on the Desktop.

5. Choose Create Shortcut(s) Here from the shortcut menu.

Dropping the folder on your Desktop and creating a shortcut...

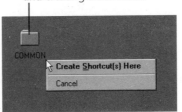

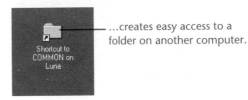

...creates easy access to a folder on another computer.

Assign a Drive Letter

1. Click the folder to select it.

2. Choose Map Network Drive from the File menu.

3. If necessary, type a different user name to access the share.

4. Click OK.

Select a different unused drive letter if you want.

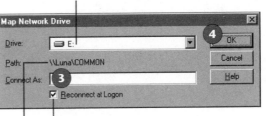

Turn on if you want to create this connection each time you log on to the network.

Check the path to verify that you've connected to the correct computer and folder.

5

Sharing Your Computer

If you need to let other people have access to some of the files that are on your computer, you can share a folder that contains the files.

TIP

You must be an Administrator or a Power User, or have similar access privileges, to change the sharing of the computer. If you're a "normal" user or a guest, you won't find the Sharing command on the shortcut menu.

TIP

Any subfolder that's contained within a shared folder is also shared.

Share a Folder

1. Locate the folder you want to share.

2. Right-click the folder and choose Sharing from the shortcut menu.

3. On the Sharing tab, click the Shared As option.

4. Type a new name for the folder if you want to further identify the shared folder.

5. Type a comment if you want one.

6. Specify how many users can connect at one time:

   ◆ Maximum Allowed, to permit as many as 10 users to be connected to your computer at the same time

   ◆ Allow, to permit a specified number of users (but not more than 10) to be connected to your computer at the same time

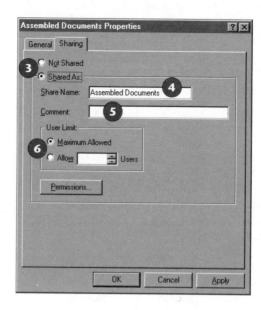

TIP

The greater the number of people who are connected to your computer and using its resources, the more slowly your computer will work. If its sluggishness becomes unbearable when several people are connected, you'll want to consider reducing the number of people who can connect at one time.

SEE ALSO

"Seeing Who's Connected" on page 92 for information about monitoring the number of connections.

TRY THIS

Organize your shared folders by content and type of permission. Create a folder named Source, and share it with Read permission. Create another folder named Feedback, and share it with Full Control permission. Place your original documents in the Source folder, and have your coworkers place their comments, changes, or any additional documents in the Feedback folder.

Set the Access Type

1 Click the Permissions button on the Sharing tab.

2 Specify the type of access:

  ◆ Read, to permit users to open files from the folder but not to allow any changes to be saved in the folder

  ◆ Change, to permit users to open files and save changes

  ◆ Full Control, to permit users to open, save, create, move, and delete files and folders

3 Click OK.

4 Click OK.

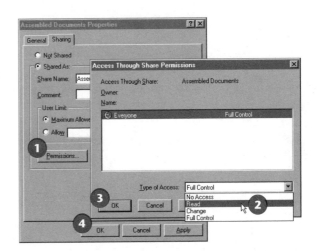

Limiting Access to a Shared Folder

A shared folder is, by default, open to anyone who has access to your computer. You can limit that access, however, by specifying which groups or individuals can access the shared folder, and you can specify the type of access each is allowed.

TIP

You must have the necessary access privileges to be able to change access to a shared folder.

TIP

To grant access to only some individuals in a group, select the group, click Members, select individuals from the group, and click Add.

Remove Global Access

1 Right-click the folder, and choose Sharing from the shortcut menu.

2 Click the Permissions button on the Sharing tab.

3 With the Everyone group selected, click Remove.

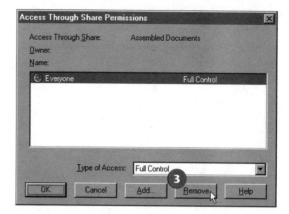

Add Groups

1 Click the Add button.

2 Select the domain or local computer that contains the individuals to be added.

3 Do either or both of the following to add access:

◆ Select a group to be added, and click Add.

◆ Click Show Users, select the names, and click Add.

4 Specify the type of access for all users.

5 Click OK.

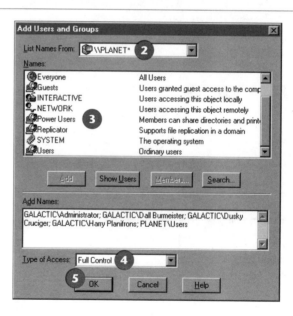

TIP

If you can't find an individual because you don't know which is his or her group or domain, click the Search button in the Add Users And Groups dialog box, and enter the user's name.

TIP

Be very careful if you need to change access to folders that you didn't set up yourself. By limiting access, you could inadvertently exclude someone who needs access to conduct remote maintenance, or you could violate network security by granting access to someone who should be excluded.

Individualize the Access

1 Select a group or an individual.

2 Specify the type of access.

3 Repeat steps 1 and 2 until you've specified the access for all groups and individuals.

4 Click OK.

5 Click OK to close the Properties dialog box for the folder.

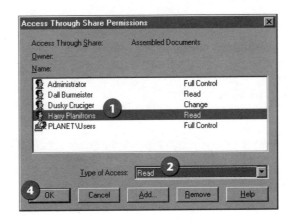

Seeing Who's Connected

If you've set up your computer to share folders with your coworkers, you can see who is connected to your computer. You'll want to monitor the connections if your computer is running sluggishly—too many connections can reduce performance substantially—or if someone can't connect because too many users are already connected. You can, for any legitimate reason (no, bad moods and power trips are *not* legitimate reasons), "pull the plug" and disconnect someone from your computer.

See Who's Connected

1. Click the Start button, point to Settings, and choose Control Panel from the submenu.

2. Double-click the Server icon.

3. Click the In Use button.

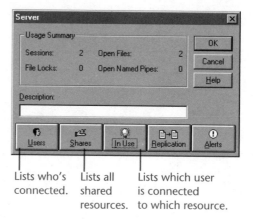

Lists who's connected.   Lists all shared resources.   Lists which user is connected to which resource.

Shows how many resources are open.

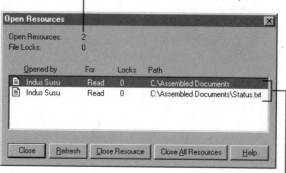

User has folder and document open.

TIP

When you disconnect someone, he or she can reconnect unless you change the access to the shared folder.

TIP

If you're wondering whether someone who's listed as being connected is actually using the connection or has left the office without disconnecting, click the Users button in the Server dialog box. Note the Idle time information for that user to see how long it's been since he or she used the connection.

Disconnect a User

1 Click the name of the user you want to disconnect.

2 Click the Close Resource button.

3 Confirm that you want to disconnect the user.

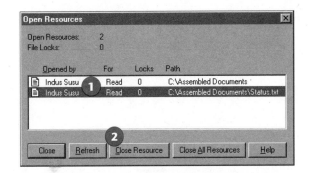

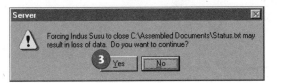

Check Your Sharing

1 Click the Shares button in the Server dialog box.

2 Click a folder to see which computers are connected to that folder.

3 Click Close when you've finished.

Lists all shared folders.

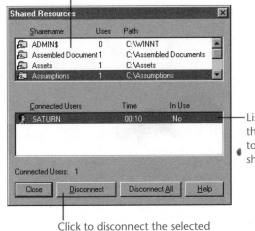

Lists computers that are connected to the selected shared folder.

Click to disconnect the selected computer from the selected resource.

Chatting Across the Net

You can have an interactive typed "conversation" with another person across your network with Chat. To use Chat, you and the other person must each have Chat running. Then it's just a matter of calling the other computer and enjoying your online chat.

TIP

The first time you start Chat, some programs that need to converse over the network are loaded. These programs continue to run even after you've closed Chat. If someone calls you after you've closed Chat, Chat will start automatically and you'll see its button flashing on the taskbar. Clicking Chat on the taskbar will display Chat and answer the call. If you don't want to answer the call, right-click the flashing button, and choose Close from the shortcut menu.

Make a Call

1. Click the Start button, point to Programs and Accessories, and choose Chat from the submenu.

2. Make sure that the person you want to call has Chat running.

3. Click the Dial button.

4. Click the name of the computer you want to connect to, and click OK.

5. Wait for the other person to answer.

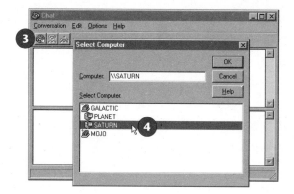

Receive a Call

1. When the phone rings on your computer, choose Answer from the Conversation menu.

2. Type your text in the top part of the Chat window.

3. Read what the other people have to say in the lower parts of the window.

4. Click the Hang Up button when you've finished chatting.

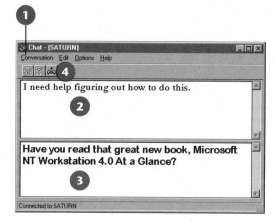

Changing Your Password

As if it's not difficult enough to remember your password, good security procedures—not to mention ruthless network administrators—require you to change your password or passwords periodically.

TIP

Some networks require you to use different tools for changing your network password. If the procedures described here don't work, consult your network administrator about any special procedures for your network.

Change Your Password

1 Press Ctrl+Alt+Delete.

2 Click the Change Password button.

3 Select the domain, network, workgroup, or computer for which you want to change your password.

4 Type your old password.

5 Type a new password.

6 Type the new password again to confirm it.

7 Click OK.

8 Click Cancel.

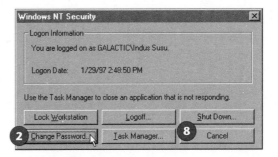

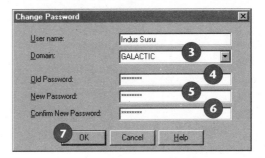

Securing Your Workstation

Computer security, and especially network security, can be easily violated by someone who has access to an unattended workstation. And who gets the blame? You do, because your user name and password were used. You can avoid such a security breach by locking your workstation when you're away from it. Your locked workstation is still running and still connected to and accessible from the network—but until you unlock it, nobody can enter anything from your keyboard or see anything on your screen.

Lock Your Workstation

1 Press Ctrl+Alt+Delete.

2 Click Lock Workstation.

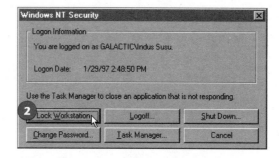

Unlock Your Workstation

1 Press Ctrl+Alt+Delete.

2 Type your password.

3 Click OK.

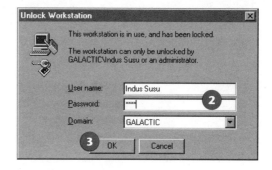

6

Printing

Whether you're printing your documents on a printer that's attached directly to your computer or on a shared printer on a company network, you're using the print services provided by Microsoft Windows NT Workstation 4.0. These services include sending the correct types of codes to the printer, organizing print jobs so that they print in an orderly succession, and managing output to different printers.

We'll cover some useful techniques in the section—for example, you'll find out how to print to a file when you can't access a printer. Then, when a printer is available, you'll be able to print your document without having to open the program it's associated with. If you can't print from an MS-DOS–based program on a network printer, you'll learn how to trick the program into "thinking" it's printing from a standard printer port.

What else you can do besides simply print a document depends on the type of permission you've been granted. Some of the procedures we'll describe in this section require that you have permission to modify the system or to take control of the printer. Even if you haven't been granted one of the higher levels of permission, you'll gain some understanding of what can be done, and you'll be able to ask a coworker who has these access rights to make the specific changes for you.

Printing a Document

When you want to print a document that is associated with a program—a Word document, for example—you can print the document directly without first starting the program. This doesn't mean that you don't need the program; it is still required for printing, but Windows NT will take care of the details for you.

TIP

Some programs require the use of the system default printer. For documents associated with such programs, you'll have to either print using the system default printer or switch the default printer designation to the printer you want to use.

Print a Document Using the Default Printer

1 Select the document to be printed.

2 Right-click a selected document, and choose Print from the shortcut menu.

Print a Document Using a Specific Printer

1 Click the Start button, point to Settings, and choose Printers from the submenu to open the Printers folder.

2 Select the document to be printed.

3 Drag the selected document to the Printers folder and drop it on the printer you want to use.

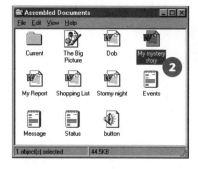

Changing the Default Printer

Some programs are set up to print only to the system default printer; other programs are initially set up to print to the default printer, but you can "target," or change to, a different printer. If you have several printers available, you can designate any one of them as the default printer.

TIP

If there's a check mark next to the Set As Default command on the shortcut menu, the printer you've chosen has already been set as the default printer.

Change the Default

1 Click the Start button, point to Settings, and choose Printers from the submenu.

2 Right-click the printer you want to use as the default printer.

3 Choose Set As Default from the shortcut menu.

4 Close the Printers folder when you've finished.

Controlling Your Printing

When you send your documents to be printed, each print job is *queued* in the order in which it's received by the print server. However, some documents might be assigned a higher printing priority than others, so the documents might not be printed in the same order in which they're received. You can see the progress of your print job in the queue, and you can temporarily suspend printing of your document or even remove your document from the queue if you want.

TIP

You can control the printing of your document but, unless you have special permission, you can't pause the printer itself, change the printing priority of a document, or pause or delete other users' documents.

View the Queue

1 Click the Start button, point to Settings, and choose Printers from the submenu.

2 Double-click the printer you're using.

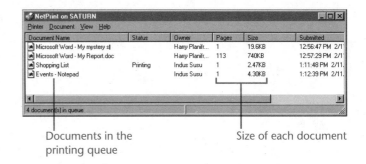

Documents in the printing queue

Size of each document

Stop the Presses

1 Click your document.

2 Choose the action you want from the Document menu:

◆ Pause, to stop your document from printing until you resume printing by choosing Resume or until you restart printing from the beginning by choosing Restart

◆ Cancel, to delete the document from the print queue

A paused document remains in the queue but doesn't print...

...while other documents continue to print.

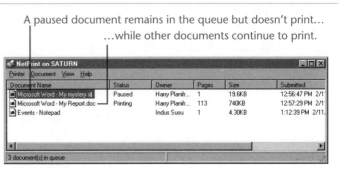

TIP

If you have the appropriate permission to change the printing priority of your document, you can move the Priority slider to the right to jump ahead of other documents in the printing queue. Use this power with discretion, however, or you'll be deafened by the howls of complaint you'll hear from those whose positions in the queue you've usurped!

Check Your Priority

1 Click your document.

2 Choose Properties from the Document menu.

3 On the General tab, take a look at the document's printing priority.

4 Click Cancel when you've finished.

5 Click a document that belongs to another user.

6 Choose Properties from the Document menu, and note that document's printing priority.

7 Complain loudly to the network administrator if someone keeps setting their documents to a higher priority than yours.

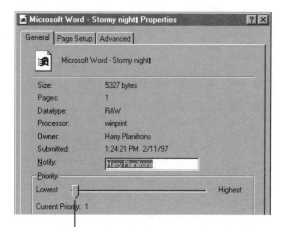

Most documents have the same low priority, and will be printed in the order in which they're received.

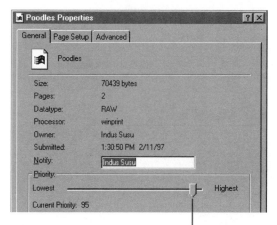

Changing the printing priority moves a document ahead of documents that have a lower priority.

6

Connecting to a Network Printer

When a printer is set up to be shared, you can easily connect to it, and you can configure your system for that printer. You need to set up the connection to the printer only once; thereafter, you can use the printer as if it were directly connected to your computer.

> **TIP**
>
> *If you're adding a new type of printer that requires additional files, you must have permission to add system files before you can install the printer.*

> **TIP**
>
> *If the printer you're installing was previously installed on your computer and then moved, you won't see the Add Printer Wizard when you reinstall that printer.*

Get the Printer

1 Click the Start button, point to Settings, and choose Printers from the submenu.

2 Use Network Neighborhood or Windows Explorer to locate the computer that has the printer, and open a window to that computer.

3 Drag the printer you want to use and drop it in your Printers folder.

4 Complete the Add Printer Wizard.

Drag the network printer from the computer it's connected to...

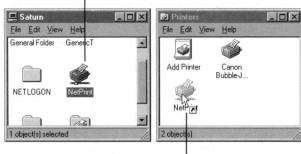

...to your Printers folder.

TIP

Use the method described here even if you're connecting to the same printer that has been moved to a different location. Because any required printer drivers will be copied from the print server to your computer, this method ensures that the drivers on your computer will match the drivers on the print server.

TIP

The Comment and Location information on the General tab of the printer's Properties dialog box is optional. However, if this information is missing, tell the owner of the printer that it would be helpful to all users of the printer if he or she completed the information.

Get the Information

1. Right-click the printer.

2. Choose Properties from the shortcut menu.

3. Click the General tab and review the information.

4. Click the Scheduling tab and review the availability of the printer.

5. Click Cancel when you've finished.

Comments and instructions from the printer's owner

Location of the printer

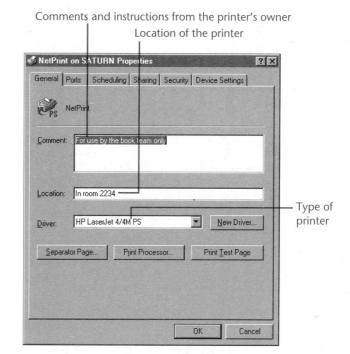

Type of printer

Times during which the printer can be used

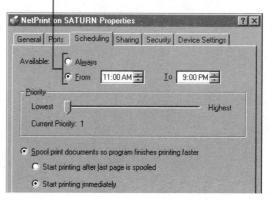

Printing a Document to a File

If you don't have access to a specific printer because it's in use, or if your access is limited to specific times, you can print a document to a file. The file contains all the special printer information from the program, so you don't need to use the program again to print—you simply send the file to the printer when the printer is available.

TIP

Many programs provide the option to print to a file without requiring you to install a new printer specifically for file output. To see whether the program you're using supports this option, choose Print from the File menu and, in the Print dialog box, turn on the Print To File option. If the program you're using has this option and the printer is installed on your computer, skip the Add Printer Wizard and use the program's option.

Create a Print File

1. Use the Add Printer Wizard to install a printer on your computer that is connected to File instead of to a printer port. Be sure to specify the same make and model specifications for the printer you will be sending the file to.

2. Use your program to print a document to the new printer.

3. Type a path and name for the output file.

4. Click OK.

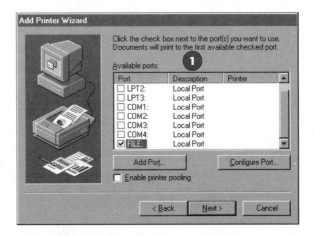

TIP

If your computer doesn't have the printer or the correct printer drivers installed, you'll need access to the Windows NT Workstation installation files, or a disk from the printer manufacturer that contains the printer-driver files for Windows NT. Of course, you'll also need the appropriate permission to modify the system.

SEE ALSO

"Adding a Printer to Your Computer" on page 107 for information about using the Add Printer Wizard.

TRY THIS

Set the printer that's connected to File as your default printer, right-click a document file (such as a bitmap image), and choose Print. Type a path and filename for the output file. Start the command prompt, and send the file to the correct printer on the print server.

Print a Print File to a Printer

1 Click the Start button, point to Programs, and choose Command Prompt from the submenu.

2 At the prompt, type *print /d:printerdevice drive:\path\filename:* where *printerdevice* identifies the location of the printer and *drive, path,* and *filename* locate and specify the print file.

3 Press Enter.

Prints the file *myfile.prn* using the printer attached to the LPT1 port.

Prints the file *myfile.prn* using the network printer HPLaserJ that's on the Saturn print server.

6

Printing from MS-DOS to a Network Printer

Many MS-DOS–based programs are set to print to a standard printer port, such as LPT1 or COM1, and these programs can't normally print to a network printer. However, you *can* print to a network printer from an MS-DOS–based program by having Windows NT reroute the program's output. The MS-DOS–based program is tricked into "thinking" it's printing to a standard port, but its output is really being sent over the network.

Reroute the Port

1. Click the Start button, point to Programs, and choose Command Prompt from the submenu.

2. At the prompt, type *net use lptx \\printserver\ printer /persistent:yes* where *lptx* is whichever parallel port you want to assign the printer to (LPT1 or LPT2), and *printserver* and *printer* identify your network printer.

3. Press Enter.

4. Run your MS-DOS program and print from the program to the parallel port you just assigned.

With this command, output sent to the LPT2 port goes to the NetPrint network printer on the Saturn server.

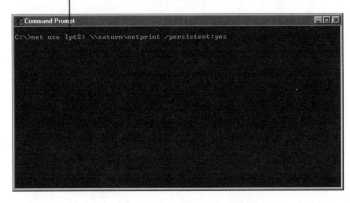

This command uses the network printer to print a list of all folders and subfolders in the Assembled Documents folder.

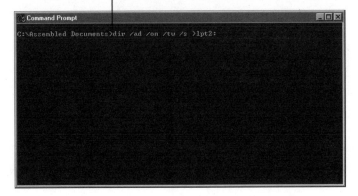

Adding a Printer to Your Computer

If you get a new printer that you're going to attach directly to your computer, you need to let Windows NT know about it by using the Add Printer Wizard.

TIP

To install a new printer, you'll need access to the Windows NT Workstation installation files, or a disk from the printer manufacturer that contains the printer-driver files for Windows NT. You'll also need the appropriate permission to modify the system.

SEE ALSO

"Changing the Default Printer" on page 99 for information about setting or changing the default printer, and "Sharing a Printer" on page 108 for information about setting up your printer so that it can be shared by others.

Add a Printer

1 Turn off your computer, install the printer, and turn your computer back on.

2 Click the Start button, point to Settings, and choose Printers from the submenu.

3 Double-click the Add Printer icon.

4 Select My Computer, and click Next.

5 Select the port to which the printer is attached, and click Next.

6 Select the manufacturer and the printer model. Click Next.

7 Complete the remaining steps of the wizard, configuring the printer for the way you'll be using it.

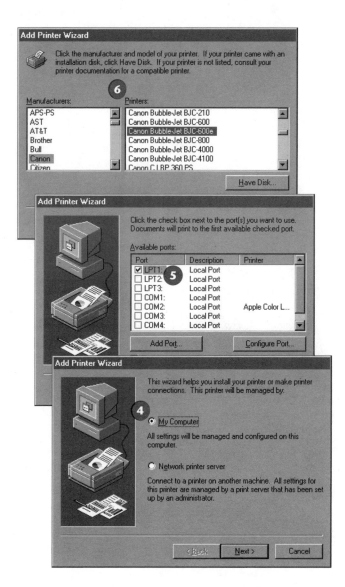

Sharing a Printer

You can set up your computer so that you can share your printer with other people in your workgroup. However, be warned that this is a situation in which you need a generous and even-tempered personality; when several people are using your printer, you'll find that your computer becomes quite sluggish.

TIP

If you install additional drivers for different systems, you'll need access to the Windows NT Workstation installation disks or folders to download the drivers. If you don't install additional drivers, any users with a different system who are setting up a connection to your printer will need to download the drivers from the installation disks or folders.

Share Your Printer

1. Click the Start button, point to Settings, and choose Printers from the submenu.

2. Right-click the printer you want to share, and choose Sharing from the shortcut menu.

3. On the Sharing tab, click the Shared option.

4. Type a name for the printer.

5. Install additional drivers if users connecting to the printer have different systems.

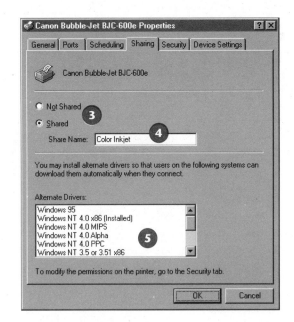

Specify the Users

1. On the Security tab, click the Permissions button.

2. Specify who has permission to print and who can modify the printer settings.

3. Click OK.

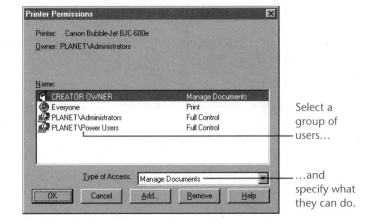

Select a group of users...

...and specify what they can do.

TIP

It's important to include the location of the printer in the information you post on the General tab. If you don't, you're likely to end up with unclaimed documents piling up in your printer, and coworkers wandering the halls looking for their printouts.

TIP

If you want to print a separator page between each print job, use the pcl.sep file for PCL-type printers, and the sysprint.sep file for PostScript-type printers. If you're feeling brave, you can edit the sysprint.sep file in Notepad, substituting the name of your computer and the printer share name for the placeholder text \\server\name.

SEE ALSO

"Sharing Your Computer" on page 88 and "Limiting Access to a Shared Folder" on page 90 for information about setting sharing permissions.

"Connecting to a Network Printer" on page 102 for information about setting up a network printer on your computer.

Post Information

1 Click the General tab.

2 Type any rules or other information about using the printer.

3 Type the location of the printer—your room number, for example.

4 Click OK.

5 Click OK to close the printer's Properties dialog box.

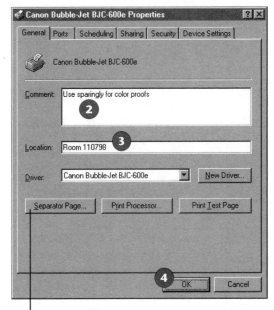

Click to insert a separator page before each print job on a PCL-type or PostScript-type printer.

6

7

Running MS-DOS

Using Microsoft Windows NT Workstation 4.0 doesn't mean that you have to abandon your MS-DOS–based programs. Most of them run extremely well in Windows NT, and some can run after you make a few adjustments to your system. Unfortunately, there *are* some MS-DOS programs that just won't run under Windows NT, and you'll need updated versions of these programs (if they're available) that allow them to run under Windows NT. If you're not sure whether your program will work in Windows NT, try it. Windows NT effectively isolates the MS-DOS program so that if it misbehaves, the rest of your system shouldn't be affected.

MS-DOS is part of the Windows NT operating system, giving you the best of both worlds. You can work at the MS-DOS prompt if that's the way you like to work. Or you can switch back and forth between MS-DOS and Windows NT as needed.

We'll cover some of the basics in this section: starting MS-DOS–based programs, working from the command line, moving or copying text between Windows NT and MS-DOS, and generally making MS-DOS–based programs perform at their top level. Our goal in this section is to help you get the most from your MS-DOS–based programs, whether you use them for work or for play.

Running MS-DOS Commands

You can start an MS-DOS program or run a single MS-DOS command directly from Windows NT, or you can open an MS-DOS window and execute all your MS-DOS activities there. After using a command, you can easily repeat the same command or modify the command line to customize the command.

Run a Single MS-DOS Command

1. Click the Start button, and choose Run from the Start menu.

2. Type the form of the command depending on the results you want (replacing the program name or command name shown below with the actual program name or command name):

    ◆ *Program name* to run the program

    ◆ *Cmd /c command* to run a command and then close the command-prompt window

    ◆ *Cmd /k command* to run a command and leave the command-prompt window open

    ◆ *Cmd /k program name* to run a program that automatically terminates and leaves the command-prompt window open

3. Click OK.

Starts the MS-DOS Edit program.

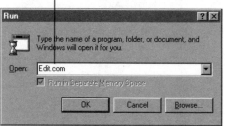

Runs the MS-DOS command, sends the results to a file, and then closes the MS-DOS window.

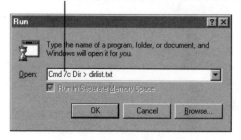

Runs the MS-DOS command Assoc and leaves the MS-DOS window open.

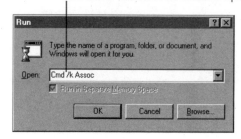

SEE ALSO

"Managing a Program Window" on page 12 for information about working with program windows, and "Arranging Windows on the Desktop" on page 28 for information about arranging your open program windows.

TRY THIS

Two for One. *Type* Dir & Mem *at the command prompt, and press Enter. Both commands are carried out. You can include more than one command on a line by using the ampersand (&) character between the commands.*

Run Multiple Commands

1. Click the Start button, point to Programs, and choose Command Prompt.

2. Do any of the following at the prompt:

   ◆ Type an MS-DOS command, and press Enter to execute the command.

   ◆ Type the name of an MS-DOS program, and press Enter.

   ◆ Type an MS-DOS command or an MS-DOS program name followed by the additional parameters allowed by the command or program to modify the actions of the command or program, and press Enter.

3. Type Exit to close the window when you've finished.

Type an MS-DOS command, and press Enter.

Use switches and additional parameters to modify a command.

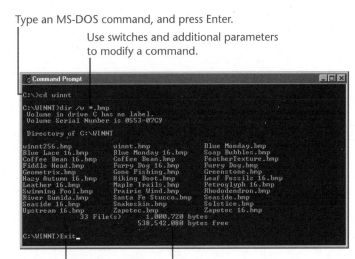

The Exit command ends the MS-DOS session and closes the Command Prompt window.

Results of commands are displayed.

Repeating an MS-DOS Command

When you're working in an MS-DOS session, you can repeat a command, regardless of how complex it is, with a single press of a key. This saves a lot of effort and helps you avoid those annoying mistyped commands. And if you want to reuse a command but make a few changes to it, MS-DOS provides editing tools that can simplify the process considerably.

> **TIP**
>
> *When you reuse a command, you are moved to that command's position in the list of commands. For example, if you move to the first command used and press Enter, pressing the Up arrow key will show only the first command. Use the Down arrow key to move through the rest of the list. If you want to cycle through the list continuously, press F8 instead of the Up or Down arrow key.*

Repeat a Command

1. Press the Up arrow key to display the previous command.

2. Continue pressing the Up arrow key to step through the previous commands. Use the Down arrow key to step back through the commands you've passed.

3. When the command you want to use is displayed, press Enter to execute it. (You can modify the command and any parameters, if necessary, before you press Enter to execute the command.)

When you press this key three times...

...this command...

...is repeated on the current command line.

TIP

To clear the command history list, press Alt+F7.

SEE ALSO

"Changing the Way the MS-DOS Window Works" on page 126 for information about adjusting the number of commands stored and starting the MS-DOS session in Insert mode instead of in Overtype mode.

TIP

Insert mode adds characters to the command line; Overtype mode replaces the current characters with the characters you type.

Select a Command to Repeat

1 Press F7 to display the list of commands.

2 Use the Up or Down arrow key to select the command you want to repeat.

3 Press Enter.

Press F7 to list the comands you've used.

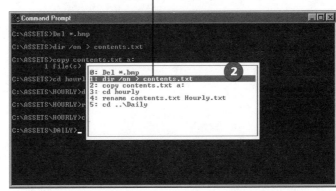

Edit a Command

1 Use the keys shown in the table at the right to edit a command.

2 Press Enter to execute the modified command or Esc to cancel the entire command line.

COMMAND LINE EDITING KEYS	
Key	**What it does**
F1	Displays the previous command one character at a time.
F2	Displays the previous command up to the character you type after pressing F2.
F3	Displays the previous command.
F4	Deletes the current command from the cursor up to the character you type after pressing F4.
Backspace	Deletes the character to the left.
Delete	Deletes the character to the right.
Insert	Switches between Insert mode and Overtype mode.
Left arrow key	Moves the cursor to the left.
Right arrow key	Moves the cursor to the right.

Exploring MS-DOS Commands

The version of MS-DOS that is part of Windows NT provides a variety of useful commands. If you're familiar with previous versions of MS-DOS, you'll find that some commands in this version are new, some have been enhanced, and some have disappeared because Windows NT has made them obsolete.

TIP

The "|" used before the word "more" is known as a pipe, and is usually typed by pressing Shift+\. This tells the system to send the output of the command through the More program, which displays the information one screenful at a time.

Get Information on a Command

1 Open a Command Prompt window if one isn't already open.

2 Type an MS-DOS command followed by a space and /? and press Enter to get information on the command.

3 If the information scrolls off the screen, press F3 to display the same command, type a space followed by */more,* and press Enter.

4 Read the information, and then press Enter to see more information.

This switch gets help on the command...

...and this parameter displays the information one windowful or one screenful at a time.

The help listing defines the function of the command and lists the alternative forms of the command.

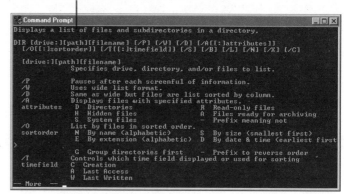

Get a List of MS-DOS Commands

1 At the command prompt, type Help.

2 Press Enter.

3 Read the description of the commands.

4 Press Enter to see the next screen.

5 Continue pressing Enter until all the commands have been displayed.

The Help command lists all the MS-DOS commands one windowful or one screenful at a time.

Sending MS-DOS Output to a File

Many MS-DOS commands and programs send a great deal of information to your screen. You can redirect the information and save it in a text file for further reference.

TRY THIS

Switch to the folder that contains your documents. On the command line, type dir /s > MyDocs.txt and press Enter. Then open the text document in Notepad. You'll see a listing of all the files in the folder and all the files in any subfolders. (To append the output to the end of an existing file instead of creating a new file, use >> instead of >.)

Redirect the Output

1. Open a Command Prompt window if one isn't already open.

2. Type the command, type a space followed by > *filename* (where *filename* is the name of the file you want the information sent to). If you want to store the output file in a folder other than the active folder, include the full path in the filename.

3. Press Enter.

4. Type *Notepad filename* (where *filename* is the name of the file), and include the path if the file isn't in the active folder.

5. Press Enter.

6. Examine the output.

7. Close Notepad when you've finished.

Starting a Program from the MS-DOS Prompt

When you're working in an MS-DOS window, you can start an MS-DOS–based program in that window or in a new window. You can even start a Windows NT program from an MS-DOS window. If you don't remember the MS-DOS path and filename, you can find the program in Windows NT and then let Windows NT insert the information for you.

TIP

You need to use only the filename, not the full path, if the program is in the currently active directory.

TIP

Some programs are designed to run only in their own window, so they will always start in a new window.

Start a Program

1. Open a Command Prompt window, type the program's path and filename, and press Enter.

2. When you've finished, use the program's menu to exit the program and return to the MS-DOS prompt.

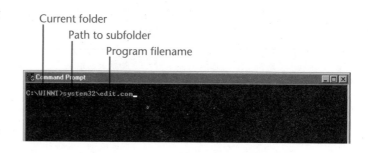

Current folder
Path to subfolder
Program filename

Find a Program to Run

1. Type *start* followed by a space and a period, and press Enter. A window for the current folder opens.

2. Navigate through the folders to find the program.

3. Drag the program and drop it in the MS-DOS window.

4. Click in the MS-DOS window if it's not the active window, and press Enter to start the program. When you've finished, use the program's menu or commands to exit the program and return to the MS-DOS prompt.

TIP

The Start command has several options, which allow you to set the title for the window and to specify whether the window should be started maximized or minimized. Type Start /? at the MS-DOS prompt for more information.

TRY THIS

At the command prompt, type CD /winnt & start "My WINNT Folder" Dir /on /w and press Enter. Substitute any folder to get its content, use the /s switch with the CD command to include subfolders, or use different switches with the Dir command to change the way the files are displayed.

Start an MS-DOS Program in a New Window

1 Type *start* at the beginning of the command line.

2 Type or drag and drop the program's path and filename, and press Enter.

Typing this command…

…starts this program in a new window.

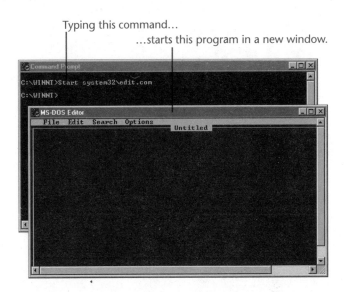

Start a Windows NT–Based Program

At the command prompt, do either of the following:

◆ Type the name of the Windows NT–based program, and press Enter.

◆ Type the path and name of a file that is associated with a Windows NT–registered program, and press Enter. The program starts with the file loaded.

Windows NT Notepad is started from the MS-DOS command prompt.

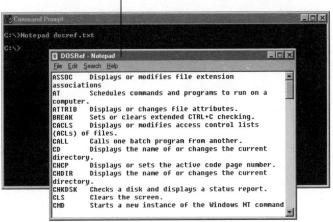

Copying Text in MS-DOS

You can easily share text among your MS-DOS output, the MS-DOS command line, MS-DOS–based programs, and even your Windows NT–based programs.

TRY THIS

MS-DOS Quick Reference.
At the command prompt, type Help > DOSref.txt *to create a text file containing explanations of all the MS-DOS commands. Then type* Notepad DOSref.txt *to display the document. When you can't remember an MS-DOS command, find it in the Notepad document, copy the command, and paste it at the command prompt. If you need additional help on the command, type* /? *after the command, and then press Enter.*

Copy MS-DOS Output

1 Run your MS-DOS command in an MS-DOS window.

2 Right-click the Command Prompt title bar, point to Edit, and choose Mark from the shortcut menu.

3 Click to position the mouse pointer where you want to start the selection.

4 Hold down the left mouse button, drag over the area to be copied, and release the mouse button.

5 Press Enter.

Paste Text into a Windows NT–Based Program

1 Switch to the Windows NT–based program.

2 Choose Paste from the Edit menu.

Text from the MS-DOS window

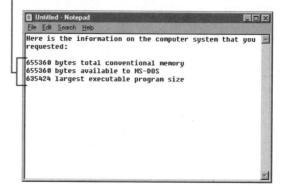

SEE ALSO

"Copying Material Between Documents" on page 70 for information about copying and pasting text.

"Running MS-DOS Commands" on page 112 for information about working at the MS-DOS prompt.

"Changing the Way the MS-DOS Window Works" on page 126 for information about using the mouse to select text without first choosing a menu command.

Copy Text from a Windows NT–Based Program into MS-DOS

1 Copy text from the Windows NT document.

2 Switch to the MS-DOS window.

3 Right-click the Command Prompt title bar.

4 Point to Edit, and choose Paste from the shortcut menu.

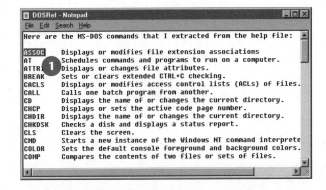

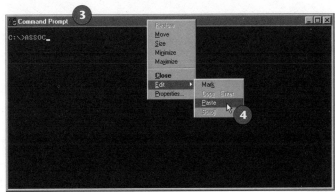

Changing the Color Scheme

Although some programs have color schemes, the MS-DOS environment tends to be monochromatic—either white on black or black on white. No more! You can adjust the colors of your MS-DOS environment to make it a little more appealing.

TIP

Some MS-DOS–based programs aren't customizable, and display only the General and Version tabs when you choose Properties.

SEE ALSO

"Setting the Appearance of All MS-DOS Windows" on page 128 for information about changing the color scheme for all your MS-DOS windows.

Change the Color

1 Start an MS-DOS session if one isn't already running.

2 Right-click the title bar and choose Properties from the shortcut menu.

3 Click the Colors tab.

4 Select the item whose color you want to change.

5 Click the color you want.

6 Adjust the RGB color values if you want to customize the color.

7 Repeat steps 4 through 6 for any other items whose color you want to change.

8 Click OK.

9 Choose to apply the changes to the current MS-DOS session only or to all MS-DOS sessions started from the same shortcut. Click OK.

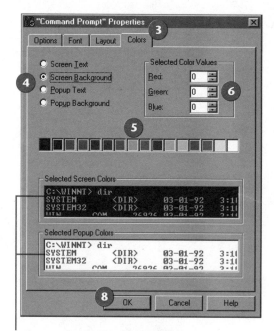

Preview your color schemes here.

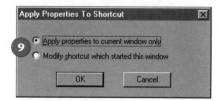

Changing the Font

The MS-DOS environment has never been renowned for attractive screen text. The characters are usually blocky, typewriter-style text that works well with data or commands but doesn't have much aesthetic appeal. You can adjust the size and the proportions of these characters or, if you really dislike the way they look, switch to a more attractive TrueType font designed specifically for the MS-DOS environment.

TIP

Different programs have different configurations on the Font tab, so be aware that you might need to be a little adaptable when changing fonts for different programs. The listed fonts also depend on the fonts that are installed on your computer.

Change the Font Dimensions

1. Start an MS-DOS session if one isn't already running.

2. Right-click the title bar and choose Properties from the shortcut menu.

3. Click the Font tab.

4. Select the font you want to use.

5. Select the dimensions of the characters in pixels, or specify a point size. If the tab lists Bitmap or TrueType fonts only, specify the type of font.

6. Click OK.

7. Choose to apply the changes to the current MS-DOS session only or to all MS-DOS sessions started from the same shortcut. Click OK.

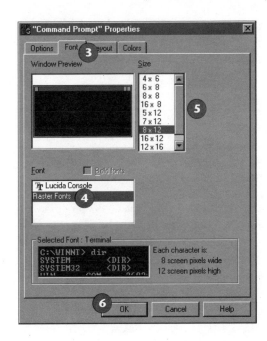

Using the Whole Screen

Miss that old familiar MS-DOS screen? You can return to it by running the MS-DOS session in a full screen. But you're not stuck with that one option. If you want to switch to your other programs or return the MS-DOS session to a window, you just need to know the right key combinations.

TIP

When you switch between a window and a full screen, the video mode changes. Some video systems don't react well to this switch and can even scramble the video output despite the fact that the program is still running correctly. If this occurs, you'll need to exit the program, configure the MS-DOS session to start exactly as you want it to, and then be sure you don't switch when the program is running.

Switch to Full Screen

1. Start an MS-DOS session if one isn't running.

2. Right-click the title bar and choose Properties from the shortcut menu.

3. Click the Options tab.

4. Select Full Screen.

5. Click OK.

6. Choose to apply the changes to the current MS-DOS session only or to all MS-DOS sessions started from the same shortcut. Click OK.

7. Do any of the following to switch between the full-screen MS-DOS session and other programs:

   ◆ Press Alt+Enter to return the MS-DOS session to a window (x86-type computers only).

   ◆ Press Alt+Tab to switch to another program and minimize the MS-DOS session.

   ◆ Click the Command Prompt button on the taskbar to return to the full-screen session.

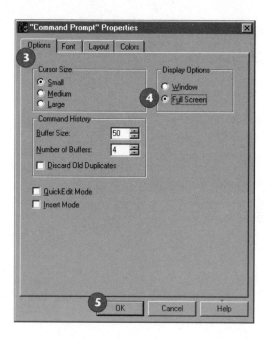

Changing the Size of the MS-DOS Window

The size of the characters you're using determines the dimensions of the MS-DOS window, so the size of the window changes automatically when you change the size of the characters. You can, however, increase the size of the window without having to increase the size of the characters by specifying how many characters wide and high you want the window to be.

SEE ALSO

"Changing the Way the MS-DOS Window Works" on page 126 for information about scrolling to see text that's no longer displayed in the window.

Change the Window Size

1 Start an MS-DOS session if one isn't already running.

2 Right-click the title bar and choose Properties from the shortcut menu.

3 Click the Layout tab.

4 Set the width in number of characters.

5 Set the height in number of characters.

6 Click OK.

7 Choose to apply the changes to the current MS-DOS session only or to all MS-DOS sessions started from the same shortcut. Click OK.

The preview shows the new size of the window in relationship to the Desktop.

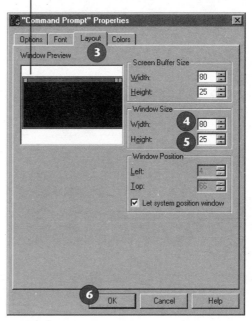

Changing the Way the MS-DOS Window Works

In addition to customizing the appearance of the MS-DOS window, you can adjust the number of previous commands that are remembered, you can change the ways editing commands and copying text work, and you can enable horizontal and vertical scrolling. You can apply these changes to an individual MS-DOS session, to a shortcut, or to all your MS-DOS sessions.

SEE ALSO

"Changing the Color Scheme" on page 122 for information about making changes to a single MS-DOS session or to a shortcut.

"Setting the Appearance of All MS-DOS Windows" on page 128 for information about making global settings.

Increase the Number of Stored Commands

1. Open the Properties dialog box:
   - ◆ For global changes, double-click the Console icon in the Control Panel.
   - ◆ For changes to a single session or to a shortcut, right-click the title bar of an MS-DOS window and choose Properties.

2. Click the Options tab.

3. Increase the number in the Buffer Size box.

4. Select to keep or to discard duplicate commands.

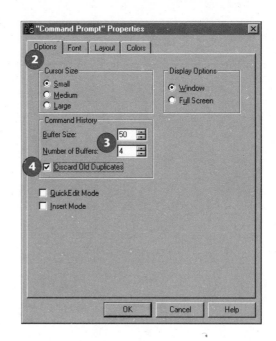

Change the Editing Mode

1. Turn on QuickEdit Mode if you always want to select text by dragging the mouse.

2. Turn on Insert Mode if you want any text you type in the command line to be inserted without overtyping the existing text.

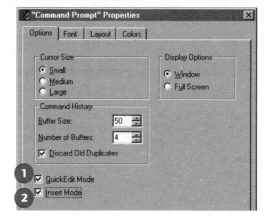

7

TIP

When you're running MS-DOS in full-screen mode, the number of lines on the screen and the number of characters on one line are determined by your screen resolution.

SEE ALSO

"Making More Room on the Desktop" on page 185 for information about changing your screen resolution.

Turn on Scrolling

1 Click the Layout tab.

2 Under Screen Buffer Size:

- ♦ Set Width to a number greater than the width under Window Size to enable horizontal scrolling.

- ♦ Set Height to a number greater than the height under Window Size to enable vertical scrolling.

3 Click OK.

4 If the changes are not global, choose to apply the changes to the current MS-DOS session only or to all MS-DOS sessions started from the same shortcut. Click OK.

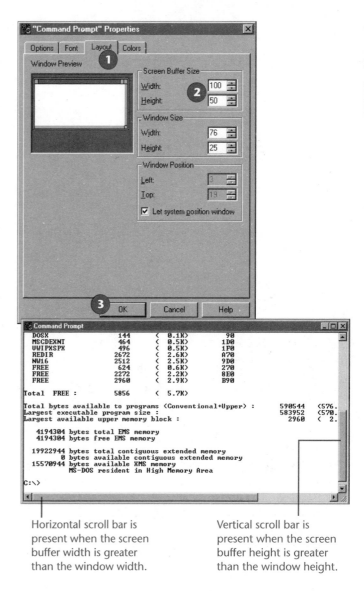

Horizontal scroll bar is present when the screen buffer width is greater than the window width.

Vertical scroll bar is present when the screen buffer height is greater than the window height.

Setting the Appearance of All MS-DOS Windows

When you adjust the appearance of an MS-DOS window, you have the option of applying the changes you've made to the current window or to all the windows you'll start from that shortcut. Instead of making changes to each type of MS-DOS window, you can make changes that apply to all your MS-DOS windows. Then you can selectively customize any MS-DOS window with settings that are different from the global settings.

> **TIP**
>
> *The global changes you make don't affect MS-DOS windows to which you've already applied custom settings.*

Make Global Settings

1 Click the Start button, point to Settings, and choose Control Panel from the submenu.

2 Double-click the Console icon.

3 Use the tabs in the Console Properties dialog box to make adjustments to

- ◆ Cursor size.
- ◆ Full screen or a window.
- ◆ Font and font size.
- ◆ Window size.
- ◆ Window position.
- ◆ Screen and text colors.

4 Click OK.

5 Open an MS-DOS window in which you want any custom settings, and adjust those settings to override the global settings.

6 Click OK.

7 Choose to apply the changes to the current MS-DOS session only or to all MS-DOS sessions started from the same shortcut. Click OK.

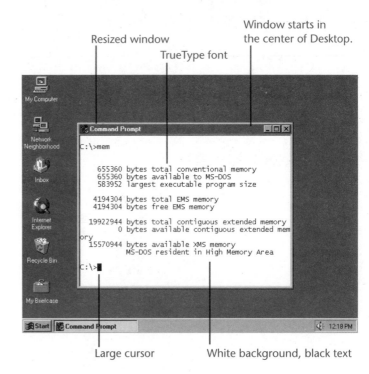

Resized window

TrueType font

Window starts in the center of Desktop.

Large cursor

White background, black text

Navigating Folders in MS-DOS

Although working in MS-DOS usually means working with paths, Windows NT makes your work a lot easier by using long filenames and folder names. You can also use Windows NT folders to help you navigate. Folders in MS-DOS have traditionally been called *directories*, but this distinction is becoming blurred as MS-DOS moves away from the traditional eight-character-plus-optional-three-character-extension naming limitations, and as MS-DOS and folder windows become more interactive.

Switch Between Folders

Use any of the Change Directory (CD) commands shown in the table at the right. Substitute the actual paths and folder names for those shown here.

MS-DOS COMMANDS FOR CHANGING FOLDERS	
Command	What it does
CD ..	Moves up one folder (to the parent folder).
CD \	Moves to the root directory (the drive folder).
CD folder name	Moves to the specified subfolder.
CD \path\folder name	Moves to the specified folder.
CD \d drive\path\folder	Moves to the specified folder on the specified drive.

Use a Folder Window

1. Type your command.

2. Switch to the folder window.

3. Drag the folder and drop it at the command prompt.

4. Press Enter.

Dropped folder shows full path.

Improving MS-DOS Program Performance

Windows NT tries to run all MS-DOS programs, but some programs perform very poorly. You might be able to improve a program's performance by making some adjustments, or you might need a new program. Try tweaking the settings to see if you can get the program up to speed.

TIP

Most companies that develop programs have Web sites. Check their pages for tips on getting the most from your programs.

Speed Up the Graphics

1. Locate the program (not a shortcut to the program) and right-click it.

2. Choose Properties from the shortcut menu, and click the Misc tab.

3. Drag the Idle Sensitivity slider all the way to the left.

4. Click the Program tab, and click the Windows NT button to display the Windows NT PIF Settings dialog box.

5. Turn off the Compatible Timer Hardware Emulation check box if it's turned on.

6. Click OK.

7. Click OK to close the program's Properties dialog box.

8. Try running the program. If it fails to run or if its performance hasn't improved, restore the settings you changed.

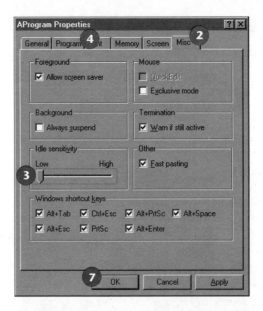

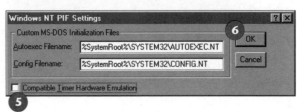

7

TIP

If you have a dual-boot system, try running the program using a different operating system, and make sure your expectations for the program's performance are realistic. You might also be able to detect whether the performance problems are associated with your hardware—a slow CD drive, for example.

TIP

The Alt+Enter combination works only on x86-type computers.

Switch Modes

1. Right-click the program, choose Properties from the shortcut menu, and click the Screen tab.

2. Select the Full-Screen option.

3. Click OK.

4. Run the program and compare its performance with the way it ran in a window. Press Alt+Tab to switch to the window mode if necessary.

5. If the program's performance hasn't improved, contact the program's manufacturer for memory settings that might improve performance.

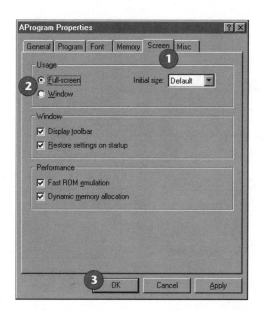

Getting an MS-DOS Program to Run

If an MS-DOS program won't run, you can make some adjustments to your system's settings that might get the program to run. However, Windows NT will not allow a program to violate Windows NT security—and many MS-DOS programs, particularly games and 16-bit multimedia titles, take direct control of parts of the system, thus violating security. If Windows NT doesn't have an automatic way to work around these violations, the program isn't allowed to run.

SEE ALSO

"Searching the Knowledge Base" on page 286 and "Getting Help from Other Windows NT Users" on page 288 for information about getting advice on problems in specific programs.

Change the Available Memory

1 Right-click the program icon and choose Properties from the shortcut menu.

2 Click the Memory tab, and try new memory settings.

3 Click OK to close the program's Properties dialog box.

4 Try to run the program. Repeat steps 1 through 3 if necessary.

Set to program specifications.

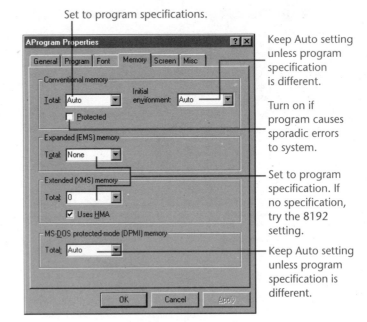

Keep Auto setting unless program specification is different.

Turn on if program causes sporadic errors to system.

Set to program specification. If no specification, try the 8192 setting.

Keep Auto setting unless program specification is different.

TIP

Changing program settings can cause some unexpected results. Check your program's documentation and, if necessary, check with the manufacturer for recommended settings.

TIP

Write down all your original settings before you make any changes so that you can restore the original settings if your changes don't solve the problem (or if they create more problems).

TIP

If the program continues to fail after you've tried everything, contact the manufacturer to find out whether there's an updated version of the program that runs in Windows NT Workstation 4.0.

Change the Timing

1 Right-click the program icon and choose Properties from the shortcut menu.

2 On the Program tab, click the Windows NT button.

3 Turn on the Compatible Timer Hardware Emulation check box.

4 Click OK to close the Windows NT PIF Settings dialog box, and click OK to close the program's Properties dialog box.

5 Try running the program. If the problem persists, return to the Windows NT PIF Settings dialog box, turn off the Compatible Timer Hardware Emulation check box, close the dialog box, and then close the Properties dialog box.

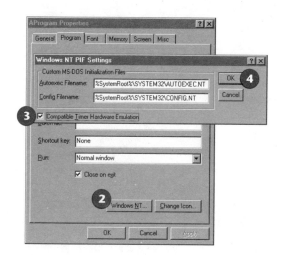

8

Working with Multimedia

Multimedia! Depending on what you use your computer for, multimedia can mean work or play—or a little or a lot of each. If you're set up to work with multimedia on your computer—if, that is, you have a sound card installed, speakers or a headset, a CD-ROM drive, and, optionally, a microphone—Windows NT is set to work with you.

You can play and create sounds, view video clips, and even play music CDs while you work. You can associate sounds with events that take place on your computer: if you'd like to hear a duck quacking every time you receive new mail, or your child's voice babbling baby language when you shut down your computer, you can make it so.

You can insert music clips into your dissertation on Beethoven or Brubeck; you can include video clips of your daughter's wedding in your e-mail to a distant relative. Provided the person on the receiving end has a similarly equipped computer, the creative possibilities are endless. And, of course, multimedia opens up a whole new realm of wonderful educational and recreational tools—multimedia encyclopedias and other reference works; foreign-language courses; cooking and gardening programs; about a zillion exciting games...

Whether you use Windows NT multimedia features for work or for play, you're going to have a lot of fun.

Playing Sound Files

Windows NT works primarily with two different types of sounds: wave sounds, which are digital recordings of sounds, and MIDI (Musical Instrument Digital Interface) sequences. A MIDI sequence contains instructions (which could be compared to sheet music) that tell your sound card how to synthesize the music.

TIP

If Media Player closes before you can make any changes, click the Start button, point your way through Programs, Accessories, and Multimedia, choose Media Player, and open the sound file from the File menu.

SEE ALSO

"Controlling the Sound Volume" on the facing page for information about changing sound levels.

Play a Sound

1 Open the folder containing the sound file.

2 Double-click the sound file. Media Player opens and plays the sound.

3 While the sound is playing, click any of the control buttons, or use the slider to stop, pause, or repeat the play.

4 If you adjusted the play, close the program when you've finished. If you didn't adjust the play, the program closes automatically when it's finished.

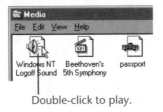

Double-click to play.

Drag slider and drop to play a different part.

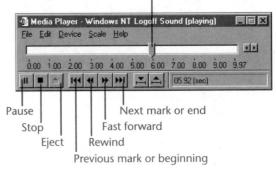

Pause

Stop

Eject

Rewind

Previous mark or beginning

Fast forward

Next mark or end

Controlling the Sound Volume

You can keep your music and other sounds muted so that you don't disturb other people, or, when you're the only person around, you can crank the sound level up and blast away! Although many programs have individual controls, you can use the volume control to set all your sound levels.

TIP

If the Volume icon doesn't appear on the taskbar, open Multimedia Properties from the Control Panel and, on the Audio tab, turn on the Show Volume Control On The Taskbar check box.

TIP

Many speakers have built-in volume controls. You can use these in conjunction with the volume control on the taskbar to fine-tune your sound levels.

Set the Master Volume Level

1. Click the Volume icon on the taskbar.

2. Drag the slider and drop it to adjust the volume.

3. Click outside the Volume icon to close it.

Set the Volume for Individual Devices

1. Double-click the Volume icon on the taskbar.

2. Adjust the settings for your devices.

Master control affects all devices.

Drag slider and drop to adjust balance.

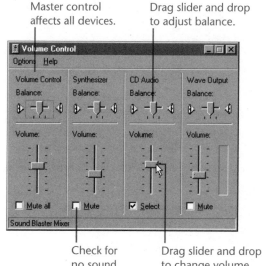

Check for no sound.

Drag slider and drop to change volume.

Playing a Video Clip

Most videos are played as part of a program and their playing is controlled by the program. You can, however, play a video directly using Media Player.

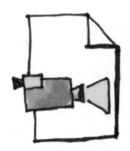

TIP

It's tempting to set your video to play in a full screen, but be aware that many videos are very grainy at that size. Experiment to find the best setting for a video on your display.

Set the Size of Video Playback

1 Click the Start button, point to Settings, and choose Control Panel from the submenu.

2 Double-click Multimedia.

3 Click the Video tab.

4 Select the size of the playback.

5 Click OK.

Multimedia

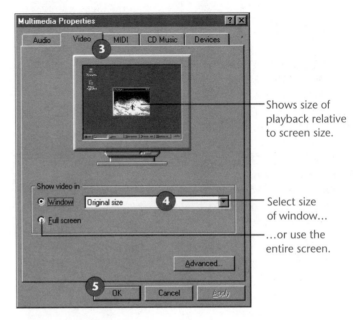

Shows size of playback relative to screen size.

Select size of window...

...or use the entire screen.

Play a Video Clip

Double-click the video file. Media Player opens, plays the video, and closes when finished.

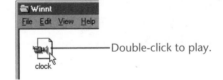

Double-click to play.

TIP

Windows NT has Video For Windows built in, so you can play AVI-type videos. You can play other video formats too, depending on the programs you've installed and provided you have the necessary hardware components.

TIP

Most—but not all—videos include sound. Make sure you have a sound card installed to get the most from your videos.

SEE ALSO

"Controlling the Sound Volume" on page 137 for information about changing sound levels.

Control the Playback

1 Click any of the control buttons, or use the slider. If the video is full screen, click the video to reveal the controls.

2 Close the window when you've finished.

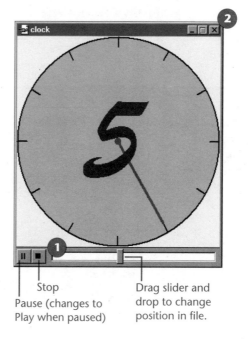

Stop

Pause (changes to Play when paused)

Drag slider and drop to change position in file.

8

Creating a Sound File

If you have a microphone—also called an *external input device*—you can create your own sound files. Even without an external input device, you can create your own sound files by combining and editing any existing sound files.

TIP

The higher the quality of the sound, the larger the file size. Use Telephone Quality to save space, Radio Quality for most uses, and CD Quality only in special cases when quality of sound is paramount. The custom options are based on the audio Codecs (compression/ decompression methods) that are installed on your system.

Set Up a Sound File

1 Click the Start button, point to Programs, Accessories, and Multimedia, and then choose Sound Recorder from the submenu.

2 Choose Save from the File menu, and save the file in the appropriate folder.

3 Choose Audio Properties from the Edit menu.

4 In the Audio Properties dialog box, choose the settings for your recording.

5 Click OK.

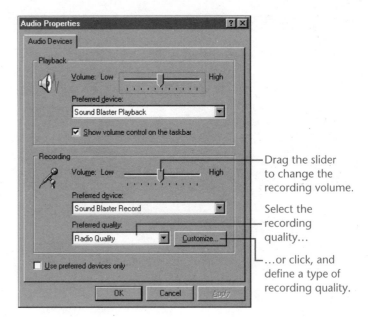

Drag the slider to change the recording volume.

Select the recording quality...

...or click, and define a type of recording quality.

Record Sounds

1 Click the Record button.

2 Speak, sing, whistle, or otherwise make sounds in front of the microphone.

3 Click Stop when you've finished.

4 Choose Save from the File menu.

TIP

The Stop button is grayed and inactive until you start recording.

TRY THIS

By combining existing files with your voice, you can create great effects. With a new Wave Sound file started, use the Insert File command on the Edit menu to insert the Wave Sound "Ding" from the Media folder (found in the Winnt folder). Click the Seek To End button and record a message, such as "I love this book!" Click the Seek To Start button and use the Mix With File command from the Edit menu to add the Wave Sound "Windows NT Logon Sound" from the Media folder. Now save your custom sound for later use.

Add Sounds and Effects

1 Move the slider to the location in the sound file where you want to add an existing sound file.

2 From the Edit menu, choose

◆ Insert File to add a file and record over any existing sound.

◆ Mix With File to merge a file with the existing sound.

3 Locate the file and click Open.

4 Choose the type of effect you want to add from the Effects menu.

5 Save the file.

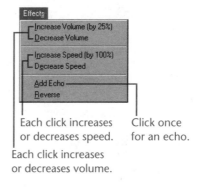

Each click increases or decreases speed.

Click once for an echo.

Each click increases or decreases volume.

Creating a Long Sound File

Windows NT's Sound Recorder limits your recording time to 60 seconds—usually more than enough time for a sound effect or a short message. If, however, you need to create a longer sound recording, you can force Sound Recorder to create a message of any length you want. Remember that sound recordings occupy a lot of space. Depending on the sound quality you use, a three-minute recording will probably take more than 3 megabytes of disk space and will be too large to send through most e-mail systems.

Set the Recording Time

1. Click the start button, point to Programs, Accessories, and Multimedia, and then choose Sound Recorder from the submenu.

2. Click the Record button and, without recording anything, wait for the full 60 seconds to be recorded.

3. Choose Save from the File menu, and save the file.

4. Choose New from the File menu.

5. Choose Insert file from the Edit menu.

6. Specify the blank 60-second file you just created.

7. Repeat steps 5 and 6 until the file contains adequate time for your recording.

8. Save the new file.

Blank saved file is 60 seconds in length.

Each time you insert the saved file, the new file becomes 60 seconds longer.

TIP

If you frequently need sound files that are longer than 60 seconds, you can preserve your long blank file by saving it under a different name before you record any sounds on it.

TIP

If you do need to transfer a large sound file via e-mail, consider using one of the numerous file-compression programs available to make the sound file smaller. Sound files can often be compressed to less than 10 percent of their original size!

Create Your File

1 Click the Record button and record the sounds.

2 Click the Stop button when you've finished recording.

3 Choose Delete After Current Position from the Edit menu to remove the remaining blank part of the file.

4 Confirm that you want to delete part of the file.

5 Save the completed file.

Shows the length of your recording.

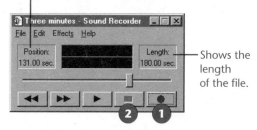

Shows the length of the file.

After you delete the unused portion, the file contains only your message.

Playing a Music CD

You can just drop a music CD into your disc drive and play it, or you can use CD Player to control how the CD is played.

SEE ALSO

"Controlling the Sound Volume" on page 137 for information about changing sound levels.

"Creating a CD Play List" on the facing page for information about programming CD Player.

TIP

If the CD doesn't start automatically, click the Start button, point your way through Programs, Accessories, and Multimedia, and then choose CD Player from the submenu. With CD Player open, click the Play button.

TIP

Choose Preferences from the Options menu to set how long each track is played when using Intro Play.

Play a CD

1 Insert the CD into the disc drive.

2 Wait for Windows NT to start playing the disc.

3 Listen and enjoy!

4 Click the CD Player button on the taskbar.

5 Choose a play option from the Options menu:

- ◆ Random Order to have CD Player decide the order in which the tracks are played

- ◆ Continuous Play to resume playing the CD after the last track has been played

- ◆ Intro Play to play the first few seconds of each track

6 Click any control button, or choose a new option from the Artist or Track drop-down list box.

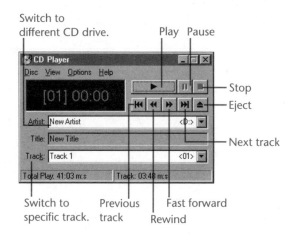

Switch to different CD drive.   Play   Pause

Stop

Eject

Next track

Switch to specific track.   Previous track   Fast forward   Rewind

Creating a CD Play List

By creating a play list, you can program which tracks are played and what order they're played in. You can create a play list for each CD and save the list. Then, whenever that CD is loaded, Windows NT will use the play list.

SEE ALSO

"Playing a Music CD" on the facing page for information about using CD Player.

TIP

Create a Mood. *If you want to play only a few tracks, click Clear All, and then add the tracks from the Available Tracks list.*

Define a CD

1. Insert the CD into the disc drive and click the CD Player button on the taskbar.

2. Choose Edit Play List from the Disc menu.

3. Type the name of the recording artist.

4. Type the name of the CD.

Create a Play List

Create your own concert:

◆ Remove unwanted tracks from the play list.

◆ Change the order of play.

◆ Name the tracks for easy identification.

Drag the track and drop it at a new location.

Select a track whose position you want to change.

Click Remove.

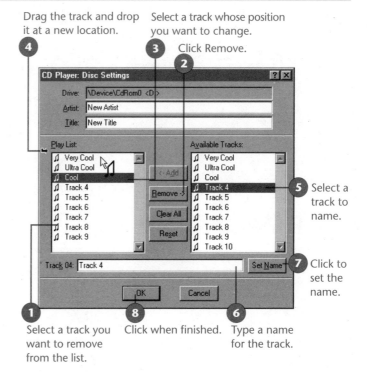

Select a track to name.

Click to set the name.

Select a track you want to remove from the list.

Click when finished.

Type a name for the track.

Inserting Part of a Multimedia File into a Document

You can use Media Player to insert a section of a wave sound, MIDI sequence, or video-clip file into a program. Although only part of the file will play from the document, the entire multimedia file must be available to the document.

SEE ALSO

"Copying Material Between Documents" on page 70 for information about copying items between documents.

Get the File

1 Click the Start button, point to Programs, Accessories, and Multimedia, and then choose Media Player from the submenu.

2 From the Device menu, choose the type of multimedia file to be used.

3 Locate and select the file, and click OK.

Define and Copy a Section

1 Drag the slider and drop it at the beginning of the section to be copied.

2 Click the Start Selection button.

3 Drag the slider and drop it at the end of the section to be copied.

4 Click the End Selection button.

5 Choose Options from the Edit menu and set the options.

6 Choose Copy Object from the Edit menu.

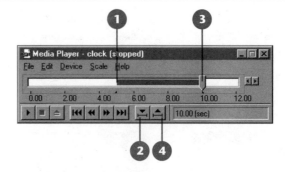

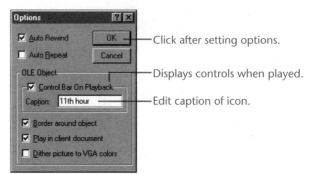

Click after setting options.

Displays controls when played.

Edit caption of icon.

TRY THIS

Add a Soundtrack. *Find a MIDI file you like. Open a document, add sound clips from selected areas of the MIDI file, and save the document. Because you used the same MIDI file as the source for all the different sound clips, you need access to only the one MIDI file to play any of the sound clips.*

TIP

If you're sending a video file or a MIDI file by e-mail, send the entire file rather than part of it; otherwise, the recipient won't be able to play it. To create a new file that contains only part of the original file, use one of the many excellent programs available for editing videos or MIDI music. To send part of a sound file, use Sound Recorder to delete the parts you don't want to include, and save the part you do want as a new file.

SEE ALSO

"Create Your File" on page 143 for information about deleting portions of a sound file.

Insert the Section

1 Switch to the document that is to contain the multimedia section.

2 Click to place the insertion point where you want the multimedia section.

3 Choose Paste from the Edit menu.

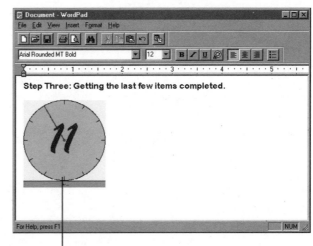

The multimedia object is placed in your document and is set to play only the section you specified.

8

Associating a Sound with an Event

If you want audio cues for events in Windows NT—closing a program or receiving new mail, for example—you can assign wave sounds to these events.

SEE ALSO

"Controlling the Sound Volume" on page 137 for information about changing sound levels.

TIP

Put any sound files that you want to use for events in the Media folder (in the Winnt folder), and the sounds will appear in the Name list.

Assign a Sound to an Event

1. Click the Start button, point to Settings, and choose Control Panel from the submenu.

2. Double-click Sounds.

3. Select an event from the Events list.

4. Select a sound from the Name list, or use the Browse button to find a sound in another folder.

5. Save the sound scheme after assigning sounds to different events.

6. Click OK when you've finished.

Sounds

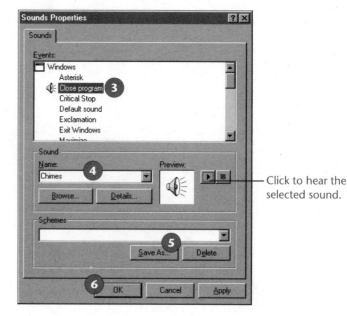

Click to hear the selected sound.

Using Mail, Phone, and Terminal

When you think about communicating with other people via your computer, you're likely to be thinking about e-mail, or electronic mail. That's what some of this section of the book is about: setting up your Inbox so that you can send, receive, and forward e-mail. But there's much more to communicating than sending e-mail. You can send enclosures, or *attachments*, with your e-mail: documents, pictures—even sound and video clips.

This section also shows you how to create and administer a post office for sending and receiving mail within your workgroup. If you have a modem, you can set up a HyperTerminal so that you can connect with bulletin boards or other types of terminal services and can transfer files between computers. You can even use your modem with an accessory program called Phone Dialer to place telephone calls for you.

Windows NT is not a static system; it's updated frequently, and there are many other services that you can add, from the powerful Microsoft Exchange Server e-mail system to the Internet service provider that delivers mail directly to your Inbox. Because you have so many choices, some of your Inbox components might look a little different from the illustrations you see in this section.

Setting Up the Inbox

When Windows NT was installed on your computer, it placed an Inbox on your Desktop. However, before you can use the Inbox to send and receive mail, you have to be set up with a mail system, whether it's a workgroup post office, a network mail server, or an online service.

TIP

Because the Inbox is designed to be a universal inbox, you can connect several mail services to your Inbox and you can have all your mail delivered to, stored in, and sent from the same location.

Specify the Services You Want

1 Double-click the Inbox on your Desktop.

2 Select the services you want to use.

3 Step through the wizard, providing information on each service you want. When you've finished, the Inbox opens.

The Inbox Setup Wizard will set up each service you select.

Set the Defaults

1 Choose Options from the Tools menu, and click the Send tab in the Options dialog box.

2 Click the Font button, and set the default font, font size, and color you want to use.

3 Make any other changes you want to the default settings.

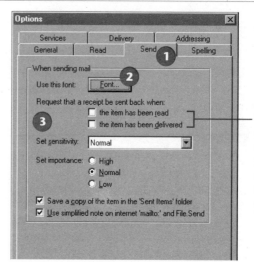

Turn on if you want a "receipt" message when mail that you've sent has been delivered or opened.

TIP

If you install Microsoft Personal Fax for Windows and you have a fax modem, you can also send and receive faxes through your Inbox.

TIP

Gather up the information you need before you start the Inbox Setup Wizard. If you're connected to a mail service on your network, ask the mail or network administrator for the procedures, locations, and passwords you need. If you're connecting to an Internet service provider to receive Internet mail, get the name of the mail server and any special setup procedures you need to set up the Internet Mail service.

SEE ALSO

"Using Microsoft Word in E-Mail" on page 164 for information about using the powerful resources of Microsoft Word—including spelling and grammar checking, AutoCorrect, and AutoFormat—when you create mail messages.

"Setting Up Your Fax" on page 240 for information about installing Microsoft Personal Fax for Windows.

Turn On the Spelling Checker

1. Click the Spelling tab. (The Inbox doesn't have its own spelling dictionary, so the Spelling tab is active only if you have a spelling checker installed from Microsoft Office or from another Microsoft 32-bit program.)

2. Turn on the spelling checking options.

3. Turn on any other spelling options you want.

4. Click OK.

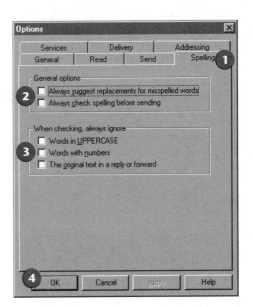

Sending E-Mail

Creating and sending an e-mail message is usually faster, easier, and more convenient than sending a letter through the U.S. Postal Service. You don't have to write an envelope, lick a stamp, or trek to the mailbox on a cold, rainy day All you do is select a name, create a message, and click a Send button. Your Inbox and your mail server do the rest. What a great idea!

SEE ALSO

"Using Microsoft Word in E-Mail" on page 164 for information about setting up Word-Mail and composing mail using WordMail.

Address a Message

1. Click the New Message button on the Inbox toolbar.

2. Click the To button.

3. Select the address list you want to use.

4. Select the name of the person you're sending mail to.

5. Click the To button.

6. Select the name of someone you want to receive a copy of the mail.

7. Click the CC button.

8. Repeat steps 4 through 7 to add other recipients to this mail.

9. Click OK when you've included everyone you want.

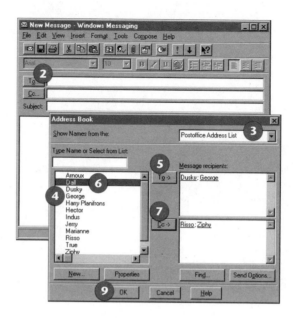

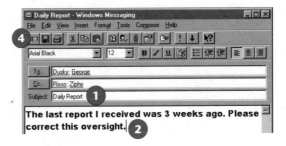

TIP

Sometimes, in a large company, several people might have the same name. If you're not certain that you've selected the correct person, right-click the name and choose Properties from the shortcut menu for detailed information about the individual.

TIP

Text formatting is often lost when a message is sent over the Internet, so don't depend on formatting to get the point of your message across.

TIP

If you're using WordMail, you won't see the delivery options buttons on the toolbar. In that case, choose Properties from the File menu and turn on the options you want.

Compose a Message

1 Click in the Subject box, type a subject, and press Tab to move into the message area.

2 Type your message, applying any formatting you want from the Formatting toolbar.

3 Click a button on the toolbar to set delivery options:

◆ Click Read Receipt to be notified when the message is opened by the recipient.

◆ Click Importance: High to mark the mail with a High Importance tag.

◆ Click Importance: Low to mark the mail with a Low Importance tag.

4 Click the Send button to send the document.

9

Reading E-Mail

Windows NT lets you know when you have received new mail, and you can specify the type of notification you prefer. You can check your Inbox and see at a glance which messages haven't been read, and you can browse through them in order or open them selectively.

TIP

You need to set the notification options only once. Whichever options you choose, a little envelope appears on the Windows taskbar when you receive mail. When you double-click the envelope icon, the Inbox becomes the active program on your Desktop.

Set the Notification

1. Choose Options from the Tools menu to display the Options dialog box.

2. On the General tab, select the type of notification you want each time new mail arrives:

   ◆ Play A Sound, if you want to hear a sound

   ◆ Briefly Change The Pointer, to have the mouse pointer change into an incoming-letter icon for a moment

   ◆ Display A Notification Message, to have a dialog box appear and stay open until you click a button

3. Click OK.

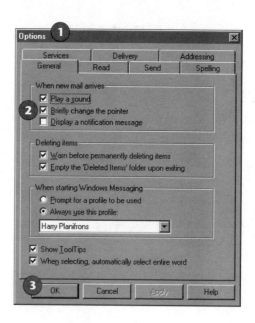

TIP

The Inbox has two views: one shows the contents of the Inbox folder, and the other shows the different mail folders. Click the Show/Hide Folder List button on the toolbar to switch between the two views.

SEE ALSO

"Associating a Sound with an Event" on page 148 for information about setting a custom sound for the new mail notification.

TIP

Unopened messages are displayed in bold type in the Inbox window. A folder that contains unread messages is also displayed in bold type.

TIP

If you want to receive mail immediately rather than wait for your system to check your mailbox at its next scheduled time, choose Deliver Now from the Tools menu.

Read Your Messages

1. Open the Inbox folder if it's not already open.

2. Double-click an unread message.

3. Read the message.

4. Click the Next or Previous button to look through the other mail in your Inbox.

5. Close the Messaging window when you've read your mail.

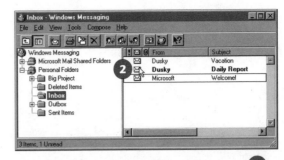

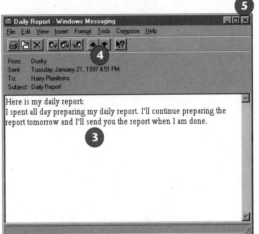

Replying to E-Mail

When you receive an e-mail message that needs a reply, you need only click a button to create a reply window that's already addressed for you. You can also have the reply window contain a copy of the original message so that the response will contain a complete record of the conversation.

TIP

You set the formatting for the original text only once; the Inbox will use those settings until you change them.

Format the Original Message

1 Choose Options from the Tools menu, and click the Read tab.

2 Specify the way you want original messages to be treated when you reply to them.

3 Click the Font button to set the appearance of the text in your reply.

4 Click OK.

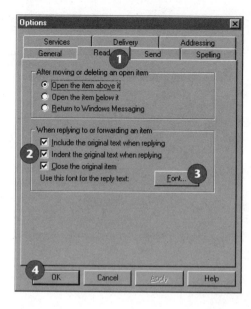

TIP

Be careful when you use the Reply To All button if the original message contained alias names for groups; you could be replying to the entire company instead of to one or two people.

TIP

If the message has a long string of replies, consider deleting some of the older ones if you feel they're not really relevant any more. It's good e-mail etiquette, however, to note in your message that you've deleted some previous messages.

Reply to the Message

1 Open the message you want to respond to.

2 Click the appropriate reply button:

◆ Reply To Sender, to send your reply to the writer of the message only

◆ Reply To All, to send your reply to the writer of the message *and* to everyone listed in the original message's To and CC lines

3 Add names to or delete names from the To and CC lines.

4 Type your reply.

5 Click the Send button.

The reply message is addressed automatically.

The original subject line is included. *RE* indicates that this is a reply.

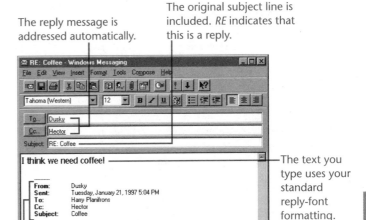

The text you type uses your standard reply-font formatting.

The original header information and message text are included and indented.

Forwarding E-Mail

Message forwarding is a great convenience: you can forward any e-mail message that you've received to one person or to many people. Or, if you've sent an original message to several people and then realize that you've left someone out, you can forward that message to the person you forgot—with your apologies, of course.

TIP

When you forward a single message, it's sent as a message. When you forward several messages, however, they become mail objects within a single message. To read each message, double-click it.

Forward a Message

1. Open the message you want to forward to someone.

2. Click the Forward button.

3. Insert the recipients' names in the To and CC lines.

4. Type your message.

5. Click the Send button.

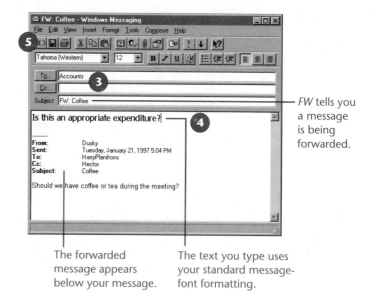

FW tells you a message is being forwarded.

The forwarded message appears below your message.

The text you type uses your standard message-font formatting.

Forward Several Messages

1. In the Inbox, select the messages to be forwarded.

2. Click the Forward button.

3. Insert the recipients' names in the To and CC lines, and the subject of the messages in the Subject line, of the new message window.

4. Type your message.

5. Click the Send button.

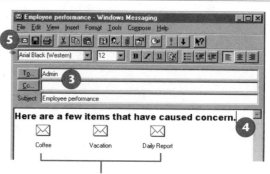

Multiple forwarded messages are inserted as message attachments. Recipient double-clicks each icon to open the message.

Mailing a File

You can send an entire file—a Word document, a sound file, a text file, or a collection of files—by including it in a mail message as an *attachment*. When you send the message, the attached file is sent as an object and is usually shown as an icon in your mail text. The recipient can double-click the icon to open the attachment, or right-click it to save it as a file.

TIP

If you see a long string of indecipherable characters instead of an icon for an attached file, the mail system has failed to decode the message. Contact your mail administrator and ask for a UUENCODE translation program.

TIP

Many mail programs can't send a file (or a group of files in one message) that's larger than about 1 megabyte.

Include a File

1. Create and address a message.

2. Type the message text.

3. Click the Insert File button.

4. Use the Insert File dialog box to find and select the file to be included.

5. Verify that the An Attachment option is selected.

6. Click OK. The file's icon appears in your message.

7. Click the Send button.

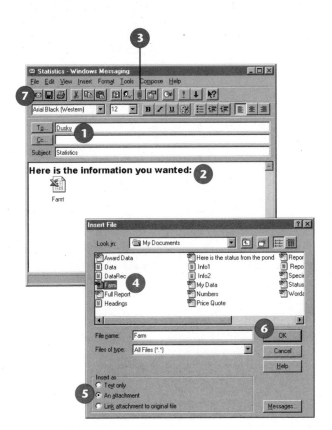

Creating a Folder System

The Inbox comes with the basic folders you need for managing your e-mail, and you can then create as many folders and subfolders as you need to organize and store your mail messages. You can also customize your Inbox window so that the columns in the right side of the window display the information you want to see at a glance when you're scanning the listings in your mail folders. You can change the number of columns that are displayed in the window, the order in which they appear, and their width.

Create a Folder System

1. Click the Show/Hide Folder List button.

2. Click Personal Folders.

3. Choose New Folder from the File menu, type a name for a new folder, and click OK.

4. Click other folders, and repeat step 3 to create additional subfolders.

5. Drag messages from one folder and drop them into a different folder to organize them.

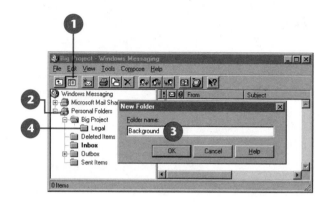

TIP

Don't go overboard creating new folders and filing the messages in the appropriate folders. No matter how you set up the folders, your new mail will be placed in your Inbox folder and will remain there until you get around to filing the messages in the appropriate folders. Instead, use the folders to archive old messages or to file messages about topics that aren't part of your usual mail traffic. With most of your messages stored in your Inbox, you can use the Find command on the Tools menu to search for a specific message, or you can click any of the column headings to sort the messages by that column.

Customize a Folder

1 Click a folder whose appearance you want to modify in the right side of your window, where the information about your messages is displayed.

2 Choose Columns from the View menu to display the Columns dialog box.

3 Modify the columns in the folder:

◆ Add new items.

◆ Remove current items.

◆ Change the order of the items.

◆ Change the width of each column.

4 Click OK.

Columns in the selected folder are changed and re-ordered.

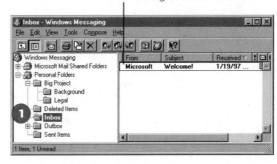

Add columns from here.   Delete or re-order columns.

Specify the width of the selected column.

Adding an Address to an Address Book

When you use e-mail, you don't need to type an address every time you send a message; you can retrieve addresses from one of your address lists. You might want to copy an address you use frequently from your company-wide address book into your Personal Address Book for quick reference.

TIP

Some additional information, such as phone numbers or office room numbers, might be displayed next to the names in your Personal Address Book. To look at all the information that's listed, select the individual's name and click the Properties button.

Add an Address

1 Click the Address Book button on the Inbox toolbar.

2 Select the address list that contains the name you want to add to your personal address list.

3 Locate and select the name you want to add.

4 Click the Add To Personal Address Book button.

TIP

You can use the Address Book for more than addressing e-mail messages. You can complete the information on the various tabs and use it to dial phone numbers automatically, and to include additional information on fax cover pages. Some programs, such as Microsoft Word, can access the Address Book as a data source for creating mail-merged documents.

Create a New Address

1 Click the New Entry button on the Address Book toolbar.

2 Select the address book in which you want the name to be stored.

3 Double-click the type of address you're adding.

4 Fill in the address information.

5 On the other tabs, fill in any additional information you'll want to refer to.

6 Click OK.

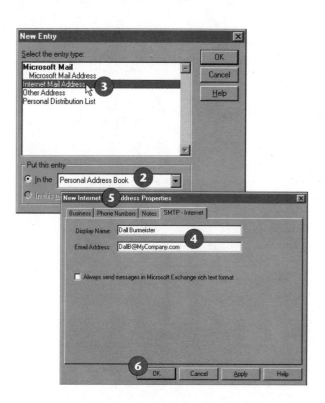

Add an Address from a Message

1 Open the message.

2 In the message header, right-click the name you want to add.

3 Choose Add To Personal Address Book from the shortcut menu.

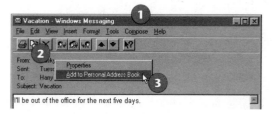

Using Microsoft Word in E-Mail

If you have Microsoft Word 95 or later installed on your computer, you can use WordMail as your e-mail editor. WordMail lets you use Word's powerful features—formatting, spelling and grammar checking, AutoFormat, AutoText, and so on—in your e-mail messages.

TIP

WordMail must be installed on your computer if you want to use it as your e-mail editor. If you don't see WordMail Options on the Inbox's Compose menu, rerun Word Setup and install WordMail.

TIP

You can use any font in an e-mail message, but if the recipient's computer doesn't have the same font installed, your message will be displayed in a default font.

Turn On WordMail

1. In the Inbox, choose WordMail Options from the Compose menu.

2. Turn on the Enable Word As E-Mail Editor option.

3. Click the template you want to use.

4. Click the Close button.

Compose a Message

1. Click the New Message button.

2. Address your message, and add the subject line.

3. Compose your mail, using any of Word's tools.

4. Click the Send button.

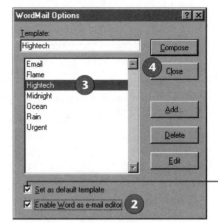

Turn on if you want to use the selected template for all your messages.

Mailing tools are included on Word's toolbar.

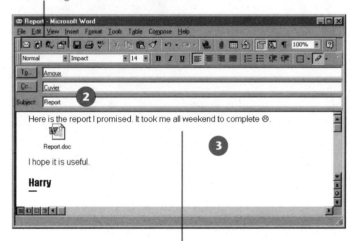

Use Word's tools—including AutoFormat, AutoCorrect, AutoComplete, spelling and grammar checking, tables, and different views—to complete your message.

TIP

WordMail using Microsoft Word 97 has more features than the Word 95 version. Word 97 is used here.

TIP

With Microsoft Word 97, you can set WordMail to format all incoming plain-text mail messages automatically.

TIP

Depending on the receiving system, formatting can often get lost when you send an e-mail message via the Internet. To ensure that you don't lose any formatting, send a formatted document as an enclosure with your mail.

TIP

Microsoft Outlook, a program that is included with Microsoft Office 97, greatly expands the functionality of the Inbox and simplifies the use of WordMail. For information about using Outlook, ask the Office Assistant to answer your questions.

Read a Message

1 Double-click a message.

2 If the message isn't formatted, click the AutoFormat button.

3 Close the WordMail window when you've finished reading the message.

Plain-text message

Click the AutoFormat button to format text.
Click to hide mail header information.

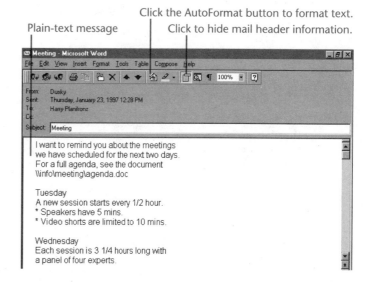

Formatted message

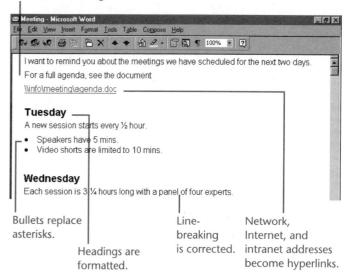

Bullets replace asterisks.

Headings are formatted.

Line-breaking is corrected.

Network, Internet, and intranet addresses become hyperlinks.

9

Setting Up Workgroup Mail

Windows NT comes with a version of Microsoft Mail that works with your Inbox so that you can create and send mail within your workgroup. To use workgroup mail, you create a post office in a location that is shared with all the people in the workgroup.

TIP

Make a note of the password and mailbox names for your post office and keep the note in a secure place. If you forget either name, you won't be able to administer the post office and you'll be stuck with the job of deleting the existing workgroup post office and creating a new one.

Create a Post Office

1 Create a shared folder that allows full access to everyone in your workgroup.

2 Click the Start button, point to Settings, and choose Control Panel from the submenu.

3 Double-click the Microsoft Mail Postoffice icon. The Microsoft Workgroup Postoffice Admin Wizard starts.

4 Select the Create A New Workgroup Postoffice option, and click Next.

5 Specify the shared folder you created for the post office.

6 Enter all the administrator information.

7 Complete the wizard.

For a small workgroup, use your own name and mailbox and tell everyone to contact you for administrative support.

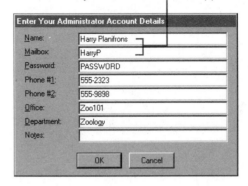

For a large workgroup, create an administrator's mailbox, and create a new profile to log on as the administrator.

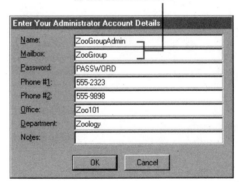

TRY THIS

If someone in your workgroup forgets his or her mail password, use the Workgroup Postoffice Admin Wizard to open the post office, select the name of the person who forgot the password, click the Details button, and type a new password. After closing the wizard, give the forgetful person his or her new password (but don't e-mail it!).

TIP

Each user you add to the post office gets an individual mailbox. The mailbox name must be unique within that post office.

Administer!

1 Click the Start button, point to Settings, and choose Control Panel from the submenu.

2 Double-click the Microsoft Mail Postoffice icon.

3 Select the Administer An Existing Workgroup Postoffice option, specify the location of the post office on your computer, and click Next.

4 Enter your mailbox and password, and click Next.

All individual mailboxes are placed in the administrator's mailbox.

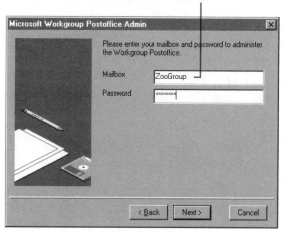

Add a New User

1 Click the Add User button.

2 Enter a user name.

3 Enter a unique mailbox name.

4 Enter a password of up to eight characters.

5 Enter any other information that you want to appear in the post office address book.

6 Click OK, and then click Close to close the Postoffice Manager dialog box.

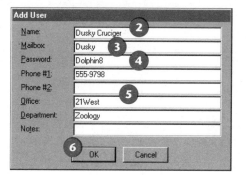

Connecting with a Terminal

When you need to connect by modem with a terminal—a bulletin board, for example—you can do so using HyperTerminal. HyperTerminal is a program provided by Windows NT that lets your computer function as a terminal. And if you have problems connecting or communicating, you can modify the settings to improve the connection.

TIP

HyperTerminal comes with some preconfigured setups for various popular services and bulletin boards. To use one of these setups, double-click the icon, and confirm and/or modify the connection information if necessary.

Set Up Your Terminal

1. Click the Start button, point your way through Programs, Accessories, and HyperTerminal, and then choose HyperTerminal from the submenu.

2. Type an identifying name for the connection, select an icon, and click OK.

3. Enter your phone information, and click OK.

4. Click the Dial button.

5. Use the sign-on information you've been assigned, and verify that the information is being displayed correctly.

6. Sign off, and click the Disconnect button.

Scroll up to see text that has scrolled off the window. Text from previous sessions is also shown.

Click to disconnect.

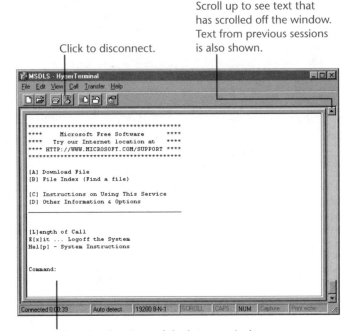

Follow the directions of the host terminal.

SEE ALSO

"Transferring Files by Modem" on page 170 for information about transferring files directly between computers.

TIP

Your connection doesn't have to be a modem connection. To connect two computers by cable, choose the correct COM port from the Connect Using list in the Phone Number dialog box that appears when you're setting up HyperTerminal.

TIP

Windows NT also provides a Telnet terminal for computers that are configured for Telnet connection. To start Telnet, click the Start button, point to Programs and Accessories, and choose Telnet from the submenu.

Modify the Connection

1. Click the Properties button on the Hyper-Terminal toolbar.

2. On the Settings tab, click the ASCII Setup button.

3. Modify the settings as shown in the table, below right.

4. Click OK.

5. Click OK.

6. Choose Save from the File menu.

7. Try your connection again.

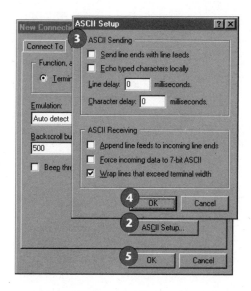

CONNECTION-SETTING TROUBLESHOOTING	
If you have this problem	Make this setting
Text you send is in one long line.	Turn on the Send Line Ends With Line Feeds option.
You don't see what you send.	Turn on the Echo Typed Characters Locally option.
Some of the text you send isn't received.	Enter 1 for Line Delay. Increase the value if necessary.
Some of the characters you send drop out.	Enter 1 for Character Delay. Increase the value if necessary.
Text you receive is in one long line.	Turn on the Append Line Feeds To Incoming Line Ends option.
Text you receive is garbled.	Turn on the Force Incoming Data To 7-Bit ASCII option.
The ends of lines are not visible.	Turn on the Wrap Lines That Exceed Terminal Width option.

9

Transferring Files by Modem

If you want to transfer files directly between computers via modem, you can transfer files the old-fashioned way—that is, from terminal to terminal. There is no limitation to file size, and you'll probably get the maximum speed from your modem. You can even use this method to transfer data between different types of computers, including mainframes and computers that aren't running Windows NT, provided the other computer has a modem and communications software. However, the procedure described here assumes that both computers are using HyperTerminal.

SEE ALSO

"Connecting with a Terminal" on page 168 for information about setting up a Hyper-Terminal connection.

Set Up the Terminals

1 On the host computer, create a new Hyper-Terminal setup, using any phone number (the number won't be used).

2 Click the Cancel button instead of dialing.

3 Click the Properties button on the toolbar, and click the ASCII Setup button on the Settings tab.

4 Turn on the Send Line Ends With Line Feeds and Echo Typed Characters Locally options.

5 Click OK.

6 Click OK.

7 On the connecting computer, set up HyperTerminal to dial the host computer, using the same ASCII Setup settings on both computers.

8 Save the settings on both computers.

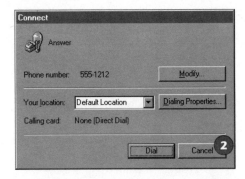

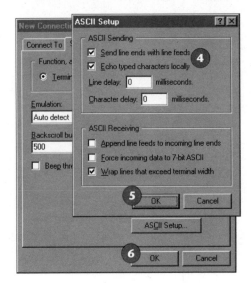

TIP

If the transmission is very slow, verify that the modem or COM port is set to work at its maximum speed. If you're getting too many errors, reduce the transmission speed. To adjust the speed, choose Properties from the File menu, and click the Configure button on the Phone Number tab.

TIP

To transfer files between two computers that are connected by a serial cable, specify the COM port instead of a modem in the Connect Using list in the Phone Number dialog box.

Connect the Computers

1. On the connecting computer, click the Connect button and then the Dial button.

2. When the phone rings on the receiving computer, type your modem's answer code, and press Enter. On many modems this code is *ATA*.

3. Type messages to each other to coordinate the transfer.

4. On the computer that will receive the file, click the Receive button on the HyperTerminal toolbar, specify the folder and protocol for the file, and click Receive.

5. On the computer that's sending the file, click the Send button on the HyperTerminal toolbar, locate the file, and click Send.

6. Wait for the file to be sent.

7. Click the Disconnect button on the Hyper-Terminal toolbar when you've finished.

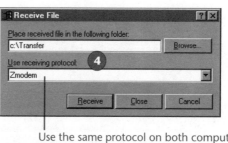

Use the same protocol on both computers.

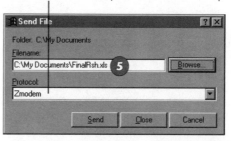

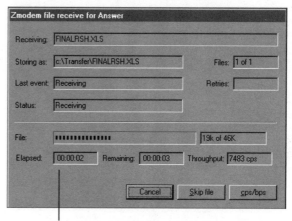

The status of the file transfer is displayed. Both computers receive the status information.

Making a Phone Call

If you have a telephone connected to your modem, you can use a Windows NT accessory program called Phone Dialer to place the call for you. You can automate the process even further by using the Speed Dial buttons.

TIP

If Phone Dialer is not listed on the Accessories submenu, you'll need to install it.

SEE ALSO

"Adding or Removing Windows NT Components" on page 232 for information about installing Windows components.

Dial a Number

1 Click the Start button, point to Programs and then Accessories, and choose Phone Dialer from the submenu.

2 Type the number or click the buttons to enter the number.

3 Click Dial.

4 When prompted, pick up the phone and click the Talk button.

5 When the conversation is over, hang up the phone.

The number you type or enter by clicking the number buttons is shown here.

TIP

To change the name and number of a speed-dial button, choose Speed Dial from the Edit menu.

TIP

You don't have to duplicate the phone numbers that are already stored in your Address Book—you can make phone calls directly from the Address Book. Here's how: open the Address Book from your Inbox, and double-click the name of the person or company you want to call. On the Phone Numbers or the Business tab, click the Dial button for the number you want to call.

Speed It Up

1 Click a blank Speed Dial button.

2 Type a name for the button.

3 Enter the phone number.

4 Click Save.

5 Repeat steps 1 through 4 to add or change speed-dial numbers.

6 Click a Speed Dial button to call that number.

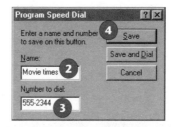

Changing the Look of Your Computer

Most of us tend to choose our clothes, our furniture, and the various other trappings of our daily lives based on personal preferences that include style, size, color, comfort, and efficiency. You love your old car because you're tall and it has enough headroom; I love my blue suede shoes because they're...blue. These preferences are part of our personalities—they might change radically over time but, for better or worse, we always have at least a few of them.

Now that computers are a part of so many people's daily lives, we want our computers to reflect our personalities, too. Whether it's your own computer or your employer's, and whether you're the only person who uses it or one of several users, you can customize your computer so that it looks exactly the way you want it to. You can change the size and color of almost everything, including your icons, your computer screen, and the Desktop itself. Try a different screen saver, or change your mouse pointer into an animated dinosaur! If you do share your computer with other people, each of you can set up your own customization and do your work in your chosen environment.

Windows NT makes it easy and fun to customize the look of your computer, whether you do it one time only or once a month.

Customizing the Taskbar

The taskbar is a really great tool for switching quickly back and forth between programs. If you want, you can alter it so that it will be even better suited to your working style. You can park it at any of the four sides of your screen, change its size, and even make it disappear when you don't need it and reappear when you do.

Move the Taskbar

1 Point to an empty part of the taskbar.

2 Drag the taskbar and drop it at the top, bottom, or either side of your screen.

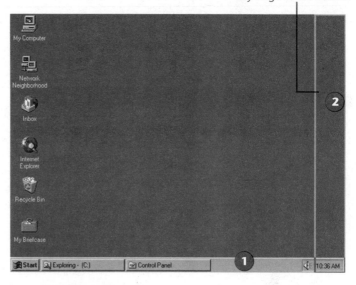

Drop the taskbar at any edge of the screen.

Resize the Taskbar

1 Move the pointer over the inside edge of the taskbar until the pointer turns into a two-headed arrow.

2 Drag the border and drop it when the taskbar is the size you want.

TIP

If you can't find the taskbar because it's hidden, or because something else is on top of it, press the Ctrl+Esc key combination. This will display the taskbar with the Start menu open.

TIP

When you right-click in an empty part of the taskbar, you can also start Task Manager.

TRY THIS

Move the taskbar to the left side of your screen. Resize it so that you can see the full names of programs and documents. Then turn on the Auto Hide and Always On Top options.

Hide or Display the Taskbar

1 Right-click in an empty part of the taskbar, and choose Properties from the shortcut menu.

2 Turn on the Auto Hide option.

3 Turn on any other options you want.

4 Click OK.

5 Move the mouse pointer to the screen edge where the taskbar is hidden. The taskbar slides into view.

6 Click the buttons you want.

7 Move the mouse pointer off the taskbar to hide the taskbar again.

Displays taskbar on top of other windows.

Hides taskbar when not in use.

Displays time on taskbar.

Shows small icons on Start menu instead of large ones.

10

Changing the Look of Icons

There are icons all over the place in Windows NT, and if you don't care for the way they look, you can give them a makeover! You can change their size, the distance between them, and even the font and font size of their captions. Any changes that you make apply to all Windows NT icons—on your Desktop, in My Computer, and in Windows NT Explorer.

SEE ALSO

"Exploring Windows NT" on page 22 and "Sorting the File Listings" on page 24 for information about arranging icons.

TIP

If you want to make the icons larger but keep the same font and font size for their captions, turn on the Use Large Icons option on the Plus! tab of the Desktop Properties dialog box.

Change the Size, Font, and Font Size of Icons

1 Right-click in a blank part of the Desktop, and choose Properties from the shortcut menu.

2 Click the Appearance tab.

3 Select Icon from the Item list.

4 Select a new point size for your icons.

5 Select a different font.

6 Select a different font size.

Standard icon

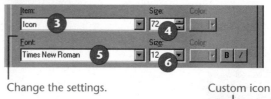

Change the settings.

Custom icon

TIP

Windows adjusts the space between icons when you change the size of an icon, but you can increase the spacing if you want. You won't see any of the changes, though, until you arrange the icons, turn on Auto Arrange, or press the F5 function key to refresh the window's contents.

TIP

By default, Windows NT sets Icon Size to 32 points and Icon Spacing to 43 points.

Increase the Spacing Between Icons

1 Select Icon Spacing (Horizontal) from the Item list.

2 Set a new size.

3 Select Icon Spacing (Vertical) from the Item list.

4 Set a new size.

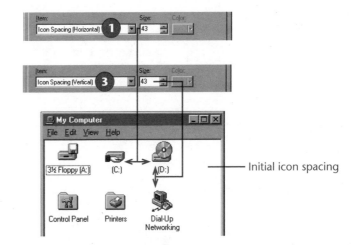

Initial icon spacing

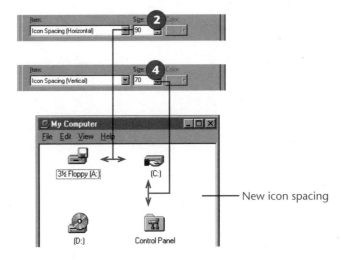

New icon spacing

10

Using a Different Icon

You're not stuck with the same old icons that were originally on your Windows NT Desktop. If you don't like them, or if you simply want a change of scenery, you can use different icons to give your Desktop a fresh and unique look.

My Computer

Network Neighborhood

Change the Icon

1 Right-click in a blank part of the Desktop and choose Properties from the shortcut menu.

2 Click the Plus! tab.

3 Select the Desktop icon you want to change.

4 Click the Change Icon button.

5 Select the icon you want to use.

6 Click OK.

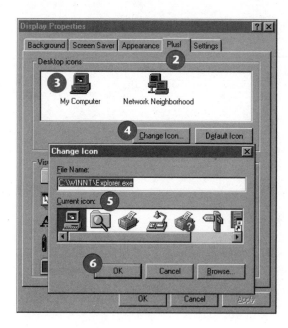

TIP

It's Everyone's Prerogative...
If you've changed an icon and then changed your mind about using it, you can easily restore the original icon by clicking the Plus! tab in the Desktop Properties dialog box, selecting the icon, and clicking the Default Icon button.

TIP

To see all the library files, some of which contain icons, make sure that the DLL files are not hidden.

SEE ALSO

"Hiding or Displaying System Files" on page 44 for information about displaying system files.

TRY THIS

Click the Change Icon button, and open the System32 folder. Examine the icons in the following files: Shell32.dll, Mplay32.exe, Comdlg.dll, Moricons.dll, Progman.exe, and Plustab.dll. Then try exploring on your own. Note that the first time you choose a file that doesn't contain any icons, Windows NT points you to the Shell32.dll file, which is loaded with icons.

Find Different Icons

1 Select the icon you want to change, and click the Change Icon button.

2 Click the Browse button.

3 Navigate through the folders to find a program file or a library (DLL) file that contains the icon you want.

4 Double-click the file.

5 Double-click the icon.

6 Repeat steps 1 through 5 to change any other icons.

7 Click OK when you've finished.

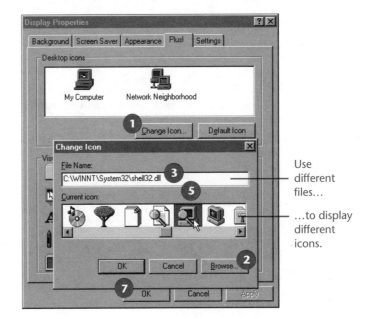

Use different files...

...to display different icons.

Changing the Look of the Desktop

Just as your physical desktop might be constructed from solid oak, printed plastic, or glass, your Windows NT Desktop can have its own uniquely patterned surface. You can add a picture for even more interest, and have it occupy the entire Desktop surface or only part of it. You can even combine a picture with a patterned background. Keep experimenting until you find the look you like—it's a lot of fun!

Add a Pattern

1 Right-click in a blank part of the Desktop and choose Properties from the shortcut menu.

2 Click the Background tab if it's not already selected.

3 Click (None) in the Wallpaper list.

4 Select the pattern that you want to use from the Pattern list.

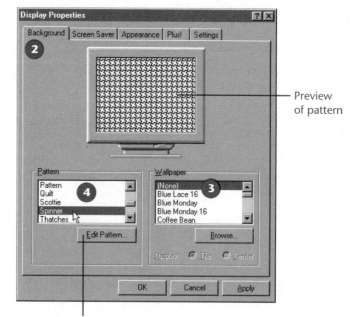

Preview of pattern

Click to customize selected pattern.

SEE ALSO

"Creating Your Own Desktop Wallpaper" on page 77 for information about creating your own wallpaper.

TIP

You can use only bitmap pictures for Desktop patterns and pictures.

TIP

The Wallpaper picture is always on top of the pattern. You'll see the pattern only if the wallpaper picture is centered rather than tiled and the picture is smaller than the whole screen. Alternatively, you can set the wallpaper to (None). If you have the wallpaper and the pattern both set to (None), the Desktop will be a solid color as set on the Appearance tab.

Add a Picture

1. Select the picture you want to use from the Wallpaper list.

2. Click the Display option you want:

   ◆ Tile repeats the image to fill the Desktop.

   ◆ Center places a single copy of the picture in the center of the Desktop.

3. Click OK.

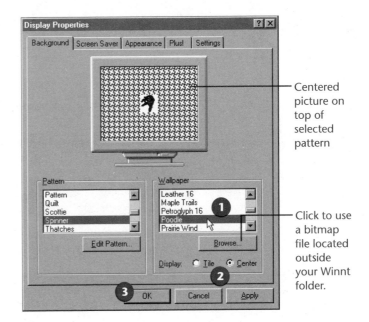

Centered picture on top of selected pattern

Click to use a bitmap file located outside your Winnt folder.

10

Cleaning Up the Desktop

If your Desktop becomes so cluttered with unused shortcuts, old scraps of text, or overlapping icons that you can't find what you want at a glance, take a minute or two to do a little housekeeping.

TIP

Some items on the Desktop—My Computer, for example—are system folders and can't be deleted.

TIP

The Auto Arrange command must be turned off before you can create your own arrangement of icons.

Delete Folders, Files, Shortcuts, and Scraps

1. Select the item or items to be deleted.

2. Drag the items and drop them on the Recycle Bin icon.

Arrange the Icons

1. Right-click in a blank part of the Desktop.

2. Point to Arrange Icons on the shortcut menu and choose the type of arrangement you want.

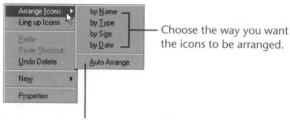

Choose the way you want the icons to be arranged.

Turn on to have Windows NT automatically arrange icons after you've moved, created, or deleted them.

Create Your Own Arrangement

1. Drag the icons to the area of the Desktop where you want them.

2. Right-click in a blank part of the Desktop.

3. Choose Line Up Icons.

Making More Room on the Desktop

If you want to squeeze more items onto your Desktop, you can change the size of the Desktop...sort of. This is one of those "virtual" realities. You "enlarge" the available space by changing the *scaling*, which lets you fit more items on the Desktop even though its area on the screen doesn't get any larger. Your gain in "virtual" area comes at a cost, though—everything will be smaller and harder to read.

TIP

If Windows NT has the proper information about your monitor and graphics card, it will display valid settings only. If all the information was not supplied, Windows NT will try any setting that you create but will cancel the setting if it doesn't work. However, some computers will have only one setting.

Increase the Screen Resolution

1 Right-click in a blank part of the Desktop and choose Properties from the shortcut menu.

2 Click the Settings tab.

3 Drag the Desktop Area slider to the right and drop it at a new setting.

4 Select a font size:

♦ Small Fonts uses the same scaling on fonts that is used on all screen elements.

♦ Large Fonts increases the readability of text.

5 Click Test to test the setting.

6 Click OK to confirm that you want to test the setting.

7 Click Yes to accept the new settings or No to revert to the original settings.

8 If you clicked No, click OK to keep the original settings.

9 Click OK to apply the changes.

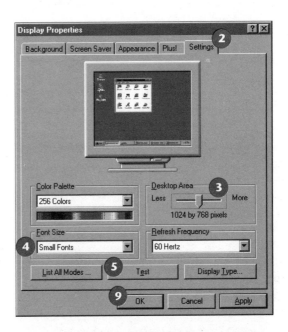

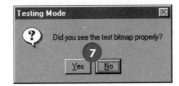

Using a Screen Saver

If you work at a computer for hours every day, it's good for your eyes—and for your mental health—to take a break and look at something different once in a while. If you work in an office with other people, you might not want your colleagues to be able to read your screen—albeit unintentionally—any time you're away from your desk for a few minutes. What you need is a screen saver to provide a nice little respite from your work, as well as some privacy. If you want to add some security you can use the password option, but then you'll need to enter your password to use the computer when the screen saver is running.

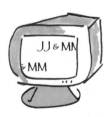

Choose a Screen Saver

1 Right-click in a blank part of the Desktop and choose Properties from the shortcut menu.

2 Click the Screen Saver tab.

3 Select a screen saver.

4 Click Settings to set options for the screen saver.

5 Set the length of time you want your computer to be inactive before the screen saver starts.

6 Click Preview to see the screen saver in full screen. Move your mouse to end the preview.

7 Turn on the Password Protected option to require your password to end the screen saver so that you can do your work.

8 Click OK.

Preview of screen-saver selection

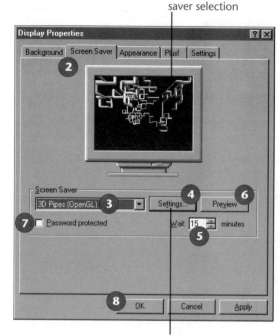

Settings are different for each screen saver.

Changing Screen Colors

If you're tired of looking at the same old colors, you can brighten up—or tone down—the colors on your screen. You can change the Windows NT color scheme to create your own custom-designed color scheme, and you'll see the new colors in your programs.

TIP

Disappearing Act! *Change your colors with caution, and make sure you keep enough contrast between a text color and its background. If, for example, you change the menu font color to the same color as the menu itself, you won't be able to see the menu items until you select them.*

TIP

Some programs have background or text colors that can't be changed, so some changes to the color scheme might not appear in all program windows.

Define a Color Scheme

1. Right-click in a blank part of the Desktop and choose Properties from the shortcut menu.

2. Click the Appearance tab.

3. Click the item you want to change, or select an item from the Item list that wasn't displayed in the preview on the Appearance tab.

4. Change the colors.

5. Repeat steps 3 and 4 to change other items.

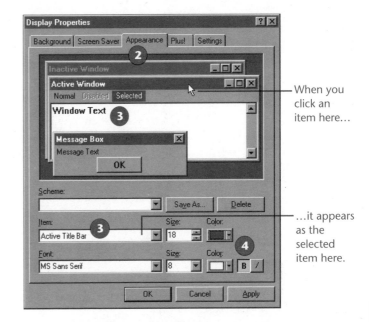

When you click an item here...

...it appears as the selected item here.

Save the Changes

1. Click the Save As button.

2. Type a name for your color scheme.

3. Click OK.

4. Click OK to apply the changes.

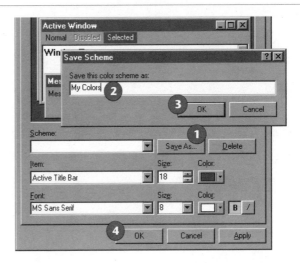

10

Making Everything More Colorful

Most computers can display different ranges of color, from a simple 16-color or 256-color palette that's fine for displaying colors in dialog boxes to a more complex true-color palette that produces photographic-quality colors. The higher levels of color use up a lot of memory, so—depending on the capabilities of your computer—you might have to work with reduced screen resolution if you need to use the highest color settings.

SEE ALSO

"Making More Room on the Desktop" on page 185 for information about setting the screen resolution.

TIP

Click List All Modes to see a list of screen-resolution, color-palette, and refresh frequencies for your monitor.

Change the Color Palette

1. Right-click in a blank part of the Desktop and choose Properties from the shortcut menu.

2. Click the Settings tab.

3. Select a setting in the Color Palette drop-down list.

4. Click the Test button.

5. Click OK to confirm that you want to test the colors.

6. Click Yes to accept the new settings or No to revert to the original settings.

7. If you clicked No, click OK to keep the original settings.

8. Click OK to apply the changes.

The colors available depend on your computer system.

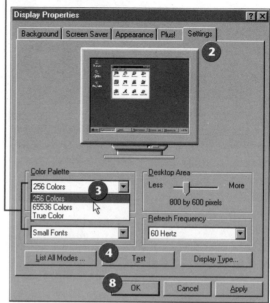

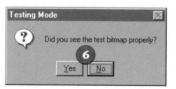

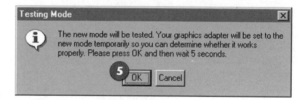

Changing the Pointer Scheme

Would you like something more exciting than an arrow as a mouse pointer? You can make your work much more entertaining by using different pointers for standard Windows NT events. Your choices are varied, from three-dimensional pointers to a frankly anthropomorphic and quite adorable animated mouse of the four-legged-and-furry variety.

SEE ALSO

"Creating a Pointer Scheme" on page 190 for information about customizing a pointer scheme.

Change the Pointer Scheme

1 Click the Start button, point to Settings, and choose Control Panel from the submenu.

2 Double-click the Mouse icon.

3 Click the Pointers tab.

4 Select a new scheme in the Scheme drop-down list.

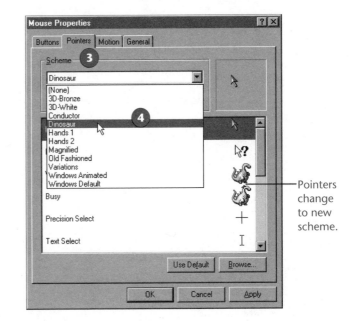

Pointers change to new scheme.

10

Creating a Pointer Scheme

You can customize your mouse-pointer scheme by replacing one or more of the existing pointers in a scheme with the pointers of your choice. In the example at the right, we changed the "Unavailable" pointer from an animated peeling banana to a metronome.

TIP

Windows NT comes with several additional mouse pointers. If these pointers were not included in your original installation, you can install them at any time.

SEE ALSO

"Changing the Pointer Scheme" on page 189 for information about changing the entire pointer scheme.

"Adding or Removing Windows NT Components" on page 232 for information about installing additional Windows NT components.

Change Individual Pointers

1. Select the event and pointer to be changed.

2. Click the Browse button.

3. Click the pointer you want for that event.

4. Click Open.

5. Repeat steps 1 through 4 to change other individual pointers.

TIP

The available mouse-pointer schemes depend on the software that you have installed. Windows NT comes with 11 pointer schemes, and Microsoft IntelliPoint mouse software provides additional schemes.

TIP

Click the Use Default button to restore the original pointer to the selected item.

Save Your Scheme

1 Click the Save As button.

2 Type a name for your scheme.

3 Click OK.

4 Click OK to apply the new scheme.

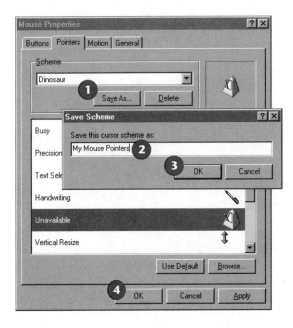

10

Improving the Look of Your Screen

You can turn on several enhancements to improve the look of your screen, especially if you are running at a high resolution and in High Color or True Color.

TIP

Using these enhancements requires considerable memory, so be selective. If, after applying them, you find that your computer is running slowly, turn off the enhancements one at a time until your computer's performance improves.

Turn on the Enhancements

1 Right-click in a blank part of the Windows NT Desktop and choose Properties from the shortcut menu.

2 Click the Plus! tab.

3 Turn on the options you want.

4 Click OK.

Places shading around screen fonts to reduce their jagged look on the screen, but doesn't affect printed fonts.

Moves the window itself when it's being dragged, instead of showing a placeholder rectangle.

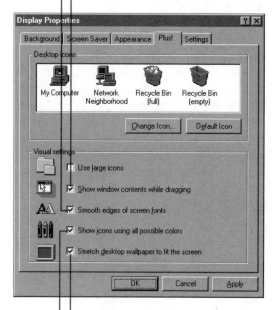

Scales a centered graphic to fill the entire screen.

Removes "dithering" from icons when system is set to High Color or True Color.

Changing the Way Your Computer Works

As time goes on, you'll probably want—or need—to do some remodeling of your system. If, for example, you always start your work day using one particular program, you can put that program in the Startup folder so that it will start automatically when you start Windows NT Workstation 4.0.

You might want to add items to or delete them from the Start menu, or make some changes to the Desktop so that it's a bit more useful.

If you're fond of the Documents menu because it's such a speedy way to access the documents you're using in your current project, you can wipe the menu clean when you start a new project so that you won't have to search through a group of out-of-date documents to find the one you want.

Perhaps you're on the move and you need to change the date, the time, and maybe even the basic setup of your computer so that you can use it in a new or alternate workplace.

Just as when you're remodeling a house, however, you need to use the right tools if you want to get the job done quickly and efficiently. Fortunately, Windows NT comes fully equipped with the tools you need, and often takes over the entire operation for you.

Starting a Program When Windows NT Starts

If you always start your work day using the same program, you can have that program start automatically when Windows NT starts. This means that Windows NT will take a little longer to load, but your program will be ready for you to start working on right away.

TIP

If you want the same document to open whenever the program starts, add the document (not the program) to the Startup folder. The document must be correctly associated with the program for this to work.

SEE ALSO

"Specifying Which Program Opens a Document" on page 210 for information about associating programs and documents.

Add a Program to Windows NT Startup

1. Right-click in a blank part of the taskbar and choose Properties from the shortcut menu.

2. On the Start Menu Programs tab, click Add.

3. Type the path and program name, or use the Browse button to locate the program. Click Next.

4. Select the Startup folder, and click Next.

5. Type the name of the program, and click Finish.

6. Click OK. The name of the program will appear on the Startup submenu, and will start up the next time you start Windows NT.

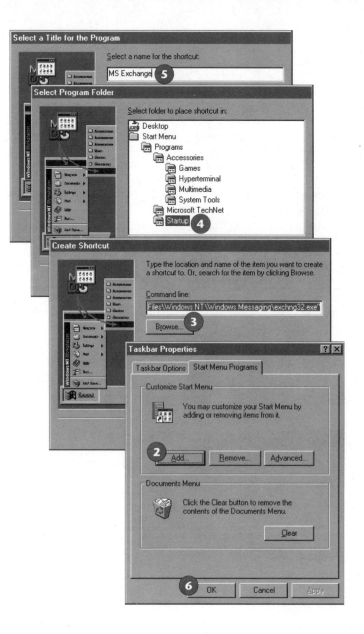

Adding an Item to the Start Menu

When you open the Start menu, the item you're looking for is usually on one of the cascading submenus. You can add items to the submenus and you can even create your own submenus. Windows NT uses folders to organize the Start menu, and each folder contained in the Start Menu folder creates a submenu. So, to add access to an item from a submenu, you add a shortcut to the item in the appropriate folder.

TIP

To add a document instead of a program to the Start menu, select All Files from the Files Of Type list in the Browse dialog box.

SEE ALSO

"Creating Shortcuts" on page 40 for information about adding shortcuts to the Start menu.

Add Access from a Submenu

1. Right-click in a blank part of the taskbar and choose Properties from the shortcut menu.

2. On the Start Menu Programs tab, click Add.

3. Click the Browse button to find the program.

4. Select the program, and click the Open button.

5. Verify the program's path and filename, and click Next.

6. Select the folder— and therefore the submenu—that will contain the program, and click Next.

7. Type the program name that you want to appear on the submenu, and click Finish.

8. Click OK in the Taskbar Properties dialog box.

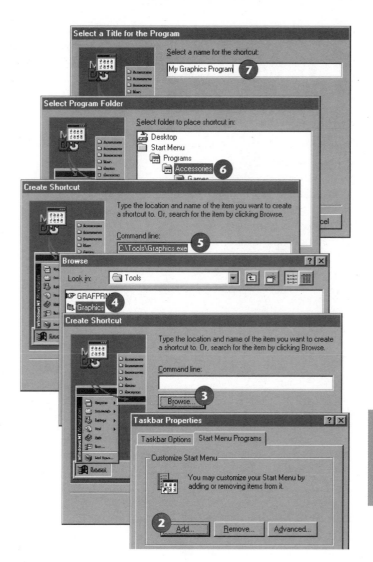

11

Removing an Item from the Start Menu

If there are shortcuts that you no longer need on the Start menu, or if you don't want to keep the shortcuts that were added during the installation of a program, you can remove them.

TIP

Removing an item from the Start menu doesn't usually remove the program itself—it removes only the shortcut to the program. If you don't want the program any longer, you should uninstall it.

You can return a deleted item to the Start menu by restoring the shortcut from the Recycle Bin.

SEE ALSO

"Recovering a Deleted Item" on page 42 for information about restoring a deleted item from the Recycle Bin.

"Removing a Software Program" on page 235 for information about uninstalling programs.

Remove an Item from the Start Menu

1. Right-click in a blank part of the taskbar and choose Properties from the shortcut menu.

2. On the Start Menu Programs tab, click Remove.

3. Open the folder containing the item to be removed.

4. Select the item.

5. Click Remove.

6. Repeat steps 3 through 5 to remove all unwanted items.

7. Click Close.

8. Click OK.

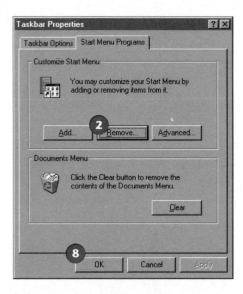

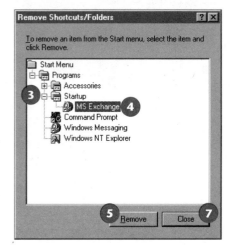

Removing the Contents of the Documents Menu

Using the Documents menu is a quick and handy way to access your most recently used documents. But sometimes—when you start a new project, for example—you don't want to sort through a menu of documents that are unrelated to your current project. You can start out with a clean slate by resetting the Documents menu.

TIP

Removing documents from the Documents menu deletes only the shortcuts to the documents, not the documents themselves.

Reset the Documents Menu

1 Right-click in a blank part of the taskbar and choose Properties from the shortcut menu.

2 On the Start Menu Programs tab, click the Clear button.

3 Click OK.

4 Click the Start button, point to Documents, and verify that the menu is empty.

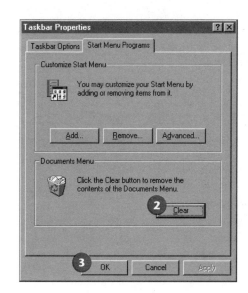

Accessing Documents from the Desktop

The first time you saw your Windows NT Desktop, it was already equipped with some icons that started programs or that led you quickly to special locations. Your systems administrator might have added other icons. You can speed up your work by placing documents that you use on a regular basis on your Desktop. Here's how.

SEE ALSO

"Creating Shortcuts" on page 40 for information about creating shortcuts and placing them on the Desktop.

Move or Copy a Document onto the Desktop

1 Double-click My Computer.

2 Navigate through the folders to find the document you want.

3 Move or copy the document onto the Desktop:

◆ To move, hold down the Shift key, drag the document, drop it on the Desktop, and release the Shift key.

◆ To copy, hold down the Ctrl key, drag the document, drop it on the Desktop, and release the Ctrl key.

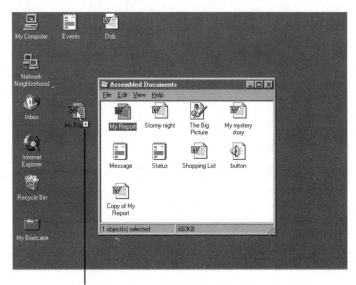

Plus sign shows that the file is being copied.

TIP

If you share your computer with other users, the documents that you place on the Desktop will not be available to your coworkers. If you want to share these documents, place them in common folders.

TRY THIS

Start WordPad and type some text. Select the text and drag it onto the Desktop. Start a new WordPad document, type some text, and then drag the Word-Pad scrap from the Desktop and drop it into the WordPad document.

TIP

Scraps can be stored in folders, so you can organize them just as you can any other files.

Save a Document to the Desktop

1 Create the document in your program.

2 Choose Save from the File menu to display the Save As dialog box.

3 Select Desktop from the Save In drop-down list.

4 Type a name for the document.

5 Click the Save button.

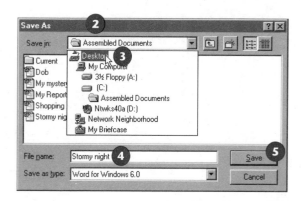

Save Part of a Document to the Desktop

1 Select the part of the document to be saved.

2 Drag the selection and drop it on the Desktop. (You'll notice that Windows NT puts a "scrap" icon on the Desktop.)

Drag content from here...

...and drop it here.

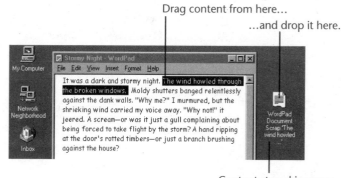

Content stored in scrap can be inserted into a document at a later time.

11

Customizing Mouse Operations

If you spend a lot of time mousing around in your programs, you can make a few minor adjustments that will substantially improve your effectiveness *and* your comfort. You can adjust the configuration of the mouse buttons for left-handed operation, as well as adjusting pointer speed and double-click speed. You can also set the mouse pointer so that it automatically points to the default button or to the default item in a dialog box or window.

Switch Mouse Buttons

1 Click the Start button, point to Settings, and choose Control Panel from the submenu.

2 Double-click the Mouse icon.

3 Click the Buttons tab.

4 Click the appropriate option.

Select the way you use the mouse.

Shows right-button functions based on button configuration.

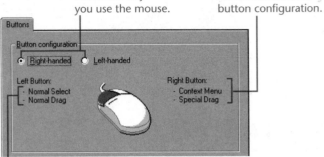

Shows left-button functions based on button configuration.

Set the Double-Click Speed

1 Drag the slider and drop it to set the speed of the double-click.

2 Double-click the jack-in-the-box.

Pops up when double-clicked. If it doesn't pop up, reset the speed and try again.

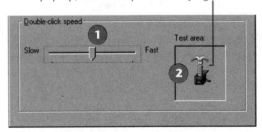

SEE ALSO

"Changing the Pointer Scheme" on page 189 and "Creating a Pointer Scheme" on page 190 for information about using different mouse pointer schemes.

"Adjusting Mouse Movements" on page 252 and "Making Mouse Dragging Easier" on page 254 for information about changing mouse actions with IntelliPoint 2.0 mouse software.

TIP

The options available might be different from those described here, depending on the mouse software that's installed on your computer.

TIP

In some programs, the Snap To feature can be a hindrance rather than a help. If you find that you often have to move the mouse to execute an action before you click the default button, turn off the Snap To option.

Set the Pointer Speed

1 Click the Motion tab.

2 Drag the slider and drop it to set the pointer speed.

3 Click Apply.

4 Move the mouse around to see if you like the speed.

5 Repeat steps 2 through 4 until you have the mouse moving at a speed you're comfortable with.

Turn On the Snap To Option

1 Turn on the Snap Mouse To The Default Button In Dialogs option to have the mouse pointer automatically positioned on the default button or the default item when a dialog box is opened.

2 Click OK.

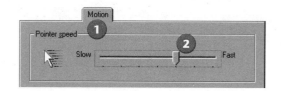

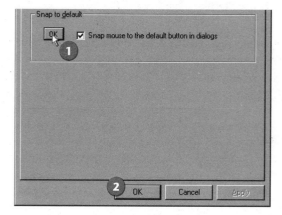

11

Fine-Tuning the Keyboard

If you sometimes end up with double characters when you want only one character or, alternatively, if it seems that you have to wait too long for a character to be repeated when you *do* want double characters, you can adjust both the length of time your computer waits before it realizes that you want to repeat the character and how fast it repeats the character.

Adjust the Repeat Rate

1 Click the Start button, point to Settings, and choose Control Panel from the submenu.

2 Double-click the Keyboard icon.

3 On the Speed tab, adjust the Repeat Delay slider.

4 Adjust the Repeat Rate slider.

5 Click in the test area and hold down a key. Note how long it takes for the first repeated character to appear and how quickly the additional characters appear.

6 Adjust the Repeat Delay and Repeat Rate settings if necessary, and repeat the test.

7 Click OK.

Sets the length of time you need to hold down a key before a character is repeated.

Sets the rate at which a character is repeated when the repeat delay has been completed.

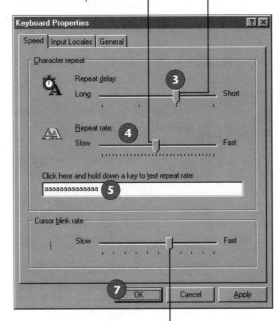

Adjusts the rate at which the cursor blinks, if necessary—that is, if its current blink rate is fast enough to be distracting or slow enough to be barely noticeable.

Adjusting the Date and Time

If you take a laptop computer with you when you travel long distances, or if the computer's battery has run down, you'll need to adjust your computer's clock to the correct time zone. If you've had your computer repaired, you'll probably need to correct the date and time. You will, however, need the appropriate permission if you want to change the system time or date.

TIP

To see whether the date is correct, point to the time on the taskbar and hold the mouse steady until the date appears.

If the Date/Time icon isn't shown on the taskbar, right-click in a blank part of the taskbar, choose Properties from the shortcut menu, and, on the Taskbar Options tab, turn on the Show Clock option.

Adjust the Time Zone

1. Double-click the time on the taskbar.

2. Click the Time Zone tab.

3. Select the time zone from the list.

4. Verify that you've selected the correct time zone by noting that your time zone is centered on the map.

Adjust the Date and Time

1. Click the Date & Time tab.

2. Select the current month from the drop-down list.

3. Select the current year from the drop-down list.

4. Click today's date.

5. Click the hour, minute, second, and AM or PM to be adjusted.

6. Use the arrows to adjust the time.

7. Verify the time on the clock face.

8. Click OK.

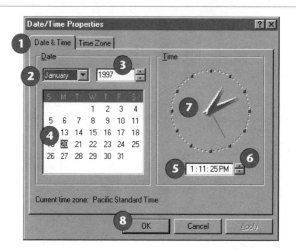

11

Adjusting Settings for a Different Region

If you are working in, or producing documents for use in, a region or country other than the one for which your computer was originally configured, you can change the region and have Windows NT automatically adjust the numbering, currency, time, and date schemes used by your programs.

Change the Region

1 Click the Start button, point to Settings, and choose Control Panel from the submenu.

2 Double-click the Regional Settings icon to display the Regional Settings Properties dialog box.

3 On the Regional Settings tab, select the language and, if necessary, the associated country.

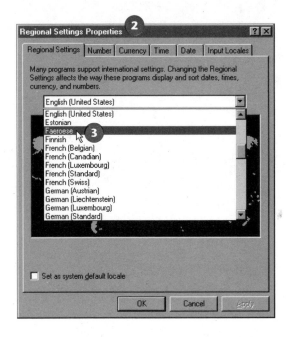

TIP

Don't get too energetic with your changes—you could end up with results that are essentially meaningless. After you select a region, all the settings change to reflect the most common usage for that region. If you need to make many changes, you might not have selected the most appropriate region. Go back, look for another locale that might be applicable, and see if the settings are correct.

SEE ALSO

"Changing the Date and Time Format" on page 206 for information about creating the date and time format you prefer.

"Using a Different Keyboard Layout" on page 208 for information about changing the keyboard layout.

TIP

If you're setting up a region that has not previously been installed on the computer, you'll need access to the Windows NT installation files. If you're setting the region up as the system default, you'll need to restart Windows NT for the new settings to take effect.

Customize the Settings

1 Use the different tabs to customize the regional settings:

- ◆ The Number tab to specify decimal, positive, and negative numbers, and number-listing formats

- ◆ The Currency tab to specify the currency symbol and positive, negative, and decimal formats

- ◆ The Time tab to set the time format

- ◆ The Date tab to set long and short date formats

2 Click Apply after each change.

3 Click OK when you've finished.

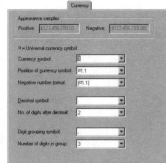

Changing the Date and Time Format

Windows NT uses the most commonly accepted ways to display date and time, but you can change the display to the format you prefer.

```
DATE FORMATS
2/5/97
or
02/05/1997
or
Feb 5, 1997

TIME FORMATS
3:05:30 P
or
03:05:30 PM
or
15:05:30
```

SEE ALSO

"Adjusting Settings for a Different Region" on page 204 for information about changing settings to the default values for different countries and languages.

Change the Date Format

1. Click the Start button, point to Settings, and choose Control Panel from the submenu.

2. Double-click the Regional Settings icon.

3. Click the Date tab.

4. Select or type a different format for the short date. See the table at the right for valid codes.

5. Click Apply.

6. Select or type a different separator for the short date.

7. Click Apply.

8. Select or type a different format for the long date.

9. Click Apply.

CODES FOR DATE FORMATS	
Code	Result
M	Month number
MM	Month number, always two digits
MMM	Three-letter month abbreviation
MMMM	Full month name
d	Day number
dd	Day number, always two digits
ddd	Three-letter day abbreviation
dddd	Full day name
yy	Year number, last two digits only
yyyy	Full year number

TIP

Many programs format the date and time using their own code; such programs might not utilize the settings shown in the tables on these two pages. If the date and time appear in a different format in one of your programs, consult the program's Help for formatting details.

TRY THIS

Select or create date and time formats and apply them. Then switch to a folder window, display file information by using the Details view, and look at the modified date and time. Change the date and time formats, and note the difference in the folder window.

Change the Time Format

1. Click the Time tab.

2. Select or type a different format for the time. See the table at the right for valid codes.

3. Click Apply.

4. Select or type a different separator for the time.

5. Click Apply.

6. Select or type a different AM symbol.

7. Click Apply.

8. Select or type a different PM symbol.

9. Click Apply.

CODES FOR TIME FORMATS	
Code	Result
h	Hour in 12-hour format
hh	Hour in 12-hour format, always two digits
H	Hour in 24-hour format
HH	Hour in 24-hour format, always two digits
m	Minute
mm	Minute, always two digits
s	Second
ss	Second, always two digits
t	AM or PM symbol, first character only
tt	AM or PM symbol, all characters

11

Using a Different Keyboard Layout

If you want to use a keyboard layout other than the current one—either a different configuration for the current language or the typical layout for a different language—you simply tell Windows NT, and all your typing will be set to that layout. Then, for programs that support regional settings, you can use your usual keyboard (or install a different one) and type using the specified layout.

TIP

If the proper keyboard driver hasn't been installed on your computer, you'll need to have (or to obtain) the appropriate permission to add system files to your computer, and you'll also need access to the Windows NT installation files.

Change the Layout

1 Click the Start button, point to Settings, and choose Control Panel from the submenu.

2 Double-click the Keyboard icon to display the Keyboard Properties dialog box.

3 Click the Input Locales tab.

4 If there's more than one locale listed, select the one you want to use with the different keyboard layout.

5 Click the Properties button.

6 Select the keyboard layout.

7 Click OK.

8 Click the Set As Default button.

9 Click OK.

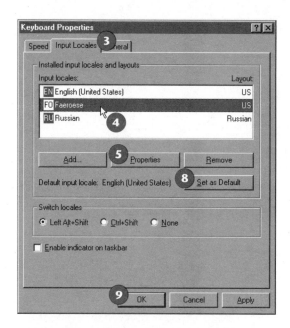

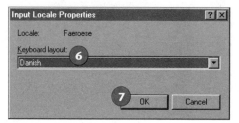

Switching Between Locale Setups

If you have more than one input locale setup on your computer, all it takes is a couple of mouse-clicks to switch easily between the configurations specified by the different locales.

SEE ALSO

"Using a Different Keyboard Layout" on the facing page for information about using different keyboard layouts and setting up different locales.

Turn On the Options

1 Click the Start button, point to Settings, and choose Control Panel from the submenu.

2 Double-click the Regional Settings icon to display the Regional Settings Properties dialog box.

3 Click the Input Locales tab.

4 Select any key combination you want to use to switch locales.

5 Turn on the Enable Indicator On Taskbar option.

6 Click OK.

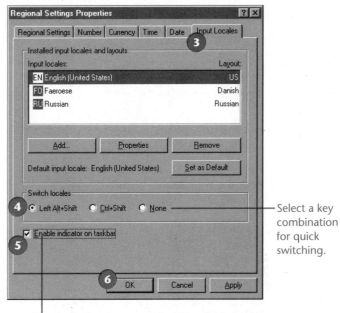

Select a key combination for quick switching.

Use the indicator to see a list of available locales.

Switch Layouts

1 Click the input locale abbreviation on the taskbar.

2 Select the keyboard layout.

11

Specifying Which Program Opens a Document

When you double-click a document, it usually opens in its associated program—a Microsoft Word document opens in Word, a bitmap image opens in Paint, and so on. Sometimes, however, you might want one type of document to open in a different program—perhaps you want text documents to open in WordPad instead of in Notepad, for example. You can make this happen by associating the file type with a program.

TIP

The types of files listed on the File Types tab depend on the programs you have installed.

Select the File Type

1 Double-click My Computer.

2 Choose Options from the View menu to display the Options dialog box.

3 Click the File Types tab.

4 Select the file type whose association you want to change.

5 Click the Edit button.

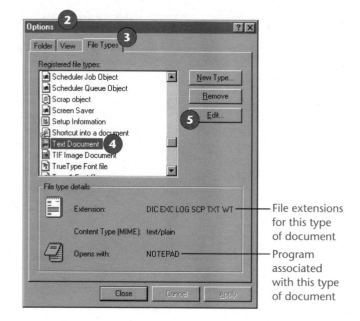

File extensions for this type of document

Program associated with this type of document

TIP

You'll need the appropriate permission if you want to modify any file associations.

TIP

Verify the association. Double-click a file of the type you just modified. If the file doesn't open, if it doesn't open where you expected it to, or if it opens but the content is corrupted, return the association to its original program.

TIP

When you double-click a file that has no registered association, the Open With dialog box appears. Use it to stipulate which program the file will be used with.

Edit the Association

1 Select Open in the Actions list.

2 Click the Edit button.

3 Click the Browse button.

4 Navigate through your folders and select the program in which you want your document to open.

5 Click Open to specify the program.

6 Click OK to set the association.

7 Click Close to end the editing.

8 Click Close to close the Options dialog box.

Click to use a different icon for this file type.

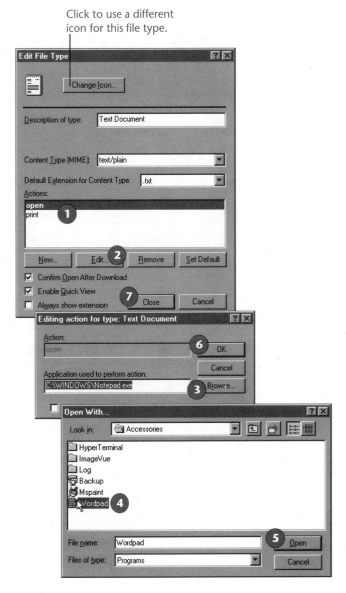

File Associations, File Extensions, and Registered Programs

Windows NT tries to let your work be *docu-centric*—that is, you concentrate on keeping your *documents* organized, and Windows NT will do the work of figuring out which *programs* your documents need to run. To do this, Windows NT needs three main pieces of information:

◆ The programs you have installed

◆ The types of documents that are to be opened in each program

◆ The file type of the document you want to use

Windows NT keeps track of all this information in a special database called the *registry*. Whenever you run Setup to install a software program, Setup adds information to the registry, including the name and location of the program and the types of documents and files the program can open.

To link a document with a program, Windows NT uses the file's extension—the three-character code that follows the document's name—to identify the document as a specific file type. The file's extension, which is usually added automatically when you save a document in a program, might or might not be visible, depending on your settings, but Windows NT is always aware of it. (See "Displaying MS-DOS Paths and Filename Extensions" on page 43 and "Hiding or Displaying System Files" on page 44 for information about displaying a file's extension.)

By recognizing the file extension, Windows NT knows the file type of the document and its associated program.

You can identify the file type of a document by its icon and, when you're in Details view, by the description in the Type column. Because a document is identified by its extension, you shouldn't change the extension when you create a document or when you're conducting any file management. Sometimes, alas, things just don't work out as they're supposed to. Some programs are installed without the use of Setup and thus might not be registered. Other programs can grab a file extension that "belongs to" another program. And sometimes, even when Setup is used, a program somehow doesn't register itself correctly.

When a program isn't properly registered, whatever the reason, you can often solve the problem by rerunning Setup for the program or by changing the file extension's program association, as described in "Specifying Which Program Opens a Document" on page 210. If neither of these methods works, contact the people who sold you the software. They might be able to supply you with updated software that properly registers the program, or they might tell you how to fix the problem with a workaround. But remember—it's *very* dangerous to edit the settings in the registry. If anyone suggests that you do this, the first thing you should do when you run RegEdit (the Registry Editor program) is to make a copy of the registry, using the Export Registry File command on the File menu. That way, if something goes wrong, you can restore the original registry.

EXAMPLES OF FILES WITH THEIR EXTENSIONS		
Document type	**Icon**	**Filename with extension**
Text document	Status	Status.txt
Bitmap image	Plans	Plans.bmp
Wave sound	My Message	My Message.wav
MS-DOS application	MyProg	MyProg.exe
Internet document (HTML)	My Home Page	My Home Page.htm

11

Changing the Way Windows NT Starts

If you have more than one operating system as a startup option on your computer, you can change which system is the default system, the order of the startup options, and the length of time the system waits for your response. If you use different hardware profiles, you can also change the way the system initiates the hardware profile at startup.

TIP

Alternative hardware profiles are a common feature of portable computers that use docking stations. Most other computer systems don't have more than one hardware profile, and on these computers you won't see this option at startup.

Change the Startup System

1 Click the Start button, point to Settings, and choose Control Panel from the submenu.

2 Double-click the System icon.

3 Click the Startup/Shutdown tab.

4 Select the default startup operating system.

5 Specify the length of time the system waits until the default system is started.

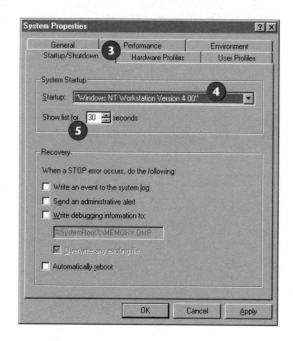

TIP

If Windows NT was installed from the Windows 95 operating system, your computer is set up with a dual-boot system—that is, you can start up in Windows 95 or in Windows NT, unless you've changed the disk's filing system (from the FAT to the NTFS system, for example). However, in a dual-boot system, Windows NT tends to take over the entire system. This means that when you start up in Windows 95, you might find that some files are missing or that you're having problems with certain programs—in short, that Windows 95 isn't working exactly the way it should. One way you can avoid such problems is to remove Windows 95 after installing Windows NT. Another way is to compress part of your hard disk to contain your Windows 95 files before you install Windows NT in an uncompressed part of your hard disk. This will make it impossible for Windows NT to read or change any of your existing Windows 95 files. Whichever method you choose, be sure to back up your files frequently so that any system conflicts won't cause the loss of valuable data.

Change the Hardware Profile Startup

1 Click the Hardware Profiles tab.

2 Select the profile you want as the default profile.

3 Click the up arrow to move the profile to the top of the list.

4 Select one of the wait options. If you select the option to wait for a specific length of time, set the time.

5 Click OK.

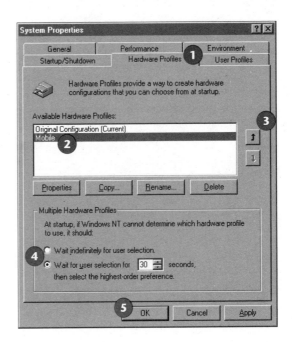

12

Being Mobile

If your work involves traveling, read this section before you take off! If you use different computers at different locations, or if you have a desktop computer at work and you travel with a notebook computer, this section of the book will help you avoid the pesky problems that can occur when you're working long distance.

You'll find out how to create one or more virtual Windows NT Briefcases, into which you can stuff a bunch of files from your main computer. You can work on the files on the road, and then update them on your main computer with a mouse-click or two. If you want to take some e-mail messages with you for reference, you can transfer them to a mail folder and include them in the Inbox of another computer. You can even send and receive e-mail automatically wherever you happen to be.

If you have a portable computer with a docking station, you'll find the information in this section useful. However, we haven't gone into any details about using a docking station, simply because Windows NT usually detects whether a computer is docked or undocked and uses the appropriate settings by automatically switching hardware profiles. To quote the oh-so-famous words of the world's software engineers, if you have a problem, "it's a hardware problem," so check with the maker of the computer system for a fix.

Using the Briefcase to Manage Files

When your work travels with you, whether it's to your home or to the other side of the world, you often need to take copies of files from your main computer and use them on a different computer. If you've done this a lot and you're aware of how difficult it can be to keep track of the most recent version of a file, you'll like the Windows NT Briefcase. Okay, so it's not made of fine Corinthian leather. You won't care when you see how easily you can synchronize the changes you make in your traveling files with the originals on your main computer.

> **TIP**
>
> *If the Briefcase isn't listed, and you don't see the My Briefcase icon on your Desktop, the Briefcase hasn't been installed and you'll need to install it.*

Copy the Briefcase onto a Floppy Disk

1 Right-click the Desktop, point to New, and choose Briefcase from the shortcut menu. Give the new Briefcase a descriptive name.

2 Drag a file or folder onto the new Briefcase icon.

3 If a welcome screen appears the first time you use the Briefcase, click the Finish button.

4 On the Desktop, right-click the Briefcase and send it to a floppy disk.

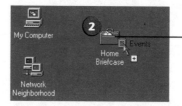

Dragging a file onto the Briefcase icon copies the file into the Briefcase.

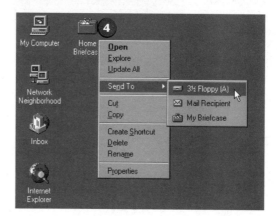

TIP

If you're copying the Briefcase onto a floppy disk, the contents of the Briefcase shouldn't be greater than the capacity of the disk—usually 1.44 megabytes. You can also use this copying procedure with larger portable storage devices, such as a ZIP drive or a removable hard disk.

TIP

To copy large files, connect to the appropriate location using a network or dial-up networking, and load the files into My Briefcase on your Desktop. When you've finished with the files, reconnect to the source computer if necessary and update all the files.

TIP

Once you've copied a file into the Briefcase, don't move or change the original file. If you do, the file in the Briefcase will become an "orphan," and you won't be able to update the original file from the file in the Briefcase. If you've orphaned a Briefcase file, you'll need to save it using a different filename.

Use the Briefcase Files

1 Insert the floppy disk into your other computer, drag the Briefcase from the disk onto the Desktop, and double-click the Briefcase icon.

2 Double-click a file to use it, and save the file to the Briefcase. When you've finished, drag the Briefcase from the Desktop to the floppy disk.

Update the Files

1 Insert the disk into your main computer.

2 Drag the Briefcase from the floppy disk onto the Desktop.

3 Double-click the Briefcase icon.

4 To update

◆ A single file, select the file, and choose Update Selection from the Briefcase menu.

◆ All files, choose Update All.

5 Click Update to confirm the updating.

The Briefcase records the location of the original files... ...and tracks which files have been changed.

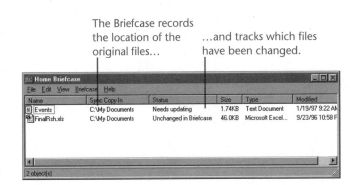

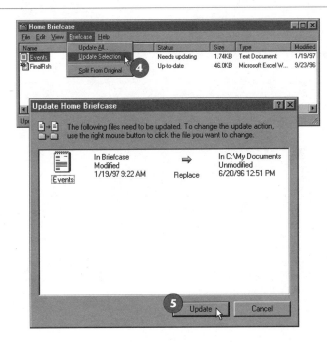

12

Taking Your Mail with You

When you're away from your office, you can take important mail messages with you. You simply copy or move the messages into a special mail folder, and then transfer the folder to your other computer.

TIP

Confused? *Aren't files usually stored in folders rather than folders being stored in files? Yes. Creating this mail folder is an unusual situation, in which you store a folder inside a file. And, to make it even more confusing, it's called a folders file!*

TIP

If you select No Encryption when you specify a security level, someone could easily hack into your messages, because they're stored as regular text. For a moderate level of security and minimum file size, use Compressable Encryption.

Create a Mail Folder

1 In your Inbox on your main computer, choose Services from the Tools menu.

2 In the Services dialog box, click Add.

3 In the Add Service To Profile dialog box, select Personal Folders, and click OK.

4 In the Create/Open Personal Folders File dialog box, navigate to where you want to store the file, type a name for the file, and click Open. This creates a PST-type file, which stores the folder you want to use.

5 Set the properties for the folder, and click OK.

6 Click OK to close the Services dialog box.

7 Select and drag messages from other folders into this folder. Hold down the Ctrl key while you drag if you want to copy the messages rather than move them.

8 Exit and log off from the Inbox.

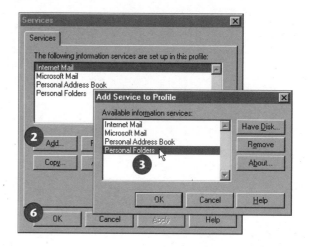

PST file is created in the Create/Open Personal Folders File dialog box.

Type a name for the folder.

Select the level of security you want. No Encryption creates a text file.

Type and verify a password. Be sure to write the password down and keep it in a safe place.

Turn on to avoid entering your password on this computer.

SEE ALSO

"Creating a Folder System" on page 160 for information about customizing the layout of your mail folders.

TIP

If you're transferring your mail to a computer that's used by other people, create a new Exchange profile for yourself before you include your transfer file. That way, you'll have your own Inbox.

SEE ALSO

"Creating Different Mail Setups" on page 226 for information about creating your own profile.

Transfer the Folder to Another Computer

1 Copy the PST file from where you stored it to the computer on which you want to use it.

2 In your Inbox, choose Services from the Tools menu, and click the Add button.

3 In the Add Service To Profile dialog box, select Personal Folders, and click OK.

4 In the Create/Open Personal Folders File dialog box, locate and select the PST file you copied, and click Open.

5 Type the password for the folder.

6 Set the properties for the folder, and then click OK.

7 Click OK to close the Services dialog box.

8 Retype the password if it's requested.

9 Click the new folder to review the mail.

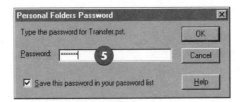

Copied mail folder with messages becomes part of the Inbox.

12

Receiving E-Mail from a Remote Location

If you download mail from different locations while you're traveling, you can choose not to download messages you don't want, and you can decide whether you want mail deleted from or retained on your mail server. Although different mail systems have different settings, most are really quite similar. This procedure is for setting up a connection using Microsoft Mail.

SEE ALSO

"Connecting to Your Network from a Remote Location" on page 228 for information about dial-up networking.

Set Up Remote Mail

1 In your Inbox, choose Services from the Tools menu.

2 Select the mail service that you'll be using from a remote location, and click the Properties button.

3 On the Connection tab, turn on the option for remote mail using a modem and dial-up networking, or the option to sense a LAN or a remote connection.

4 On the Remote Configuration tab, turn on the remote mail option.

5 On the Remote Session tab, turn on the options you want for the mail session.

6 Click OK, and then click OK to close the Services dialog box.

7 Exit and log off from your Inbox.

Turn on to connect to the service automatically when the Inbox is first started.

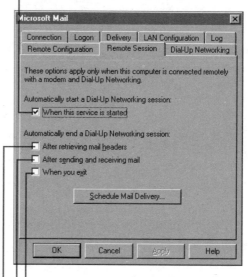

Turn on to disconnect from the service when you exit from the Inbox.

Turn on to disconnect from the service after all new mail has been received and all mail in your Outbox has been sent.

Turn on to disconnect from the service after remote mail has retrieved the latest mail headers.

TIP

If the service you selected doesn't provide a tab for setting remote options, either the service doesn't support remote mail or you don't have Dial-Up Networking installed. Check with your system administrator if you have problems using remote mail.

TIP

If more than one service is set for remote mail, point to Remote Mail on the Tools menu. The services will be listed on the Remote Mail submenu.

TIP

Unmarked message headers are retained in the Remote Mail window, and no action is performed until you mark the header for downloading or deletion.

Connect

1 Open the Inbox.

2 Choose Remote Mail from the Tools menu.

3 On the Remote Mail toolbar, click the Connect button.

4 Turn on the options you want, and click OK.

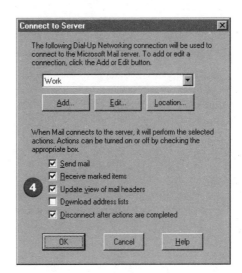

Send and Receive Mail Messages

1 Mark your message headers for the actions you want.

2 On the remote Mail toolbar, click the Connect button.

3 Specify what you want to be sent and retrieved, and click OK.

4 Check your Inbox for delivered messages.

Marks message to be downloaded and deleted from the server.

Marks message to be downloaded and for a copy to be retained on the server.

Marks message to be deleted from the server without being downloaded.

Scheduling Remote Mail Delivery

If you're set up to use remote mail away from your office, you can have your computer automatically dial in to your mail server at set intervals, connect to your network, and send and receive mail for you. Why do it yourself when Windows NT can do it for you?

TIP

You can schedule more than one remote mail delivery by clicking the Add button again.

Set Up an Automatic Connection

1 In your Inbox, choose Remote Mail from the Tools menu.

2 In the Remote Mail window, open the Tools menu and point to the menu item for mail service (Microsoft Mail Tools, for example). Choose Schedule Remote Mail Delivery from the submenu.

3 In the Scheduled Remote Mail Delivery dialog box, click Add.

4 Specify the dial-up connection.

5 Specify the interval.

6 Click OK four times to close all the dialog boxes.

7 Open your Inbox.

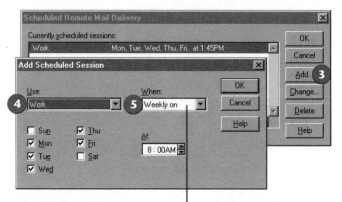

Select Every to specify a time interval between connections, select Weekly On to specify the days and the time for the connection to be made, or select Once At to specify the date and the time for the connection to be made.

Connecting from Different Locations

If you travel around a lot—breakfast in New York, lunch in Chicago, and dinner in Seattle, perhaps—and you dial in or send faxes from your computer from each location, you need to tell Windows NT where you're calling from so that it can use the correct dialing properties for that location.

TIP

Many modem-based services, such as Remote Mail and HyperTerminal, have buttons or menu commands that take you directly to the Dialing Properties dialog box.

Create a New Location

1 Click the Start button, point to Settings, and choose Control Panel from the submenu.

2 Double-click the Modems icon.

3 In the Modem Properties dialog box, click the Dialing Properties button.

4 Click the New button, type a name for the location, and click OK.

5 Specify the settings for this calling location.

Set Up a Calling Card

1 Turn on the Dial Using Calling Card option, and click Change.

2 Select the calling card you want to use.

3 Enter your calling-card number.

4 Click OK.

5 Click OK to close the Dialing Properties dialog box.

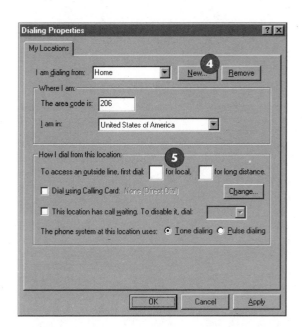

Creating Different Mail Setups

If you have different mail configurations available to you depending on where you are—a network fax, your own modem, a network mail server, or a remote service—you can create a different profile for each and switch to the appropriate one when you start up Microsoft Exchange.

Create a Profile

1 Exit and log off from your Inbox.

2 Click the Start button, point to Settings, and choose Control Panel from the submenu.

3 Double-click the Mail icon.

4 Click the Show Profiles button.

5 Click the Add button.

6 Step through the Inbox Setup Wizard, specifying the services and settings for the new profile. Type a name for the profile.

7 Select the profile you want to use.

8 Click the Close button.

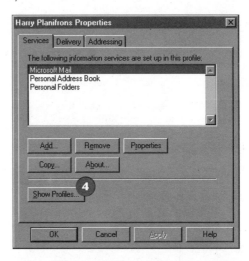

TIP

If none of the profiles in the Choose Profile dialog box is appropriate, click the New button and create a new profile.

TIP

If you want to adjust each service every time you start the Inbox, click the Options button in the Choose Profile dialog box, and turn on the Show Logon Screens For All Information Services check box.

Switch Your Profile

1 Open your Inbox, and choose Options from the Tools menu.

2 On the General tab, turn on the option to be prompted for a profile when Windows NT Messaging starts up.

3 Click OK.

4 Exit and log off from your Inbox.

5 Reopen the Inbox.

6 Select the profile you want to use.

7 Click OK.

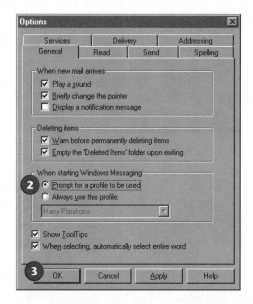

Connecting to Your Network from a Remote Location

If your network has dial-up network services and you have been granted permission to connect from a remote location, you can establish a dial-up connection to your network and connect to it by phone using a modem. Once you're connected, you have access to your network just as if you were in the office.

TIP

You need to set up the dial-up location only once. After it's set up, you just select the connection and click Dial.

Set Up Your Computer

1 Set up your computer to have the same network protocols and configurations that it would have if it were directly attached to the network.

2 Open My Computer, and double-click the Dial-Up Networking icon.

3 Click New.

4 Type a descriptive name for the connection.

5 Enter the number of the direct line to the server.

6 Complete the information on the different tabs, based on the information provided for the connection by the network administrator.

7 Click OK.

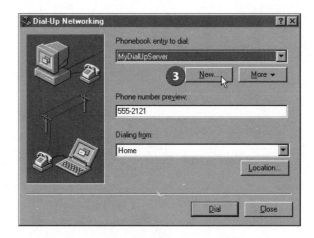

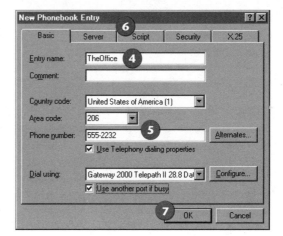

TIP

The network administrator can restrict your access to a single computer or give you full access to the entire network. Contact the network administrator before you try to connect. He or she should supply you with all the network-configuration information and the passwords you need to log on. Use the Network icon in the Control Panel to configure the network settings.

TIP

If you spend your entire work session connected to your network, you can log on directly with dial-up networking. To do so, simply turn on the Logon Using Dial-Up Networking check box when you log on, and select the dial-up networking connection.

TIP

Dial-Up Networking is useful for more than just connecting to your corporate network. You can use Dial-Up Networking to connect to services such as CompuServe, to connect to the Internet, and when you're connecting two computers with a serial cable.

Connect to the Network

1 With the new connection selected, click Dial.

2 Enter your user name, password, and the domain to which you're connecting. Be sure to use the correct logon information for the network you're connecting to.

3 Click OK.

4 Wait for the connection to be made.

5 Work on the network as usual.

6 When you've finished, use your network's standard logoff procedure, if one is required.

7 Right-click the Dial-Up Networking Monitor on the taskbar to hang up.

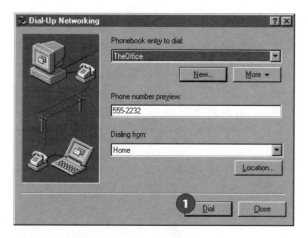

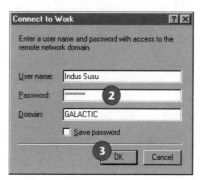

12

Adding On to Your System

By now, you've probably had enough experience with Windows NT to appreciate many of the great features and refinements that are built into the system. However, a computer rarely has all the Windows NT features installed, so you'll be able to enrich your system by installing additional components. Windows NT isn't a static system, and there are many *add-on* features available to enhance its functionality. Two of those add-ons are Microsoft Personal Fax and IntelliPoint 2.0 software. And what system would be complete without an assortment of programs installed?

Microsoft Personal Fax provides a group of powerful tools that let you send and receive faxes directly through your computer—if you have a fax modem. We were able to look at the *beta* software (software that's still under development) for these tools just before this book went to the printer, so what you see on your screen might look a little different from what we show in this section.

IntelliPoint 2.0 software lets you use the newest of pointing devices: the IntelliMouse, or *wheel mouse,* with its unique little wheel and wheel button, both of which provide you with a variety of helpful features. You'll also find out how IntelliPoint 2.0 software can relieve your "mouse-finger" woes by providing alternative ways to use the mouse.

Adding or Removing Windows NT Components

As you work, you might find that some Windows NT components you'd like to use aren't installed on your computer. Or perhaps there are Windows NT components installed that you never use, and they're just occupying valuable disk space. You don't have to rerun the rather lengthy Windows NT Setup program—you can use one of the tools Windows NT provides to install or remove any Windows NT components.

TIP

To install components, you'll need the appropriate permission—that is, you'll need to have been granted either Administrator or Power User rights—and access to the installation software.

Add or Remove a Component Group

1 Save any documents that you're working on, and close all your running programs.

2 Click the Start button, point to Settings, and choose Control Panel from the submenu.

3 Double-click the Add/Remove Programs icon.

4 On the Windows NT Setup tab, turn check boxes on or off to add or remove all the items in the component group.

Click a checked box to turn off the option and remove all items from the group.

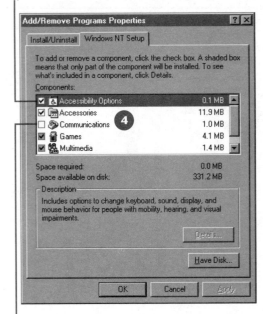

Click an unchecked box to turn on the option and add all items to the group.

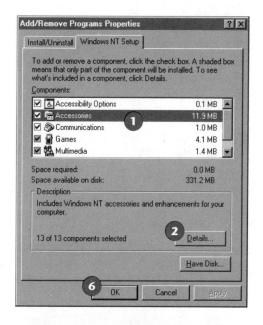

TIP

Sometimes an item in a component group also contains items you can select individually. If, when you select an item, the Details button becomes available (not grayed), you can click it and then select the items you want to include or exclude.

TIP

A grayed check box indicates that some (but not all) items in the group are selected.

Add or Remove an Item in a Component Group

1 Select the component group in which you want to add or remove an item.

2 Click Details.

3 Click a checked box to remove the item, or click an unchecked box to add the item.

4 Click OK when you've finished adding or removing the item or items.

5 Repeat steps 1 through 4 for each component group you want to change.

6 Click OK.

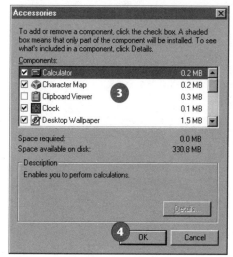

Installing a Software Program

Most software programs have an installation program that copies the required files to the hard disk and tells Windows NT which files are installed, where they are, and what they do. Windows NT simplifies the installation of most Windows NT–based programs and of many MS-DOS–based programs with the helpful Installation Wizard. Before you start, look at the program documentation for installation instructions. It's better to avoid problems in the beginning so that you don't have to fix them later.

TIP

Caught in the Net. *If you're installing a program over a network, check with your network administrator first. Some programs can't be installed over a network, and others require that special software be run by the network administrator.*

Install a Program

1. Save any documents that you're working on, and close all your running programs.

2. Click the Start button, point to Settings, and choose Control Panel from the submenu.

3. Double-click the Add/Remove Programs icon.

4. Click Install.

5. Place the installation disk or the CD in your drive, and click Next.

6. If the correct Setup program filename is displayed, click Finish. If not, click Browse, locate the Setup program, and then click Finish.

7. Follow the Setup program's instructions.

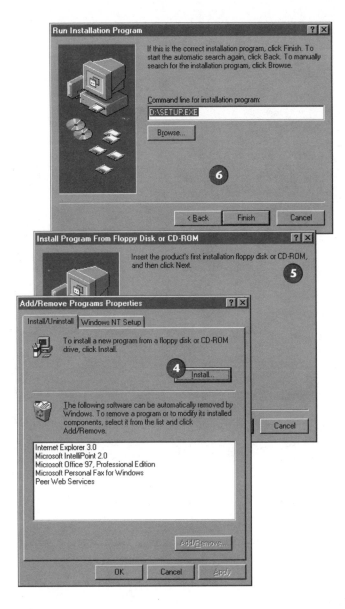

Removing a Software Program

Most programs are *registered* with Windows NT when you install them. You can—and should—use Windows NT tools to remove programs. If you simply delete the files, you might leave accessory files you don't need, or delete files you need for other programs. When you use Windows NT tools to uninstall a program, Windows NT keeps track of the files you need. When a file is no longer needed by any of your programs, Windows NT deletes the file.

SEE ALSO

"File Associations, File Extensions, and Registered Programs" on page 212 for information about registered programs.

"Adding or Removing Windows NT Components" on page 232 for information about removing programs that are part of Windows NT.

Uninstall a Program

1. Save any documents that you're working on, and close all your running programs.

2. Click the Start button, point to Settings, and choose Control Panel from the submenu.

3. Double-click the Add/Remove Programs icon.

4. On the Install/Uninstall tab, select the program to be uninstalled. (Programs that are components of Windows NT—Paint and WordPad, for example—aren't listed here. You can remove them using the Windows NT Setup tab.)

5. Click Add/Remove. If the program you want to remove isn't listed, see the program's documentation for removal instructions.

6. Follow the instructions that appear on the screen.

7. Click OK when you've finished.

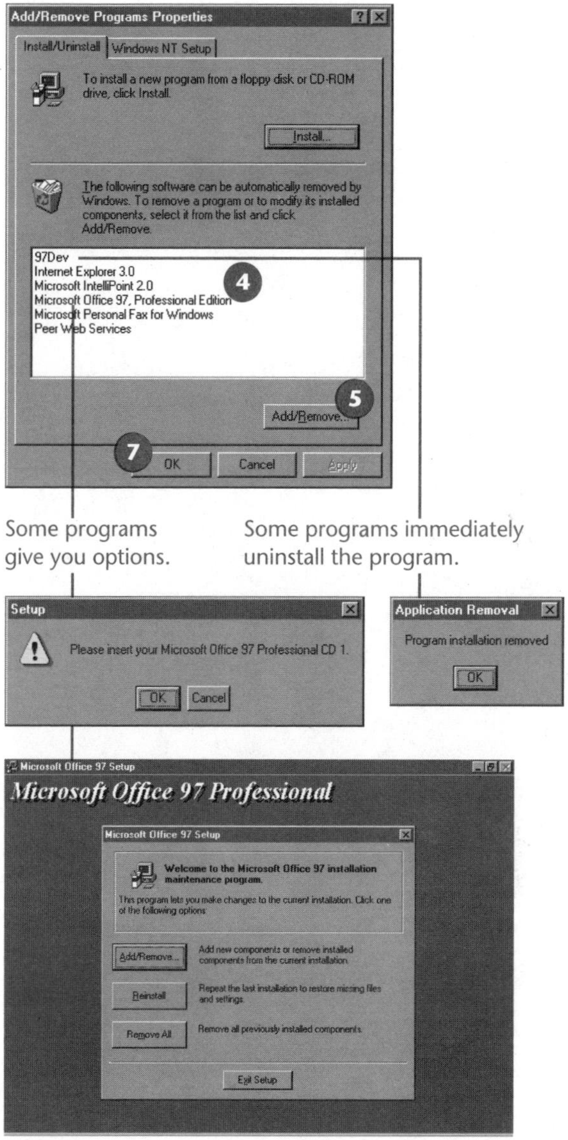

13

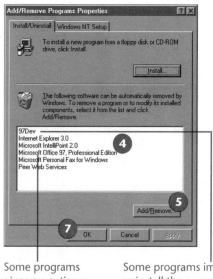

Some programs give you options.

Some programs immediately uninstall the program.

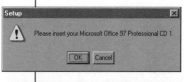

Adding Fonts to Your System

Fonts are styles of lettering whose different designs add personality and feeling to our words. Some programs offer many fonts on CD that you can install as you need them. Windows NT makes it easy to install fonts, and to view them on screen. If you want to, you can print very nice sample sheets and store them in a binder—a handy reference tool when you're trying to decide which fonts to use.

Add a Font

1 Click the Start button, point to Settings, and choose Control Panel from the submenu.

2 Double-click the shortcut to the Fonts folder.

3 Choose Install New Font from the File menu.

4 Navigate to the drive and folder containing the font to be installed.

5 Select the font or fonts. (To select several fonts, hold down the Ctrl key and click each font.)

6 Click OK.

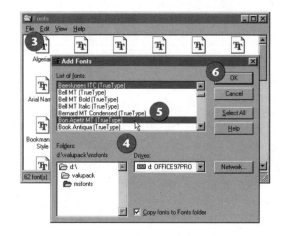

TIP

Some programs require you to use that program's Setup to install the fonts that come with the program.

SEE ALSO

"Hooked on Fonts" on page 238 for information about the different types of fonts that you can install.

View and Print a Font

1. Double-click the font name to view a font sample.

2. Click Print to print a font sample sheet.

3. Click Done.

4. Repeat steps 1 through 3 to view and print additional font samples.

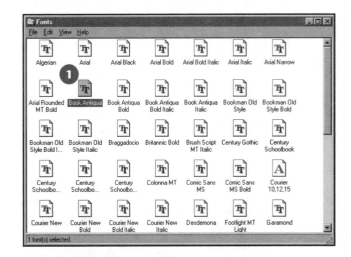

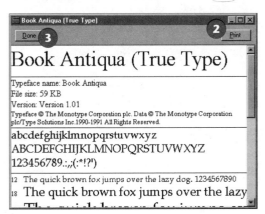

Hooked on Fonts

When you open the Font drop-down list on a program's toolbar, you might be surprised to see how many fonts you already have. Where did they all come from? Well, Windows NT comes with quite a few fonts, and if you've installed other programs, you've probably installed their font collections too. Depending on where your fonts came from, you'll see various icons—or in some cases no icon at all—next to their names in the Font list. The two icons you'll see most frequently represent *TrueType fonts* and *printer fonts*. (Windows NT also includes a few other fonts that are provided for compatibility with some older programs.)

◆ TrueType fonts are WYSIWYG (what-you-see-is-what-you-get) fonts, which means that the printed output looks exactly the same as what you see on your screen. TrueType fonts are outline fonts: the shapes of the letters are drawn with lines and curves rather than with patterns of dots. TrueType fonts were designed to print well at any size on almost any printer, even at low resolutions.

◆ Printer fonts are stored in your printer, not in your computer's Fonts folder. When you install a printer, these fonts are made available to your programs, and their names appear in your Font list. Be aware, if you're using a printer font, that what you see on your screen might not exactly match your printed output—sometimes you'll see a look-alike font instead.

What these rather dry facts don't tell you is what a delight it is to be able to transform the look and the personality of your text with a few mouse-clicks. Try it! Select some text, open your Font drop-down list, click a font name, and see what you get. Open the Font Size list and click to change the size. For a real surprise, try one of the picture fonts. Your words will change into a series of little pictures (called *dingbats*), and you can enlarge them, italicize them, and so on, just as you can words. It can be a lot of fun.

If you feel like a kid with a new toy, just keep in mind that you *can* have too much of a good thing. A document with too many different fonts can be very difficult to read, and instantly marks you as an amateur in the world of graphic design. Keep things simple. Professional designers seldom use more than two or three different fonts in a document—a *display font* for headlines or anything that's meant to attract attention, a *text font* for the body of the document, and perhaps a third font for elements such as captions, pull quotes, sidebars, and so on.

There are literally *thousands* of fonts, and new ones are being created all the time. To learn more about fonts and their history, you'll find the shelves of your local library or bookstore overflowing with fascinating books.

A discussion about the best fonts to use for display or text is beyond the scope of this book, but you won't go wrong if you use a big, bold font for display and a plain, readable font for text.

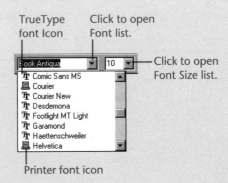

TrueType
font Icon

Click to open
Font list.

Click to open
Font Size list.

Printer font icon

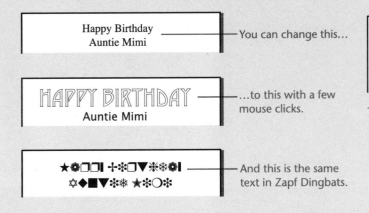

You can change this...

...to this with a few
mouse clicks.

And this is the same
text in Zapf Dingbats.

Stormy Night

It was a dark and stormy night. The wind howled through the broken windows. Moldy shutters banged relentlessly against the dank walls. "Why me?" I murmured, but the shrieking wind carried my voice away. "Why not!" it jeered. A scream—or was it just a gull complaining about being forced to take flight by the storm? A hand ripping at the door's rotted timbers—or just a branch brushing against the house?

Stormy Night

It was a dark and stormy night. The wind howled through the broken windows. Moldy shutters banged relentlessly against the dank walls. "Why me?" I murmured, but the shrieking wind carried my voice away. "Why not!" it jeered. A scream—or was it just a gull complaining about being forced to take flight by the storm? A hand ripping at the door's rotted timbers—or just a branch brushing against the house?

Stormy Night

It was a dark and stormy night. The wind howled through the broken windows. Moldy shutters banged relentlessly against the dank walls. "Why me?" I murmured, but the shrieking wind carried my voice away. "Why not!" it jeered. A scream—or was it just a gull complaining about being forced to take flight by the storm? A hand ripping at the door's rotted timbers—or just a branch brushing against the house?

Three different looks created with display and text fonts

Setting Up Your Fax

If your computer has a fax modem and if Microsoft Personal Fax for Windows has been installed, you can send faxes directly from your computer to another computer or to a fax machine. When you first install Microsoft Personal Fax for Windows, the Installation Wizard makes certain settings. Over time you'll probably want to customize these settings.

TIP

In some locations, the law requires you to include the Transmitting Subscriber ID (TSID) number in your fax. If you elect not to include this number, the fax number from your User Info tab will be included in the banner. The TSID or your fax number might appear on the receiving fax machine's display as an identifier of the incoming fax.

Enter Your Data

1 Click the Start button, point to Settings, and choose Control Panel from the submenu.

2 Double-click the Fax icon.

3 Click the User Info tab.

4 Fill in any missing information that should be included on the fax cover page.

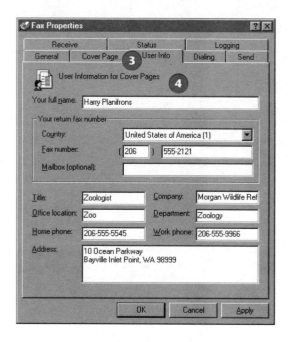

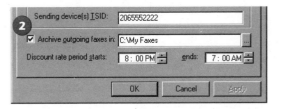

Archive the Faxes

1 Click the Send tab.

2 Specify where you want to keep copies of your sent faxes.

TIP

The fax cover pages that come with Microsoft Personal Fax have fields that obtain information from the User Info tab and add it to the fax cover page automatically. By filling in the User Info tab, you'll save yourself the time and effort of completing the cover page manually.

SEE ALSO

"Connecting from Different Locations" on page 225 for information about specifying your location.

"Sending a Fax with an Attachment" on page 244 for information about sending a fax directly from the Inbox.

"Creating Your Fax Cover Page" on page 248 for information about modifying a fax cover page.

Set Up the Dialing

1 Click the Dialing tab.

2 Specify how often and at what interval any faxes that didn't go through are to be sent, or retried, again.

3 Identify any phone prefixes in your area code that require the area code to be included when you dial.

4 Specify whether you want a banner that includes contact information at the top of each page.

5 Click OK.

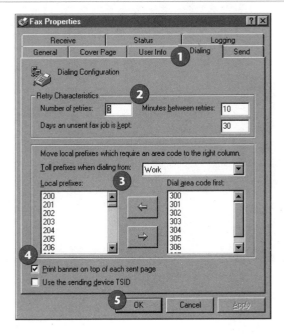

TIP

If you're using your computer at a new location, create the location information before entering all your dialing settings, and then select the location on the Dialing tab.

Faxing a Note

If you want to fax a note that you haven't yet typed, the Fax Send Utility provides an easy way to send your message. You specify the person or people who will receive the fax, you select a cover-page style, and then you type your note.

TIP

After you complete the fax, Microsoft Personal Fax will take a little while to process the information and create the fax before actually sending it.

TIP

If you're not going to include a cover page with your fax, be sure that the first page of the document contains the name of the person you're sending the fax to, as well as your name, fax number, and telephone number for callback if there are any problems when you're sending the fax.

Create Your Fax

1. Click the Start button, point to Programs and then to Fax, and choose Fax Send Utility from the submenu.

2. Add the recipients' addresses. Click Next.

3. Specify whether you want a cover page included and, if so, which one. Also specify when you want the fax sent, and enter the billing code if it's required. Click Next.

4. Type the subject of the fax.

5. Type your note.

6. Click Finish to send the fax.

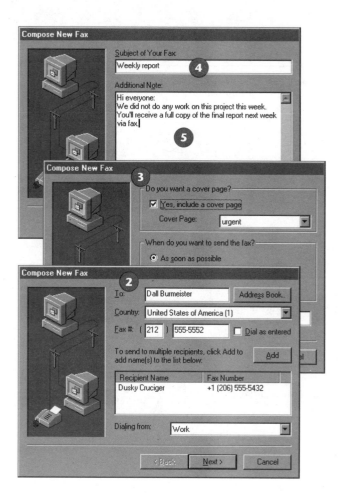

Faxing a Document

With Microsoft Personal Fax for Windows, you can fax any document that you can print. You do this by sending the document to a fax printer instead of to a standard printer.

TIP

If the program is designed to print only to the default printer, set the fax printer as your default printer before faxing the document. Remember to switch back to your standard default printer after sending the fax.

TIP

Billing codes are recorded in the fax log. Use the Event Viewer (on the Administrative Tools submenu of the Start menu) to view the log. Use the Logging tab of the Fax Properties dialog box to specify which items are logged and how they're logged.

Fax a Document

1. Create and save your document.

2. Choose Print from the File menu.

3. In the Print dialog box, select the Fax printer.

4. Click Properties.

5. Specify when you want to send the fax.

6. Specify the paper size, resolution, and orientation for the fax.

7. Enter any appropriate billing information.

8. Click OK.

9. Click OK in the Print dialog box.

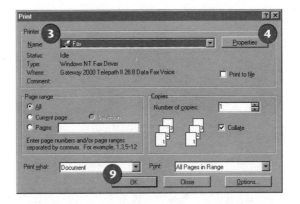

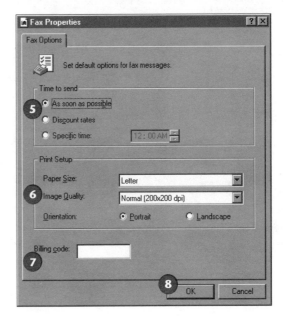

Sending a Fax with an Attachment

If your computer is set up with Windows Messaging, you can create a message to be faxed, and you can attach files whose contents will be included in the fax, just as you would send an attachment with your e-mail. For example, you can create an introductory text message and include a spreadsheet document or a large word-processed document. You do this by sending the fax from your Inbox.

> **TIP**
>
> *To set Send properties, such as time sent, type of cover page, and inclusion of an identifying banner on each page, set the default fax properties from the Control Panel.*

Set Up Your Inbox

1 Open the Inbox if it's not already open.

2 Choose Services from the Tools menu.

3 Click the Add button.

4 Select Fax Address Book, and click OK. Click OK when you're advised that you'll need to restart Windows Messaging.

5 Click Add again.

6 Select Fax Mail Transport, and click OK. Click OK when you're advised that you'll need to restart Windows Messaging.

7 Click OK to close the Services dialog box.

8 Choose Exit And Log Off from the File menu.

9 Open your Inbox.

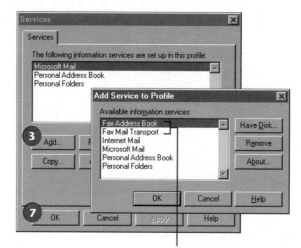

Add both the Fax Address Book and the Fax Mail Transport services.

TIP

By including both e-mail addresses and fax addresses in the To and CC lines, you can send the same message to some people by e-mail and to others by fax. Windows Messaging will figure out which system to use from the type of address you provide.

TIP

You don't have to include a file—you can send an unaccompanied message too. If you prefer the environment provided by the Inbox to that of the Fax Send Utility—and especially if you're using WordMail—you can send all your faxes through the Inbox.

TIP

You need to enter a fax address only once. Thereafter, simply select the recipient's name in your Address Book, and click the To button.

Create a Message

1 Click the New Message button.

2 Click the To button.

3 Click the New button to create a fax address.

4 Double-click Fax Address.

5 Complete the fax address information.

6 Click the To button.

7 Type the fax message. Include any files you want to send.

8 Click the Send button.

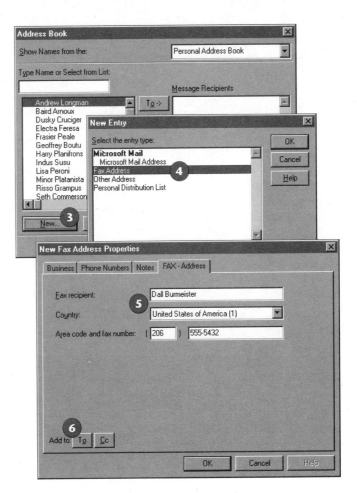

Receiving a Fax

If your computer is equipped with a fax modem, you can set the computer to receive an incoming fax, print it, and store it in a folder or in your mailbox. The received fax is a graphics image, and you can view it on your computer and even manipulate the image for easier reading.

TIP

You can connect to other fax modems on your network. Check with your network administrator for details and security procedures.

Specify Your Receiving Setup

1 Click the Start button, point to Settings, and choose Control Panel from the submenu.

2 Double-click the Fax icon.

3 Click the Receive tab.

4 Turn on the check box for your fax modem if it's not already checked.

5 Specify whether you want to print an incoming fax and, if so, which printer to use.

6 Specify where you want to store the fax.

7 Specify whether you want it stored in your mailbox.

8 Click OK.

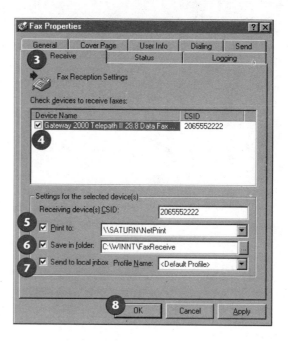

TIP

Windows NT comes with imaging software that you can use to view your faxes, but the Fax Viewer that's included with Microsoft Personal Fax for Windows is an updated version and does a better job.

TIP

Faxes, both sent and received, are stored as TIF images. You can use other programs that can read TIF files to view and manipulate your faxes too.

TIP

The Fax Viewer works just like many other graphics programs—that is, you can rotate the graphics image (the contents of the fax), change the level of magnification, select specific areas, and add your own annotations.

View a Fax

1. Click the Start button, point to Programs and then to Fax, and choose Fax Viewer from the submenu.

2. Use the toolbar buttons to view or to print the fax.

3. Choose Exit from the File menu when you've finished.

4. If you made changes, choose Yes to save them or No to discard them.

Turn on to change your view of the fax by dragging it.

Turn on to show a thumbnail image of the fax.

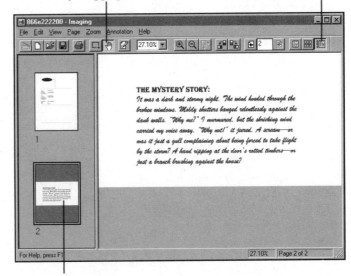

Click a thumbnail to jump to that page.

Creating Your Fax Cover Page

When you send a fax using Microsoft Fax, you can include a cover page that merges data from your Address Book with your own user information (which you supplied when you set up your fax services). Microsoft Personal Fax for Windows includes some general cover-page styles, which you can modify to your own design using the Fax Cover Page Editor program.

TIP

The Fax Cover Page Editor works just like most drawing-editing programs, except for the inclusion of the data fields. You can stack and group items, and you can even use the area at the right of the page as a scrap area for storing items that you don't necessarily want to include on every cover page.

Modify a Cover Page

1 Click the Start button, point to Programs and then to Fax, and choose Cover Page Editor from the submenu.

2 Click the Open button, select the cover page you want to modify, and click the Open button.

3 In the Fax Cover Page Editor program, choose Save As from the File menu, and save the file under a different filename.

4 Modify the cover page as desired:

◆ Delete any elements you don't want.

◆ Use the Drawing tools to add visual elements.

◆ Use the Insert menu to add data fields that insert information about the sender, the recipient, or the message.

◆ Use the Alignment tools to arrange the elements.

5 Click the Save button.

6 Choose Exit from the File menu.

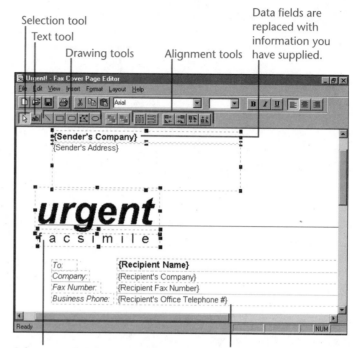

Selection tool

Text tool

Drawing tools

Alignment tools

Data fields are replaced with information you have supplied.

Select several elements by dragging the Selection tool over them, and then position them using the Alignment tools.

Drag an existing data field into a new position or delete it. Add a new data field using the Insert menu.

Hiding and Finding the Mouse

If you have Microsoft IntelliPoint 2.0 software installed on your computer and you have an Intelli-Mouse, you're using the newest generation of pointing devices. On some computer screens, or when you're running certain programs, you might find that the mouse pointer is too obvious and gets in your way. In other situations, the opposite is true—it can be frustratingly difficult to find the mouse pointer when it hides among the *t*s and *l*s in a document, for example. With Microsoft IntelliPoint 2.0 software installed, you can hide the pointer until you need it and then have it reappear with just a touch of the mouse. If you can't find the pointer on your screen, Windows Sonar will show you where it is.

Set Up the Pointer

1. Double-click the mouse icon on the taskbar.

2. Click the Visibility tab.

3. Turn on the Sonar option.

4. Turn on the Vanish option.

5. Click OK.

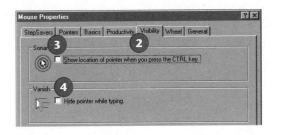

Hide and Find the Pointer

1. In a program window, start typing. The mouse pointer disappears.

2. Move the mouse to make the pointer reappear.

3. Press the Ctrl key to locate the pointer.

With the Vanish option turned on, the mouse pointer disappears when you type.

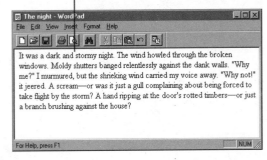

Sonar finds the mouse pointer for you.

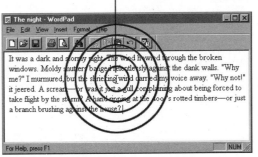

Wheeling with the IntelliMouse

Windows NT is designed to work with the IntelliMouse, but only the most recently designed programs currently have the ability to work with the wheel. The wheel works in two ways: you can press it to use it like a mouse button, and you can rotate it to use the special wheel properties. The functionality of both the wheel and the wheel button in the Intelli-Mouse is determined by the individual program.

TIP

The wheel button functions in the same manner as a third mouse button, so if the pro-gram has features that work with a third mouse button, those features will work with the wheel button. Rotating the wheel, however, is a feature unique to the IntelliMouse, so the program must be designed to work with an IntelliMouse.

Set Up the Wheel

1. Click the Start button, point to Settings, and choose Control Panel from the submenu.

2. Double-click the Mouse icon.

3. Click the Wheel tab, and turn on the Turn On The Wheel option if it's not already checked.

4. Turn on the Turn On The Wheel Button option if it's not already checked.

5. Select Default for the button assignment if it's not already selected.

6. Click OK to close the Mouse Properties dialog box.

Click to set scrolling to a specific number of lines or to scroll one windowful at a time.

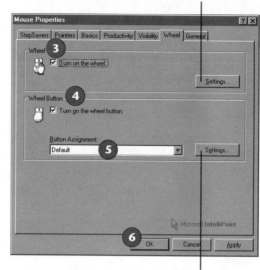

Click to set the speed of the mouse pointer when the wheel button is pressed.

Start Internet Explorer 3.0, and size the window so that the horizontal and vertical scroll bars are both visible. Rotate the wheel in one direction and then in the other direction to scroll horizontally. Press the wheel and hold it down. Move the mouse to the right until the arrow points to the right and the window scrolls. With the wheel button still pressed, move the mouse in different directions and watch the way the window scrolls. Release the wheel button when you've finished playing.

If you change the functionality of the mouse but it doesn't work as expected, try double-clicking the wheel button.

Find Out What the Wheel Does

1 Read the program's documentation and online help.

2 If the information is inadequate, experiment! Try the methods shown in the table at the right and see how your program responds to the wheel actions.

Change the Wheel Button's Function

1 Click the Start button, point to Settings, and choose Control Panel from the submenu.

2 Double-click the Mouse icon.

3 On the Wheel tab, select a new function for the wheel button.

4 Click OK.

EXAMPLES OF USING THE WHEEL	
Action	**What it does**
Rotate the wheel.	In a My Computer window: scrolls up or down.
Shift+rotate the wheel.	In Windows NT Explorer: opens the folder being pointed to or closes an open folder.
Ctrl+rotate the wheel.	In Word 97: increases or decreases zoom.
Click the wheel button and move the mouse.	In Internet Explorer 3.0: scrolls in the direction the mouse is moved. Click again to turn off scrolling.

Acts as a standard third mouse button in a program.

One click is the same as a double-click of the left mouse button.

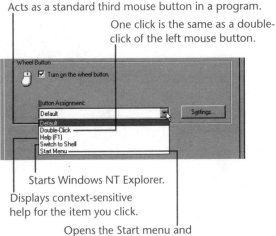

Starts Windows NT Explorer.

Displays context-sensitive help for the item you click.

Opens the Start menu and displays the Windows NT taskbar.

Adjusting Mouse Movements

Microsoft IntelliPoint 2.0 software provides several options that allow you to customize the way the mouse works to fit your working style. You'll probably want to be a bit selective, however, in the options you use. Some are real time-savers; others can cause unexpected problems. The best thing to do is turn on a few options, try them out, and decide whether or not you like them.

Speed Up Your Work

1. Click the Start button, point to Settings, and choose Control Panel from the submenu.

2. Double-click the Mouse icon.

3. Click the StepSavers tab, and turn on the SnapTo, ClickSaver, and Focus options.

4. Click the Productivity tab, and turn on the ClickLock option.

5. Click the Settings button.

6. Set the duration for which the button must be held to activate the ClickLock feature, and click OK.

Positions the pointer over the default button or default item when you open a window or a dialog box. If no default is set, positions the pointer in the center of the window.

Activates a window or a dialog box when you point at the title bar instead of clicking it.

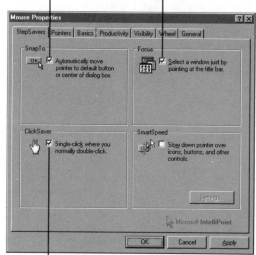

A single click acts as a double-click for items that require a double-click, but acts as a single click for items that respond only to a single click.

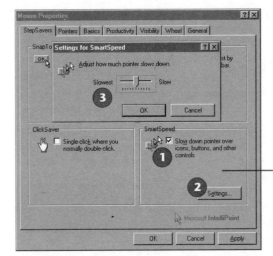

13

TIP

TIP

Experiment with a balance between the speed of the mouse and the acceleration of the mouse pointer. Both have an effect on the way the mouse moves, but it's the way you work that determines the best settings for each.

TIP

You can test the speed of the mouse while the Mouse Properties dialog box is still open—just move the mouse pointer around on the screen to test the speed and acceleration of the mouse.

Change the Mouse Speed

1 On the StepSavers tab, turn on the SmartSpeed option.

2 Click the Settings button.

3 Adjust how much the mouse slows down when approaching an item, and click OK.

4 On the Basics tab, adjust the speed of the mouse pointer.

5 Click the Advanced button.

6 Specify whether, and at what rate, you want the mouse pointer to accelerate when you move the mouse quickly, and then click OK.

7 Click OK to close the Mouse Properties dialog box.

Decreases the mouse speed as the pointer approaches any item that can be clicked.

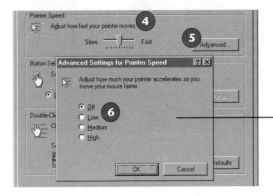

Sets how fast the pointer moves in relationship to how quickly you move the mouse.

Making Mouse Dragging Easier

Dragging items around in Windows—files between folders, text in a document, part of a picture in a drawing program, for example—is simple and convenient, but it can be hard on your "mouse finger," your wrist, and your patience. To simplify dragging, Microsoft IntelliPoint 2.0 software gives you the option of "locking" your click so that you can drag without holding down the mouse button. If you do a lot of dragging, you'll like this feature.

> **TIP**
>
> *If the pointer moves without dragging the item, hold the mouse button down longer and try again, or adjust the duration in the Settings For ClickLock dialog box.*

Turn On Dragging

1 Double-click the mouse icon on the taskbar.

2 Click the Productivity tab.

3 Turn on the ClickLock option.

4 Click the Settings button.

5 Set the length of time you need to hold down the mouse button to turn on the dragging.

6 Click OK.

7 Click OK.

Click and Drag

1 Point to the item you want to drag.

2 Hold down the left mouse button, release the mouse button, and move the mouse.

3 Move the item to where you want to drop it, and click the left mouse button.

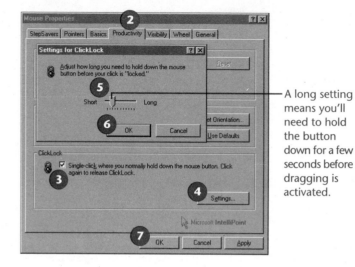

A long setting means you'll need to hold the button down for a few seconds before dragging is activated.

With the ClickLock option, this document is being dragged...

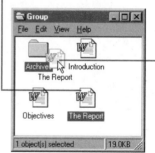

...by clicking, not by holding down, the mouse button.

What is "the net"? Briefly (*very* briefly!), the net is two main things: it's the Internet, where you can wander the world accessing information about everything imaginable, and it's your company intranet—a communications system set up on a corporate network. What can the net do for you? Whatever you want—more than we can possibly describe here. But we can help you explore some of the tools that Microsoft has made available for your travels on the net.

With the release of Windows NT 4.0, Microsoft has included a version of Internet Explorer. We'll look at the latest version, Internet Explorer 3.0, which can serve as your interface to the net. It's called a *browser* because you use it to browse through the different pages on the Internet. Internet Explorer is built to work closely with Windows NT, and with programs such as Microsoft Office 97. In this section, we'll also take a look at several *add-ons*—programs and tools that you can purchase or that you can download from Microsoft's Internet site. Many of these tools work whether you're using the Internet or your corporate intranet.

Using Internet Explorer and all its tools is a subject for an entire book. Our purpose here is to get you comfortable with basic operations and confident enough to go out and enjoy your explorations.

Going to a Net Site

To Internet Explorer, the only differences between the Internet and your company intranet are the connection and the type of address you use to connect. In either case, you can go directly to a specific site—provided you have its address or a shortcut to it—or you can "surf" the net, gathering the information you need.

TIP

If you've copied an Internet address from a document to the Windows Clipboard, you can paste the address into the Address box—just click in the box and press Ctrl+V.

SEE ALSO

"Changing Internet Explorer Links" on page 258 for information about changing the destinations of the buttons on the Links toolbar.

"Returning to Your Favorite Sites" on page 260 for information about saving addresses for future use.

Jump to a Site

1. Start Internet Explorer, and connect to the Internet if you're not already connected.

2. If the toolbar isn't displayed, choose Toolbar from the View menu.

3. Click the Links toolbar if it's not fully displayed.

4. Click a button to go to a site.

Click to display the hidden Links toolbar.

The Links toolbar contains links to several locations.

Use an Address

1. Click the Address toolbar.

2. Click the current address to select it, and insert the address you want to go to. (If you're using an intranet whose network has a gateway to the Internet, jumps from your intranet might take you to the Internet without your being aware of it. Use the Back button or the drop-down list on the Address toolbar to return to your intranet.)

3. Press Enter.

Click to display the hidden Address toolbar.

When you enter this address...   ...you go to this site.

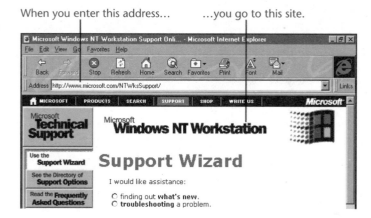

TIP

If you access the Internet from a corporate network that uses a proxy server, the network administrator can block your access to certain sites and can even record the sites you visit.

TIP

If Internet Explorer is not set up to start at your company's intranet home page, type the name of the intranet server in the Address box. To go to a computer that's using the Personal Web Server to publish pages on the intranet, type that computer's name in the Address box.

TIP

The Personal Web Server lets you use your computer as an intranet server instead of having to post Web pages and resources on the main Web server. Use the Personal Web Server in a small network or workgroup, or to test pages you're creating before you post them on the main Web server.

Surf the Net

1 From your current page, do any of the following:

- ◆ Click the Search button, and use a service to locate a site by name or location.

- ◆ Click a relevant jump on the page to go to a new site.

- ◆ Click the Back button to return to a previous site.

- ◆ Click the Forward button to return to a site you left using the Back button.

- ◆ Open the Address list to select and jump to a previously visited site.

- ◆ Click the Stop button to stop downloading a page, and then jump to a different location.

2 If you get lost, click the Home button to return to your start page, or click the Search button to conduct another search.

Move backward and forward through sites you've already visited.

Find sites that fit your search criteria.

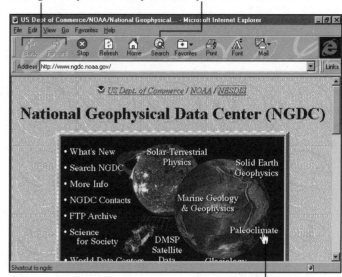

When the mouse pointer changes into a tiny hand, it's pointing to a jump that will take you to a different location.

14

Changing Internet Explorer Links

When you install Microsoft Internet Explorer, it has a preinstalled start page and it already contains links to other pages. Depending on your needs, you might want to have a different Internet start page. If you're using an intranet, you might want to set the start page to the main intranet page. And by customizing the other links, you can create quick and easy access to other pages with a click of a button.

TIP

If you want to reset a button on the Links toolbar to its original destination after you've changed it, select the link on the Navigation tab, and click the Use Default button.

Set a New Start Page

1. Navigate to the page you want to use as your start page.

2. Choose Options from the View menu, and click the Navigation tab in the Options dialog box.

3. With Start Page selected, click the Use Current button.

4. Click OK.

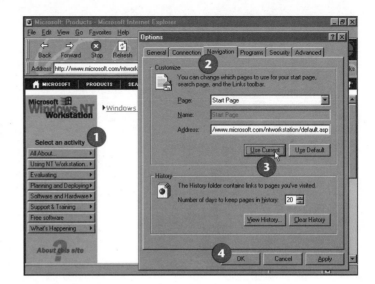

TIP

When you click the Use Current button, the address of the page you've navigated to is shown in the Address box.

TRY THIS

On the Navigation tab, click the View History button. Click the Cancel button to close the Options dialog box, and then use the History folder to locate a site you've visited and will revisit frequently. Double-click the shortcut to go to that page, and use the Navigation tab of the Options dialog box to add the site to the Links toolbar.

Set New Links Destinations

1. Navigate to the page you want to use as a link.

2. Choose Options from the View menu, and click the Navigation tab in the Options dialog box.

3. Select a link. These links correspond to the buttons on the Links toolbar.

4. Type the caption you want to use to identify the button.

5. Click the Use Current button.

6. Click OK.

7. Repeat steps 1 through 6 to redefine links to other buttons.

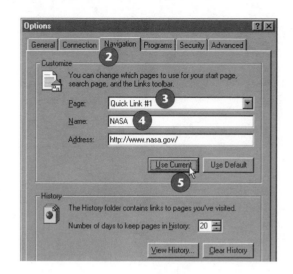

14

Click a redefined button...

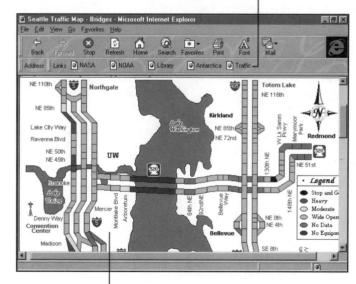

...to go to that site.

Returning to Your Favorite Sites

When you find a good source of information or entertainment, you don't need to waste a lot of time searching for that site the next time you want to visit it. You can simply add the site to your Favorites list, and Internet Explorer obligingly creates a shortcut to the site for you.

SEE ALSO

"Sharing a Site" on the facing page for information about saving shortcuts to or addresses of Internet sites.

Save a Location

1. Navigate to the site whose location you want to save.

2. Click the Favorites button on the Links toolbar, and choose Add To Favorites from the drop-down menu.

3. Type a name for the site, or use the proposed name.

4. Click OK to add the site to your Favorites folder.

Return to a Location

1. Click the Favorites button.

2. Click the name of the site you want to return to.

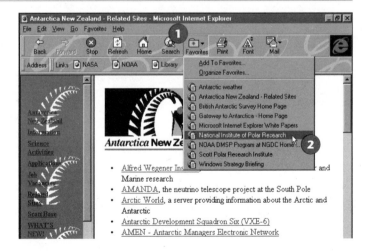

Sharing a Site

Don't keep all the good sites to yourself! You can share a great site with friends and colleagues by sending them a shortcut to the site. If you prefer, you can send the entire address rather than a shortcut.

TIP

Documents created in Microsoft Office 97 programs can contain hyperlinks to Internet or intranet sites. This capability provides a very friendly and powerful way to share Web sites.

TIP

To share a site that you've visited before, find the shortcut in your Favorites folder (in your individual profile folder) or in the History folder (in the Winnt folder).

Get the Shortcut

1. Navigate to the site you want to share with someone.

2. Choose Create Shortcut from the File menu.

3. Drag the shortcut to the site from your Desktop to copy it into an e-mail message or into any appropriate document.

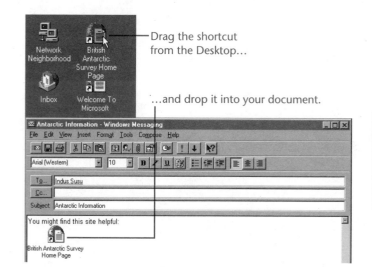

Drag the shortcut from the Desktop...

...and drop it into your document.

Get the Address

1. Right-click the shortcut to the site, and choose Properties from the shortcut menu.

2. Click the Internet Shortcut tab.

3. With the Target URL text selected, press Ctrl+C to copy it.

4. Click Cancel.

5. Click in the document where you want to place the address, and press Ctrl+V to paste the address.

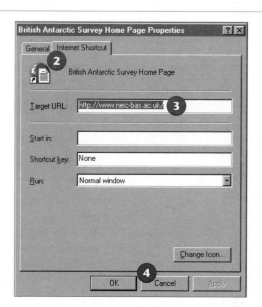

Protecting the Innocent

Microsoft Internet Explorer provides a system that lets you screen access to sites based on their content. Powerful as this sounds, the system depends on sites having been rated, and many sites currently remain unrated. By limiting your access only to sites that have specific ratings, you'll be severely restricting your access to the Internet.

TIP

If Content Advisor doesn't provide the security you need, you might want to check out the software programs available that give you more advanced methods of controlling access to specific sites or types of sites.

Set Up the Control

1 With Internet Explorer open, choose Options from the View menu.

2 On the Security tab, click the Settings button to start Content Advisor.

3 Enter your password. If this is the first time you're making any settings, confirm the password.

4 On the General tab, set access options.

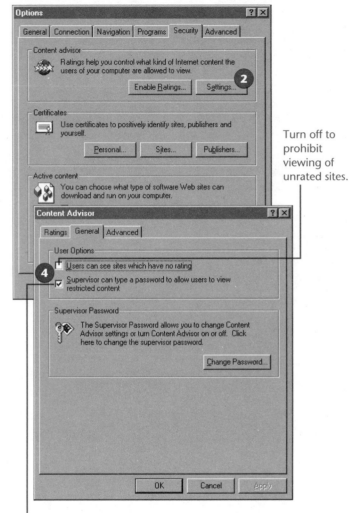

Turn off to prohibit viewing of unrated sites.

Turn on to be able to use your password to access unrated sites and rated sites that exceed your settings.

TIP

The Description section of the Ratings tab provides rather graphic information about the type of material that can be accessed at each level.

TIP

To turn off Content Advisor, choose Options from the View menu, click Disable Ratings on the Security tab, and supply your password.

Set the Ratings

1 On the Ratings tab, select a category.

2 Drag the slider to set the rating level.

3 Continue selecting categories and setting the ratings until all ratings have been set.

4 Click OK.

5 Click Enable Ratings.

6 Enter your password, and click OK. Click OK when notified that Content Advisor is running.

7 Click OK to close the Options dialog box.

14

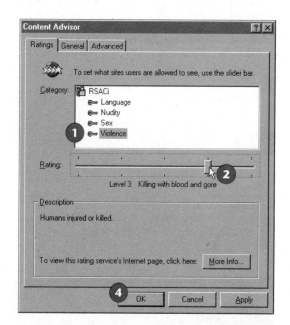

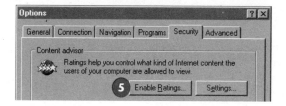

Chatting over the Internet

Microsoft Comic Chat provides an entertaining way to have a conversation over the Internet. The chat must be hosted by a chat server (called an Internet Relay Chat server), and your fellow chatterers need to be using Comic Chat too; otherwise, the graphics won't do much.

TIP

Mother Knows Best! *When you were little, she said, "Don't talk to strangers!" Now she says, "Don't tell strangers in chat rooms anything important about yourself!" Chat rooms often have strange characters lurking in corners. Unless you know whom you're dealing with, it's a good idea to remain anonymous.*

TIP

You can change the number of horizontal panels in the comic strip by adjusting Page Layout on the Settings tab of the Options dialog box.

Set Up Your Comic Strip

1. With Comic Chat running, choose Options from the View menu, and click the Character tab.

2. Select the character you want.

3. Click the Background tab.

4. Select a background for the comic.

5. Click the Personal Info tab.

6. Make any changes to your information.

7. Click OK.

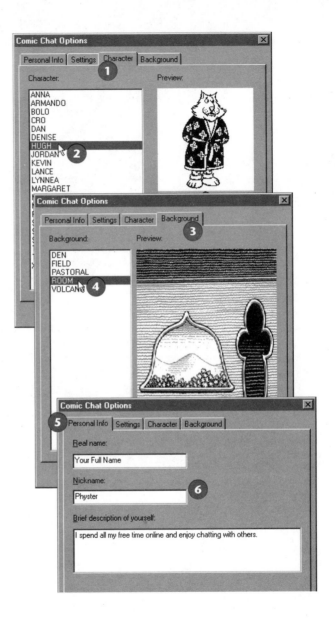

Your text can affect the gestures of your character. Either in a chat session or when you're practicing offline, start your comment with the word "I." In another comment, use "You" as the first word. Note the way your character points. If you're angry, type in all caps and you'll see that your typing can change your character's emotions. Experiment with e-mail "shorthand," such as LOL and :).

TIP

To practice working with the characters, save a Comic Chat session when you've finished chatting, disconnect, and then choose Open from the File menu. Open the saved chat session, move to the end of the chat, and then type your new dialog and adjust your character's emotions and gestures.

TIP

If the drawing of the comic strip on your screen is too slow or too distracting, or if you're the only person in the conversation who's using Comic Chat, you can turn off the graphics and view text only. To do so, choose Plain Text from the View menu.

Chat Away

1 When you're connected to the Comic Chat server, choose Chat Room List from the View menu.

2 Select a Chat Room, and click Go To.

3 Select an emotion.

4 Type your comment.

5 Click a button for the way you want your comment posted:

◆ Click Say to place your text in a voice balloon.

◆ Click Think to place your text in a thought balloon.

◆ Click Whisper to have your text sent only to the character whose name you've clicked.

◆ Click Action to display a text frame with your name and some text at the top of the panel.

Other characters participating in the chat
Your character, with selected emotion

Type your text here.   Your character with your text

Drag the dot to change your character's expression.

Reading the News

One of the add-ons to Internet Explorer is Microsoft Internet Mail And News. With it, you can connect to newsgroups from the news server provided by your Internet service provider or from news servers provided by others. When you connect to a newsgroup, you can read and post messages. When you subscribe to a newsgroup, you have the fastest and easiest access to that newsgroup.

TIP

Internet News supports offline reading and replying. You designate messages or a newsgroup to be downloaded while you're connected, and then you disconnect and review the material. Your replies are stored in the Outbox until you reconnect.

Select Your Newsgroups

1 With the news reader connected, click Newsgroups.

2 If you have more than one news server, select the one you want to use.

3 Search for the newsgroups you want to access.

4 Double-click a newsgroup to subscribe to it. The groups to which you've subscribed will appear on the Subscribed tab and in the Newsgroups list in the Internet News window.

5 Select the newsgroup you want to visit.

6 Click Go To.

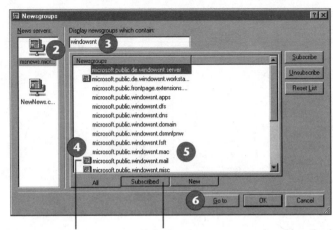

The newspaper icon shows you've subscribed to that newsgroup.

Only the newsgroups you've subscribed to are listed on the Subscribed tab.

SEE ALSO

"Designating a News Server" on page 270 for information about specifying your news server.

TIP

To customize the toolbar, right-click it and choose Customize to change the buttons; or choose Align to move the toolbar to the left side of the window.

TIP

To place the message header and the message text pane side by side, point to Preview Pane on the View menu and choose Split Vertically from the submenu.

TIP

A newsgroup rarely contains very much "hard" news. Newsgroups are used mostly as interactive bulletin boards for the exchange of information between users of the newsgroups.

Read the News

1 Click the message you want to read. If you want to see the message in a whole window rather than in a pane of the news reader, double-click the message.

2 Read the message. If you opened a separate window for the message, close the window when you've finished.

The regular font shows that the message has been read.

The Bold font shows that the message hasn't been read.

All the newsgroups you've subscribed to are listed.

A plus sign means there are additional messages related to the first message. A minus sign means all the messages in the series are displayed. A series of messages is called a *thread*.

Posting a Newsgroup Message

Newsgroups are interactive—that is, you can read and reply to messages and post your own messages. When you reply to a message, you can post your response in the newsgroup or you can mail your response directly to the author of the message. You can also customize your signature and have it added automatically to your messages.

TIP

Where Did It Go? *If you post a message and then open it from the newsgroup to review it, you might not see that message the next time you go to the newsgroup. The message is still there, but you probably have your news reader set to display unread messages only. To display your message, choose All Messages from the View menu.*

Set Up Your Response

1. With the news reader open, choose Options from the News menu, and click the Server tab.

2. Add to or change any of your personal and contact information.

3. Click the Signature tab.

4. Turn on the Text option.

5. Type the signature text you want to add to your messages.

6. Select which types of message you want the signature to be added to automatically.

7. Click OK.

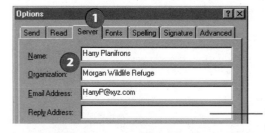

Complete if you want messages sent to an e-mail address other than the one from which you're sending your message.

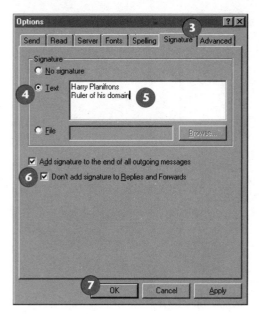

TIP

Most newsgroups have specific rules of conduct. Make sure that your messages are compatible with each newsgroup's etiquette; language or topics that are acceptable in one newsgroup might be offensive in another. Also, be cautious about creating long messages, especially when you're including text from a message you're responding to.

Post Your Message

1 Click the appropriate button:

- ◆ New Message to post a new message

- ◆ Reply To Group to post a response to the message you've selected

- ◆ Reply To Author to send an Internet Mail message to the author of the message you've selected

2 Type your message.

3 Click the Post Message button or the Send button.

Click, and type a subject.

Signature is inserted automatically.

Designating a News Server

When you first set up the news reader, you need to designate a news server. You can add other news servers or replace the existing one.

TIP

You can start the news reader from the Start menu by choosing Internet News, or from Internet Explorer by clicking the Mail button on the toolbar and choosing Read News from the drop-down menu.

SEE ALSO

"Getting Help from Other Windows NT Users" on page 288 for information about connecting to the Microsoft newsgroups and getting help on Windows NT or other products from other Windows NT users.

TIP

Turn on the logon option only if you've been instructed to do so by the news-server administrator. Many news servers don't require this information.

Add a News Server

1 With Internet News open, choose Options from the News menu, and click the Server tab.

2 Click Add.

3 Type the name of the news server and, if required for connection, your account name and password.

4 Click Set As Default if you want this to be the server to which News Reader automatically connects.

5 Click OK.

6 Click OK.

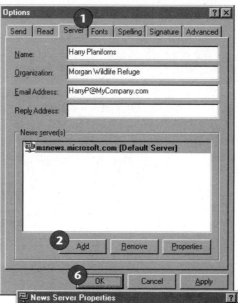

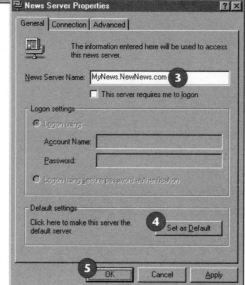

Using Internet Mail

If you're connected directly to the Internet, you can use the Internet Mail part of Internet Mail And News to send and receive messages. When your Internet mail is configured based on information provided by your Internet service provider, you can compose messages, respond to messages you've received, and forward messages.

TIP

If you want to use Internet Mail, the server you use to access the Internet must support the necessary services (PPP, SMTP, and POP3). Check with your Internet service provider or with your network administrator for information about these services. You'll also need the names of the SMTP and POP3 servers for your setup.

Read Your Mail

1. With Internet Mail open and connected to the Internet, click Send And Receive.

2. Click the message you want to read.

3. Read your message.

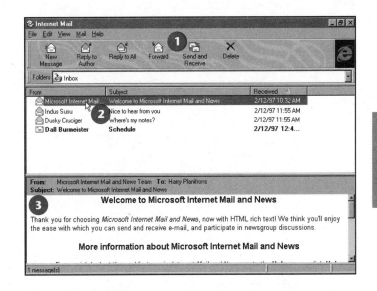

Send a Message

1. Select a message, and click the Reply To Author or the Reply To All button. Or click the New Message button to create a new message.

2. Complete or modify the To, CC, and Subject lines.

3. Type your message.

4. Click the Send button.

5. Click the Send And Receive button to send all your messages and to receive any waiting messages.

Click to open your Address Book.

If you don't complete this line, it will be blank in the message.

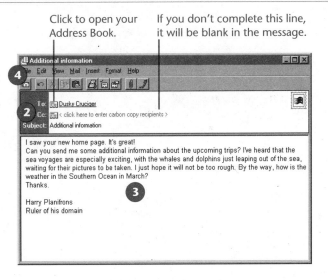

Connecting to a Meeting on the Net

With Microsoft NetMeeting 2.0, you can hold a productive meeting on the net. You can "chat" online, have voice conversations, share programs, illustrate your ideas on a "whiteboard," and—provided you have the correct equipment—even share video images. You can run NetMeeting over a network, over the Internet, or by modem. When the date and time for the meeting are announced, the person who's hosting the meeting should supply all the participants with the necessary connection settings and the address.

TIP

If someone is simply sending you video images, you don't need any extra equipment to be able to view them—just turn on the option to receive video images on the Video tab of the Options dialog box.

Set Up the Connection

1. With NetMeeting running, choose Options from the Tools menu.

2. On the Protocols tab, turn on the protocol that you'll be using if it's not already turned on.

3. On the Directory tab, supply information about yourself as you want it listed in a directory.

4. If you use a directory server, turn on the option to log on to the directory server.

5. Turn on the Do Not List My Name option if you don't want unsolicited calls.

6. Select or type the name of any directory server.

7. Click OK.

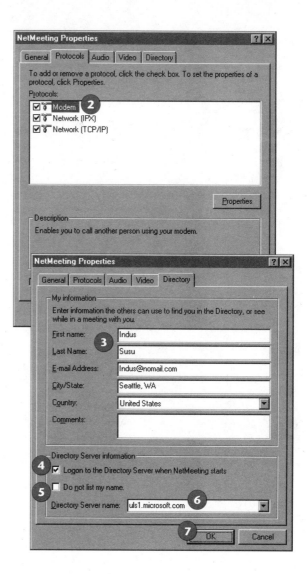

TIP

Nyet Meeting. *If you're troubled by incoming telephone calls when NetMeeting is running, choose Do Not Disturb from the File menu to ignore all incoming calls until you choose Do Not Disturb again.*

Connect to a Meeting

1 If you're using a locator server, click the name of the person you want to call.

2 Click the Call button. If it isn't already shown in the Address box, type the address:

- ◆ If you're using the Internet, type the computer identifier provided by the person you're connecting to.

- ◆ If you're using your network, type the name of the computer.

- ◆ If you're using a modem, type the phone number.

3 In the Call Using box, select the connection method.

4 Click Call.

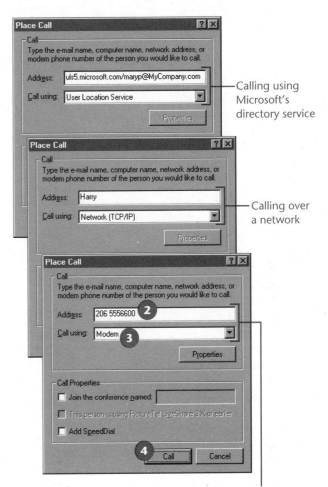

Calling using Microsoft's directory service

Calling over a network

Calling a computer for a modem-to-modem connection

Hosting a Meeting

When it's your turn to host a meeting, everyone connects to your computer. All you need to do is set up NetMeeting so that all participants in the meeting will be automatically connected.

TIP

The order in which participants' computers connect determines which computer can have voice or video communications with the host computer. Always establish the voice and/or video connections before having any other computers connect with the host computer.

Receive a Call

1. Choose Options from the Tools menu.

2. On the General tab, specify the way you want to receive calls.

3. If you're receiving calls by modem, click the Protocols tab, select the modem, click Properties, and turn on the option to answer incoming calls. Click OK.

4. Click OK to close the Options dialog box.

5. Choose Host Conference from the Call menu to start the meeting.

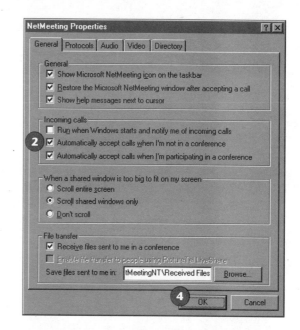

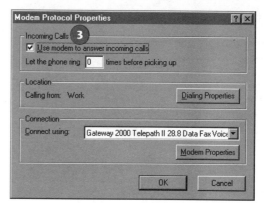

Talking on the Net

With NetMeeting, a sound card, and a microphone, you and a similarly equipped colleague can hold voice conversations through your computers. Depending on the connection and the equipment, the conversation can be as clear as a bell or it can be slow and scratchy. You might also experience a slight delay in the voice transmission as the digital sound is compressed and then decompressed.

TIP

You'll probably hear about full- and half-duplex modems when NetMeeting is mentioned. The more common half-duplex modem restricts conversation to one person at a time, rather like a two-way radio. A full-duplex modem lets both people talk simultaneously. If your modem is full duplex but NetMeeting only lets you set it up as half duplex, check with the modem manufacturer for updated files that work with Windows NT 4.0.

Make a Call

1 Verify that your speakers are turned on and that your microphone is in place.

2 Connect to the person you want to talk to. Make sure that neither of you is in conference with other computers— only two computers can share audio (or video) at one time.

3 Speak into the microphone.

4 Use the speaker and microphone volume controls to adjust the volume as needed.

5 Use any of the other NetMeeting tools.

6 Hang up when your conversation is over.

Drag to adjust the volume of your microphone.

Drag to adjust the volume of your speakers.

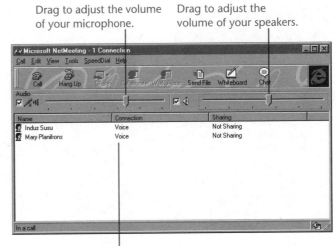

NetMeeting shows that you have voice communications enabled.

Conferring on the Net

When you are part of a NetMeeting, you can sit back and be an observer, or you can be an active participant by displaying items on the Whiteboard and making comments in a chat. When you do participate, whatever you contribute is viewed by everyone participating in the conference.

TIP

The Whiteboard can have multiple pages; use the buttons at the bottom right of the window to move among the pages and to add new pages.

TRY THIS

Before you connect to a meeting, add a page to the Whiteboard, move to that page, and add the elements you want to present at the meeting. When you connect, that Whiteboard page will be available for your presentation.

Brainstorm on the Whiteboard

1. Click the Whiteboard button.

2. Use any of the following tools to convey information:

   ◆ The Pen, Line, or any shape tool to draw on the Whiteboard

   ◆ The Text tool to type text

   ◆ The Eraser tool to select and remove an element

   ◆ The Remote Pointer or the Highlighter to emphasize an area

   ◆ The Selection tool to select and drag elements to new locations

3. Use any of the following methods to insert additional information:

   ◆ The Select Area or Select Window tool to select and paste part of the screen or a whole window

   ◆ The Paste command to copy material from the Clipboard

Use the Select Area tool to add clip art from a document.

Use the Select Window tool to add a program window.

Highlight text for emphasis.

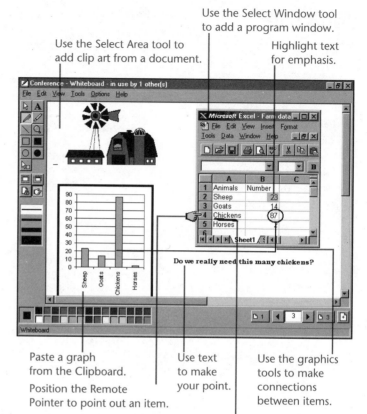

Paste a graph from the Clipboard.

Position the Remote Pointer to point out an item.

Use text to make your point.

Use the graphics tools to make connections between items.

Use the Pen tool for freehand drawing.

SEE ALSO

"Talking on the Net" on page 275 for information about using voice communications.

"Sharing a Program on the Net" on page 278 for information about displaying and working with programs in the conference.

TIP

You can save the contents of the Chat and Whiteboard windows for later review by choosing Save from the File menu.

TIP

Your network must be configured correctly to support Net-Meeting. Check with your network administrator if you have any problems running NetMeeting on your company's network. When you're connecting by modem, type the phone number of the computer's modem. That modem must be set to answer calls. When you're using the Internet, use the directory server provided by Microsoft, or use any other server to which you have access.

Chat It Up

1 Click the Chat button on the NetMeeting toolbar.

2 Type your text. Press Enter to send your message.

3 Read what other people have to say.

The name of the person making the comment...   ...and the comment

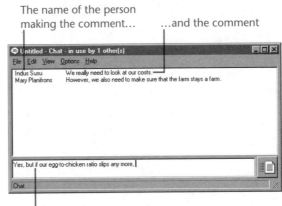

Type your comment here.

Sharing a Program on the Net

Sometimes it's difficult to follow what someone is talking about when he or she is working with a program in a meeting. With NetMeeting, you can see and understand the program as the person is working with it. And if you have a bright idea during the meeting, you can go in and work with the program yourself.

> **TIP**
>
> *The final version of NetMeeting 2.0 was not available at the time this book went to the printer, so what you see might look different from what we've shown here. In our beta version, we could share programs in NetMeeting 2.0 when it was running in Windows 95, but not in Windows NT.*

> **TIP**
>
> *The person who is running the program "owns" it, so he or she can take control of the program or stop sharing it at any time.*

View a Program

1 Ask the person who's running the program to share it.

2 On the taskbar, click the button for the shared application.

3 Click the Collaborate button.

4 Click in the document to take control of it.

5 Type your information.

6 Click the Work Alone button when you no longer want to contribute.

Tab shows who owns the program.

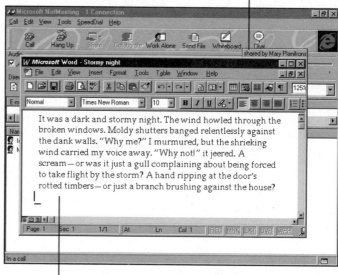

Shared program is viewed by all, but only one person at a time can work on it.

Taking Care of Problems

What if you have a problem and you can't find the information you need in this book? Although we've tried really hard to cover a broad range of problems, from the most common to the not so common, you still might have a question or two about Windows NT that we haven't answered here. If so, we'll direct you to the place where you're the most likely to find an answer. Read on.

The simplest and most logical place to look for an answer is in the Windows NT Help system (or in the Help system for a specific program if your problem is with a program rather than with Windows NT). The Windows NT Start button provides instant access to the Help system, and you can read the Help topics or use the Troubleshooter to help you identify and solve your problem.

If you're still stuck, and if you have access to the Internet, you can go further afield. For example, you can visit the Windows NT Support page, you can search the Microsoft Knowledge Base, and you can get help from other Windows NT users by posting your question in one of the Microsoft newsgroups. We'll show you how to find out whether you need an upgrade to your version of Windows NT and where to get it if you do.

And maybe there's no free lunch, but there *is* free software...and we'll tell you where to get it!

Using Help to Solve Problems

The Windows NT Help system contains many Troubleshooter topics that provide interactive support for common problems. These topics will help you narrow down the possible causes for the problem you're experiencing, and in many cases they'll provide jumps that take you directly to the Windows NT dialog box in which you can fix the problem.

> **TIP**
>
> *Many individual Help topics give you direct access to the appropriate troubleshooting topic. However, if you look up an item but you don't find the information you need, see whether there's a troubleshooting entry in the Help index. Fore example, if you look up "modems" in the Help index, one of the many subentries is "troubleshooting."*

Start the Troubleshooter

1 Click the Start button, and choose Help from the Start menu.

2 Click the Index tab.

3 Type *trouble* to display the troubleshooting topics.

4 Double-click the topic that's the most relevant to your problem.

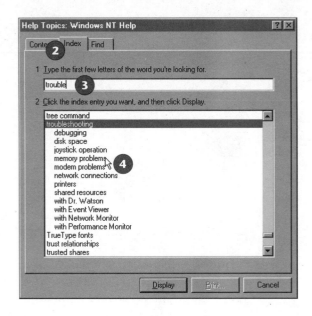

The troubleshooting questions are arranged in a logical manner to help you diagnose your problem, but they sometimes require more information than you have, and they can lead you down a dead-end route. If you think you've chosen the wrong answer, use the Back button to backtrack, and try again. If you need to supply more information, minimize the Help window, step through the procedure that's giving you a headache, and then return to the Troubleshooter with your detailed notes in hand.

Step Through the Troubleshooter

1. Read the text, and click the option that best describes the problem.

2. Continue reading the text, taking the recommended actions, and clicking the most appropriate options.

3. Use the jump button to open the folder, dialog box, or program that will help you fix the problem.

15

Getting System Information

When your system isn't working properly and you need to contact someone for help, you're going to have to supply that helpful person with some information about your system. It's quick and easy to get a comprehensive listing of your system settings. Although most of the information is indecipherable to the average person, there is some valuable information you can use, and there are useful details for the support person.

Get System Settings

1 Click the Start button, point to Programs and then to Administrative Tools, and choose Windows NT Diagnostics from the submenu.

2 On the Version tab, click the Print button.

3 Select the All Tabs option to print the information from all the tabs.

4 Click to print a summary.

5 Click to send all the information to a text file.

6 Click OK.

7 In the Save WinMSD Report dialog box, specify the location in which the file is to be stored. Click Save.

8 Click OK to close the Diagnostics dialog box.

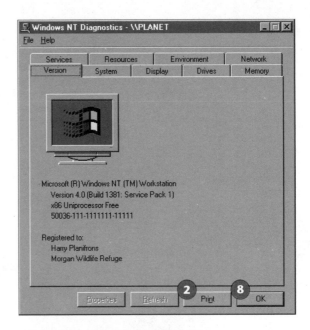

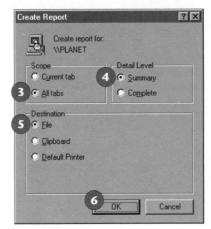

TIP

To see different types of logged information in Event Viewer, choose System from the Log menu to see system information or choose Application to see information logged by programs—for example, your incoming and outgoing faxes logged by the Microsoft Personal Fax for Windows.

TIP

You start Event Viewer and Performance Monitor from the Administrative Tools submenu of the Start menu. You start Task Manager by right-clicking the Windows taskbar.

TIP

Dr. Watson generates a log file intelligible only to those well-versed in technical jargon. To use Dr. Watson for assistance, just copy and send the Drwtsn32 log file (located in the Winnt folder) to your support person.

TIP

Task Manager provides a very useful Help file that explains the meaning of many of the techno-jargon terms used in the statistics.

Review the Information

1 Open the text file you just created.

2 Find any information that seems usable and copy it into another document. Extract the following:

- ◆ Version information, including type of processor and whether any service packs are installed

- ◆ Processor information

- ◆ System BIOS type and date

- ◆ Video BIOS type and date

- ◆ Video-adapter settings and memory

- ◆ Physical memory

3 Print the extracted information for reference, and save the document for future use.

4 If you need additional information, use any of the tools listed in the table at the right.

5 Get help, and supply any information that's needed.

USEFUL DIAGNOSTIC TOOLS	
Tool	**What it does**
Dr. Watson	Automatically generates a report in a log file when a program causes an error.
Event Viewer	Views logs of events for the system or for programs.
Performance Monitor	Displays graphs showing utilization of the items you specify.
Task Manager	Lists running programs, running processes, and memory usage.

15

Obtaining Information from Microsoft

If you have access to the Internet, you have immediate access to a vast amount of information and product support, as well as free software, from Microsoft.

TIP

Internet pages change their looks all the time, so the pages shown here might look quite different when you connect to them. It's a good idea to check the pages frequently for updated information.

SEE ALSO

"Getting Free Software" on page 290 for information about downloading free software from Microsoft Internet sites.

Get Connected

1. Use an Internet browser to connect to *http://www.microsoft.com/ ntworkstation.*

2. Click the item you want information about.

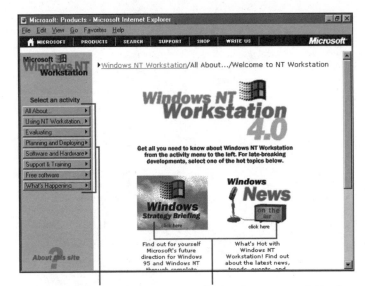

Click a button and choose an area of interest from the menu.

Click to jump to special topics.

TIP

Microsoft maintains support for all Microsoft products. To locate information about specific products, or about Microsoft itself, start at the main Web page address: http://www.microsoft.com.

TIP

The Support Wizard is a great tool for locating resources, but, because it covers so much ground, it can sometimes be a bit frustrating. If you have any idea as to which resource might be the most helpful— Frequently Asked Questions or Downloading A Driver, for example—try that one first.

Get Support

1 Click the Support & Training button, and choose Getting Technical Support from the menu.

2 Select the Get Support Online option.

3 Use the Support Wizard to find what you need, or click one of the buttons to go directly to an item.

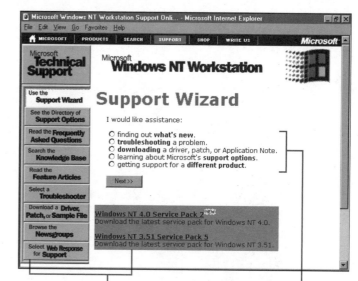

Click to go to a specific resource...   ...or use the Support Wizard to navigate through the available sources to find the information you want.

15

Searching the Knowledge Base

Microsoft has gathered all documented Windows NT–related problems—and, in many cases, the techniques for solving them—and placed them in the Microsoft Knowledge Base. This is the same tool that's used by Microsoft's support engineers, and it's also the "secret weapon" of many consultants. By using good keywords and a couple of search techniques, you should find the solutions to most of your problems in the Knowledge Base—and it's free (except for any connection-time fees charged by your Internet service provider)!

Access the Knowledge Base

1. Use an Internet browser to connect to *http://www.microsoft.com/kb.*

2. Select the product you want information about.

3. Type your keyword or key phrase.

4. Specify whether you want the title only or the title and a brief excerpt.

5. Click Next.

6. Review any articles relevant to your problem that are returned by the search.

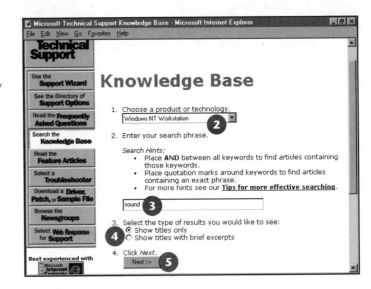

The Microsoft Knowledge Base is also available from other sources, including some online services and information programs such as Microsoft TechNet. If you use an online service, however, make sure the Microsoft Knowledge Base has been updated recently.

If you're not sure of the exact order of the words in a key phrase but need to narrow your search, use the operator NEAR between each word in the key phrase.

Refine the Search

1 Click the New Search button or use the Back button to return to the main search page.

2 Select the product if necessary.

3 Use more precise keywords, and use any of the operators shown in the table at the right to create a more specific search. (Replace the examples with your own keywords.)

4 Click Next.

SEARCH STATEMENTS

Statement	What it does
keyword1 AND keyword2 (sound AND volume)	Finds article that includes both keywords.
keyword1 OR keyword2 (sound OR volume)	Finds article that includes either keyword1 or keyword2 or both keywords.
keyword1 keyword2 (sound volume)	Finds article that includes keyword1 followed immediately by keyword2.
keyword1 NEAR keyword2 (sound NEAR volume)	Finds article in which keyword2 occurs within 50 words of keyword1.
"keyphrase" (Q&A)	Finds article that contains the entire keyphrase, even if it contains special characters.
startofkeyword* (count*)	Finds article that contains words that start with the startofkeyword characters (country, countenance, counting).
keywordstem (sit**)	Finds article that contains any word form of the keywordstem (sit, sat, sitting).

15

Getting Help from Other Windows NT Users

If the Help topics and the Microsoft Knowledge Base haven't solved your problem, there's yet another resource you can use. Microsoft maintains a number of newsgroups that are available to anyone who needs them. Microsoft doesn't support the newsgroups by having its own engineers answer questions, but there are many knowledgeable people—including an ever-expanding group of MVPs—prowling the newsgroups in search of unanswered questions.

TIP

MVPs (Most Valuable Professionals) volunteer their time to answer questions posted in the newsgroups and are recognized by Microsoft for their expertise and efforts. They're happy to help, but they're not there to do all the work for you.

Post Your Question

1 Set your Internet newsreader to use the news server *MSNews.Microsoft.com*. If you don't have a newsreader installed, download Internet Mail And News from *http://www.microsoft.com/ntwkssupport/default-news.htm*.

2 Search for newsgroups that contain the keyword *windowsnt*.

3 Select the newsgroup whose name seems the most relevant to your problem.

4 Go to that newsgroup.

5 Post a message with full details of the problem, including information about your system, if relevant.

6 Check back periodically for a reply. Most questions are answered within a day or two.

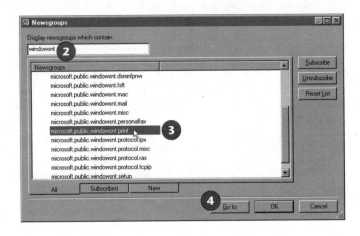

Patching Up Your System

Special service packs for early releases of the Windows NT operating system are available from Microsoft. These service packs fix some known problems and add a few enhancements to Windows NT. If you encounter any problems with your system, and the Knowledge Base or other information source suggests you upgrade Windows NT, you can either download the service packs and install the programs or ask your network administrator about installing the service packs.

SEE ALSO

"Getting Free Software" on page 290 for information about obtaining software and software patches.

See Whether You Need an Upgrade

1 Click the Start button, point to Programs and then to Administrative Tools, and choose Windows NT Diagnostics from the submenu.

2 On the General tab, look at the version number of Microsoft Windows NT. Any services packs that have been installed are listed.

3 Close the Windows NT Diagnostics dialog box.

4 If there are no service packs installed, obtain and install the recommended service packs.

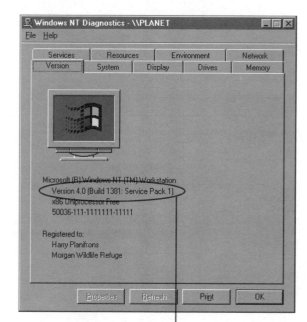

This computer has a service pack installed.

15

Getting Free Software

Microsoft posts updates, fixes, add-on files, and programs that you can download from the Microsoft Internet sites. You might be surprised at what you can find when you prowl around in these sites. And once you find out about new software that you can download, it's easy to jump to that site and download a variety of new products.

SEE ALSO

"Working with Beta Software" on page 292 for information about taking precautions to avoid problems when you're using beta software.

Look for New Software

1. Using your Internet browser, connect to the Microsoft site and read about new releases, patches, program previews, and available beta software.

2. Go to the appropriate home page for the product you're interested in, and follow the links to the download page.

ADDRESSES OF SOME USEFUL MICROSOFT SITES	
Address	What you'll find there
http://www.microsoft.com	Central site: announcements, and links to any Microsoft location
http://www.microsoft.com/ corpinfo/	Microsoft press releases, including new-product and public-beta announcements
http://www.microsoft.com/ ie/default.asp	Internet Explorer news, listing of new releases, and access to all Internet Explorer add-ons
http://www.microsoft.com/ products/	Links that take you to the home page for each Microsoft product
http://www.microsoft.com/ download/	Links to all Microsoft software products available for download
http://www.microsoft.com/ ntworkstation/	Windows NT home page, with links to software download
http://www.microsoft.com/ workshop/	Advanced tools designed for Web publishing

TIP

Read the download and installation instructions carefully, and follow the procedures exactly to avoid problems later.

TIP

Some software items, including most service packs, are quite large. If you're downloading using a modem, be prepared to spend a long time connected.

TIP

If the newly installed program causes problems, use Add/Remove Programs in the Control Panel to uninstall the software. If it's a service pack, contact your support person to find out what went wrong. If it's a beta product, wait for the next release!

Download the Software

1. Create an empty folder in which to store the downloaded file.

2. Read the download instructions.

3. If you're given the option, download the item as a file into your new folder.

4. If you're downloading beta software—that is, software that's still under development—take precautions against losing data.

5. Install the software as instructed on the Internet download page.

Choose Product Updates from the Free Software menu…

…to get jumps to software that will fix problems and improve your system.

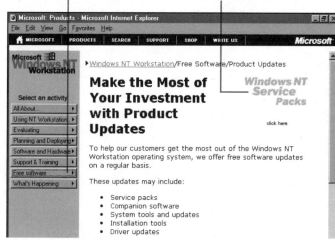

Choose Shareware And Utilities from the Free Software menu to get access to software that expands your system.

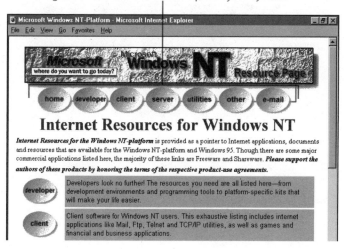

15

Working with Beta Software

Although the software that's available for download has usually been through a rigorous testing program, beta software *is* still under development, and has the potential to cause problems that run the gamut from minor to major. Whenever you use beta software, you can prevent such problems by taking a few simple precautions.

TIP

When they've finished working with beta software, many beta-software testers routinely reformat their computer's hard disk to get rid of all the junk that beta software can leave behind; then they reinstall all their software. As extreme as it sounds, this is often the best way to avoid software problems.

SEE ALSO

"Removing a Software Program" on page 235 for information about removing a program.

Install the Software

1. Back up all your files to a location external to your computer.

2. If you have an earlier version of the beta software installed, remove it.

3. Close all running programs except Windows NT, Windows Explorer, or any folder windows you have open.

4. Double-click the file to start the installation, and follow the directions on the Setup screens.

5. When the setup is completed, restart Windows NT.

6. Play with the program, but do *not* use it for any work you can't afford to lose. Back up all the files from all your programs frequently.

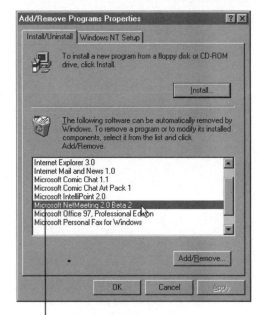

Use Add/Remove Programs in the Control Panel to remove a previous version of a software program or to remove beta software that's causing problems.

Index

Italicized page numbers refer you to information you'll find in a Tip or a Try This entry.

Jerry Joyce has had a long-standing relationship with Microsoft: he was the technical editor on 23 books published by Microsoft Press, and he has written manuals, help files, and specifications for numerous Microsoft products. You might also find him prowling around online bulletin boards and newsgroups, answering questions about getting work done with various software products. Jerry's alter ego is that of a marine biologist; he has conducted research from the Arctic to the Antarctic and has published 18 scientific papers on marine-mammal and fisheries issues. In his spare time he enjoys traveling, birding, and disappearing into the mountains.

Marianne Moon has worked in the publishing world for many years as proofreader, editor, and writer—sometimes all three simultaneously. She has been editing and proofreading Microsoft Press books since 1984 and has written and edited documentation for Microsoft products such as Flight Simulator, Golf, Publisher, the Microsoft Mouse, and Greetings Workshop. In another life, she was chief cook and bottlewasher for her own catering service and wrote cooking columns for several newspapers. When she's not chained to her computer, she likes gardening, cooking, traveling, writing poetry, and knitting sweaters for tiny dogs.

Marianne and **Jerry** own and operate **Moon Joyce Resources**, a small consulting company. They've had a 16-year working relationship and have been married for the last 6 years.

The manuscript for this book was prepared and submitted to Microsoft Press in electronic form. Text files were prepared using Microsoft Word 7.0 for Windows. Pages were composed using QuarkXPress 3.32 for the Power Macintosh, with text in ITC Stone Serif and ITC Stone Sans and display type in ITC Stone Sans Semibold. Composed pages were delivered to the printer as electronic prepress files.

Cover Design and Illustration
Tim Girvin Design
Gregory Erickson

Interior Graphic Designers
designlab
Kim Eggleston

Interior Graphic Artist
WebFoot Productions

Interior Illustrator
s.bishop.design

Typographer
Kari Becker Design

Proofreader
Alice Copp Smith

Indexer
Bero-West Indexing Services

Things are looking up!

Here's the remarkable, *visual* way to quickly find answers about the powerfully integrated features of the Microsoft® Office 97 applications. Microsoft Press® *At a Glance* books let you focus on particular tasks and show you with clear, numbered steps the easiest way to get them done right now.

Microsoft® Excel 97 At a Glance
Perspection, Inc.
U.S.A. $16.95   ($22.95 Canada)
ISBN 1-57231-367-6

Microsoft® Word 97 At a Glance
Jerry Joyce and Marianne Moon
U.S.A. $16.95   ($22.95 Canada)
ISBN 1-57231-366-8

Microsoft® PowerPoint® 97 At a Glance
Perspection, Inc.
U.S.A. $16.95   ($22.95 Canada)
ISBN 1-57231-368-4

Microsoft® Access 97 At a Glance
Perspection, Inc.
U.S.A. $16.95   ($22.95 Canada)
ISBN 1-57231-369-2

Microsoft® Office 97 At a Glance
Perspection, Inc.
U.S.A. $16.95   ($22.95 Canada)
ISBN 1-57231-365-X

Microsoft® Windows® 95 At a Glance
Jerry Joyce and Marianne Moon
U.S.A. $16.95   ($22.95 Canada)
ISBN 1-57231-370-6

Microsoft Press® products are available worldwide wherever quality computer books are sold. For more information, contact your book retailer, computer reseller, or local Microsoft Sales Office.

To locate your nearest source for Microsoft Press products, reach us at www.microsoft.com/mspress/, or call 1-800-MSPRESS in the U.S. (in Canada: 1-800-667-1115 or 416-293-8464).

To order Microsoft Press products, call 1-800-MSPRESS in the U.S. (in Canada: 1-800-667-1115 or 416-293-8464).

Prices and availability dates are subject to change.

Microsoft*®*Press

Get
quick,
easy
answers—
anywhere!

Microsoft Press® Field Guides are a quick, accurate source of information about Microsoft® Office 97 applications. In no time, you'll have the lay of the land, identify toolbar buttons and commands, stay safely out of danger, and have all the tools you need for survival!

Microsoft® Excel 97 Field Guide
Stephen L. Nelson
U.S.A. $9.95 ($12.95 Canada)
ISBN 1-57231-326-9

Microsoft® Word 97 Field Guide
Stephen L. Nelson
U.S.A. $9.95 ($12.95 Canada)
ISBN 1-57231-325-0

Microsoft® Outlook™ 97 Field Guide
Stephen L. Nelson
U.S.A. $9.99 ($12.99 Canada)
ISBN 1-57231-383-8

Microsoft® PowerPoint® 97 Field Guide
Stephen L. Nelson
U.S.A. $9.95 ($12.95 Canada)
ISBN 1-57231-327-7

Microsoft® Access 97 Field Guide
Stephen L. Nelson
U.S.A. $9.95 ($12.95 Canada)
ISBN 1-57231-328-5

Microsoft Press® products are available worldwide wherever quality computer books are sold. For more information, contact your book retailer, computer reseller, or local Microsoft Sales Office.

To locate your nearest source for Microsoft Press products, reach us at www.microsoft.com/mspress/, or call 1-800-MSPRESS in the U.S. (in Canada: 1-800-667-1115 or 416-293-8464).

To order Microsoft Press products, call 1-800-MSPRESS in the U.S. (in Canada: 1-800-667-1115 or 416-293-8464).

Prices and availability dates are subject to change.

Microsoft Press

Keep things **running** smoothly around the **Office.**

These are *the* answer books for business users of Microsoft® Office 97 applications. They are packed with everything from quick, clear instructions for new users to comprehensive answers for power users. The Microsoft Press® *Running* series features authoritative handbooks you'll keep by your computer and use every day.

Microsoft Press® products are available worldwide wherever quality computer books are sold. For more information, contact your book retailer, computer reseller, or local Microsoft Sales Office.

To locate your nearest source for Microsoft Press products, reach us at www.microsoft.com/mspress/, or call 1-800-MSPRESS in the U.S. (in Canada: 1-800-667-1115 or 416-293-8464).

To order Microsoft Press products, call 1-800-MSPRESS in the U.S. (in Canada: 1-800-667-1115 or 416-293-8464).

Prices and availability dates are subject to change.

Running Microsoft® Excel 97
Mark Dodge, Chris Kinata, and Craig Stinson
U.S.A. $39.95   ($53.95 Canada)
ISBN 1-57231-321-8

Running Microsoft® Office 97
Michael Halvorson and Michael Young
U.S.A. $39.95   ($53.95 Canada)
ISBN 1-57231-322-6

Running Microsoft® Word 97
Russell Borland
U.S.A. $39.95   ($53.95 Canada)
ISBN 1-57231-320-X

Running Microsoft® PowerPoint® 97
Stephen W. Sagman
U.S.A. $29.95   ($39.95 Canada)
ISBN 1-57231-324-2

Running Microsoft® Access 97
John Viescas
U.S.A. $39.95   ($53.95 Canada)
ISBN 1-57231-323-4

Microsoft *Press*

Take
productivity
in stride.

Microsoft Press® *Step by Step* books provide quick and easy self-paced training that will help you learn to use the powerful word processor, spreadsheet, database, desktop information manager, and presentation applications of Microsoft Office 97, both individually and together. Prepared by the professional trainers at Catapult, Inc., and Perspection, Inc., these books present easy-to-follow lessons with clear objectives, real-world business examples, and numerous screen shots and illustrations. Each book contains approximately eight hours of instruction. Put Microsoft's Office 97 applications to work today, *Step by Step*.

Microsoft Press® products are available worldwide wherever quality computer books are sold. For more information, contact your book retailer, computer reseller, or local Microsoft Sales Office.

To locate your nearest source for Microsoft Press products, reach us at www.microsoft.com/mspress/, or call 1-800-MSPRESS in the U.S. (in Canada: 1-800-667-1115 or 416-293-8464).

To order Microsoft Press products, call 1-800-MSPRESS in the U.S. (in Canada: 1-800-667-1115 or 416-293-8464).

Prices and availability dates are subject to change.

Microsoft® Excel 97 Step by Step
U.S.A. $29.95   ($39.95 Canada)
ISBN 1-57231-314-5

Microsoft® Word 97 Step by Step
U.S.A. $29.95   ($39.95 Canada)
ISBN 1-57231-313-7

Microsoft® PowerPoint® 97
 Step by Step
U.S.A. $29.95   ($39.95 Canada)
ISBN 1-57231-315-3

Microsoft® Outlook™ 97 Step by Step
U.S.A. $29.99   ($39.99 Canada)
ISBN 1-57231-382-X

Microsoft® Access 97 Step by Step
U.S.A. $29.95   ($39.95 Canada)
ISBN 1-57231-316-1

Microsoft® Office 97 Integration
 Step by Step
U.S.A. $29.95   ($39.95 Canada)
ISBN 1-57231-317-X

Microsoft® Press